Robin Hood
home
baking

Robin Hood

home baking

from cookies & cakes to pizza, pot pies & more

Robert
ROSE

Disclaimer

National Library of Canada Cataloguing in Publication Data
    Robin Hood home baking: from cookies & cakes to pizza, pot pies & more.

Includes index.
ISBN 0-7788-0074-1

1. Baking. I. Robin Hood Multifoods Inc.

TX765.R6256 2004   641.8'15   C2004-902890-1

Cover: Marbled Cream Cheese Brownies (see recipe, page 84)
Photo page 2: Chicken Pot Pie (see recipe, page 234)
Photo page 6: Bumbleberry Cream-Filled Crêpes (see recipes, page 184)

Design & Production: PageWave Graphics Inc.
Editor: Judith Finlayson
Copy Editor: Christina Anson Mine
Index: Barbara Schon
Photography: Robert Wigington
Food Stylist: Jill Snider
Prop Stylist: Maggi Jones, Sue Florian

We acknowledge the financial support of the Government of Canada through the
Book Publishing Industry Development Program (BPIDP) for our publishing activities.

Published by: Robert Rose Inc.
120 Eglinton Ave. E., Suite 800, Toronto, Ontario, Canada M4P 1E2
Tel: (416) 322-6552   Fax: (416) 322-6936

Printed in Canada

1 2 3 4 5 6 7 8 9 10   FP   09   08   07   06   05   04

Robin Hood has been a household name in Canada since 1909 when our first flour mill went into operation in Moosejaw, Saskatchewan. Since then, Robin Hood has become Canada's favorite flour, milled from the very best Canadian wheat in our mills in Montreal, Port Colborne, Ontario and Saskatoon.

Much of our success has come from the long-term relationships we have developed with generations of Canadian home bakers. Every year, thousands of people contact our Consumer Services Department for baking advice. Each year our Test Kitchen develops, modifies, adjusts and triple-tests hundreds of baking recipes that meet your home baking needs. And over the years, Robin Hood recipes have woven themselves into the fabric of daily life, creating memories and traditions for family and friends.

In *Robin Hood Home Baking,* we have created a complete baking book for novice and experienced bakers alike. With a comprehensive introduction to home baking, 150 easy-to-follow recipes ranging from snacks to desserts and savory dishes, as well as mouthwatering photographs, it's the only baking book you will need. It will be your inspiration and guide. And Robin Hood will continue to provide you with the finest flour and our supportive team of home baking experts.

It's what you've come to expect from Robin Hood.

Wishing you the very best of *Home Baking.*

CONTENTS

Acknowledgments

I'd like to express sincere thanks to the many talented and devoted people who helped put this book together: the publisher, Bob Dees, who convinced us to do another cookbook following the success of our *Baking Festival Cookbook;* Andrew Smith, Joseph Gisini and Kevin Cockburn, who designed and laid out the book; Brenda Venedam, who accurately input the recipes; and Judith Finlayson and Christina Anson Mine for their eagle eyes in editing.

At Robin Hood, thanks to all the staff for their support and understanding of the demanding workload required to meet deadlines; the large number of employees who critically tasted and evaluated every recipe until it was perfect; and Michelle, Sarah and Thérèse of Consumer Services, who pleasantly answer endless consumer calls regarding our recipes.

I also want to thank Robert Wigington, the outstanding photographer I've worked with for the past 27 years, who always manages to make even the most difficult shots jump off the page; Carol Wigington, who organized photography meetings and schedules and kept everyone on track; and Sue Florian, our creative prop stylist.

JILL SNIDER

Introduction

Whenever thoughts turn to home, they inevitably gravitate toward baking. Nothing epitomizes domestic comfort more than freshly baked pies, breads, warm puddings, crisp buttery cookies or crunchy healthy snacks. But more than that, home baking is central to our everyday lives. From morning toast or muffins to coffee-break cake and evening dinner followed by a dessert, these ultimate comfort foods have woven themselves deeply into the fabric of daily life. Plain or fancy, old-fashioned or elegant, decadent or healthy — almost everyone cherishes a memory linked with freshly baked goods. So, not surprisingly, creating these mouthwatering treats to share with family and friends can be one of life's great pleasures.

Whether you are a novice or an experienced baker, the *Robin Hood Home Baking Book* will inspire you to explore the wonderful world of baking. The basic ingredients couldn't be simpler, but the endless ways they can be varied make baking a great adventure. Fruit, nuts, grains, chocolate, dairy products and a wide range of flavorings can be mixed and matched with the essential components to create an array of delectable tastes and textures. Savory sensations cover a wide range, from vegetables to poultry, meats and fish.

With a 150 easy-to-follow recipes and an abundance of mouthwatering photographs, this book is destined to become an indispensable resource in kitchens from coast to coast. There's something here for every occasion. Intended for home cooks, the *Robin Hood Home Baking Book* is filled with dependable and delicious recipes that use basic ingredients. If they aren't already in your pantry, they will be readily available at your grocery store. We hope these recipes will inspire you to create delicious homemade treats that are uniquely yours.

Baking Basics

Baking is a science as much as an art, a basket of skills and techniques that create the foundation upon which artistry can build. With its orientation toward detail and dependence upon the chemical reactions of ingredients, baking is far less forgiving than cooking. Adding too much liquid to a stew may produce a watery result that lacks flavor, but the less-than-ideal dish may still be enjoyable. On the other hand, too much liquid in a cake batter is likely to produce a result that can't be salvaged.

Despite its exacting nature, it would be a mistake to assume that baking is, by definition, difficult. Some baked goods — for instance, drop cookies — are among the easiest home-cooked products to make, and many outstanding cooks got their start as toddlers baking cookies with Mom. The issue with baking is that, unlike cooking, it demands strict adherence to the rules. Because the basic ingredients are so simple — flour, mixed with some combination of salt, eggs, sweetener, leavening agent and fat, such as oil, butter or shortening — how they are combined and in what proportion are particularly important. Baking recipes are so rooted in science — the way ingredients react and the principles of how heat is transferred — they are more than guidelines: they are formulae that document how to measure, combine and cook ingredients to achieve particular results. Tinker with the formula and you're tempting disaster.

To achieve success, home bakers need four basic things: reliable recipes written to accommodate their level of skill, good equipment, quality ingredients and an attentive mind-set. Usually, poor results can be traced back to a fault in one of these components.

All too often, the problem lies with the recipe. Some recipes are vaguely written and don't provide clear instructions that can be easily followed. Others assume a level of skill that a home baker is unlikely to have and use terms that are unintelligible to inexperienced cooks. All these factors increase the possibility of error. It has always been important to have confidence in your recipe source, but this is especially true today, when so many recipes are taken off the Internet, often from sites that lack quality control. The simple truth is that some recipes just don't work. And you don't want to invest valuable time and costly ingredients only to discover your recipe was a dud.

Because the recipes in this book originated in the Robin Hood Test Kitchen, you can be confident they have been properly formulated and thoroughly tested. In addition, we've included an abundance of tips to help you improve your baking skills and avoid potential pitfalls. We hope you will be able to achieve outstanding results every time you bake.

ACHIEVING BAKING SUCCESS

To ensure success every time you bake:

- choose the best ingredients;

- use a reliable recipe;

- follow it closely; and

- pay attention to information about equipment, measurements and ingredients.

Baking Equipment

Using the right equipment is an important part of successful baking. In order to produce satisfactory results, good-quality dishes and pans, accurate measures, mixing bowls, spoons, spatulas and wire racks are essential. Depending upon how much you bake and what you're making, you may also need an electric mixer, a food processor, cutting boards, a strainer, a rolling pin, a pastry board and parchment paper.

Oven Temperature

Your oven is probably the single most important piece of baking equipment you own. Oven temperature plays a critical role in baking. If your oven is too hot, your baked goods will be overly brown on the surface and possibly not completely cooked through. If it is not hot enough, you will need to overcook the interior to achieve a desirable degree of browning.

Ideally, when you set the temperature, that's how hot your oven will be once it has finished preheating. The problem is, most ovens are 25°F (10°C) hotter or cooler than their setting. One solution is to have your oven calibrated by a professional to ensure that the setting and the temperature align. The flaw in this solution is that it's expensive to have an oven professionally calibrated, and unless you do it routinely, it's likely to fall out of alignment. A simpler and more cost-effective approach is to familiarize yourself with how your oven bakes. You will gain a sense of whether your oven is hotter or cooler than the setting by observing how quickly or slowly it cooks in relation to the recipes you use. A more accurate solution, which we recommend, is to purchase an oven thermometer. This simple, inexpensive device will tell you exactly what your oven temperature is and allow you to adjust the setting accordingly.

Convection Ovens

If you are using a convection oven to bake the recipes in this book, check your manual and follow the instructions. Because convection ovens are more energy efficient than traditional models, you can either reduce your baking time by about 25 per cent or lower the oven temperature by 25°F (10°C). As a rule of thumb, if you are baking anything for less than 15 minutes — cookies, for example — reduce the oven temperature rather than the baking time. Preheat your oven to the desired temperature before baking.

Pans

Good-quality, shiny metal pans and baking sheets are a great invest-ment because they bake evenly and do not rust. However, heatproof glass pans also work well for many recipes. Since the quality of your pan can make a big difference to baking results, it's worth doing research before buying, particularly since expensive pans aren't necessarily the best. Ask for advice at a good kitchen-supply store or read cooking magazines, such as *Cook's Illustrated,* which test and rate equipment.

Pay Attention to Size

Today's baking pans are not as standardized as they once were; they differ in size and shape from older ones and they also vary from one manufacturer to another. In addition, the labeling may show a mixture of imperial and metric measurements, which can be confusing. You'll likely have several standard-size pans in your pantry that you can readily identify for use in these recipes. But if you're using a pan that isn't a standard size, you'll need to estimate the volume and dimensions yourself. To confirm the volume of a pan, fill liquid measuring cups with water and pour liquid into the pan until it reaches the brim. The quantity you used is the volume measure of the pan. Use a ruler to measure the length and depth, taking measurements on the inside across the top of the pan. Measure depth on the outside of the pan, vertically from the bottom to the brim.

ALL PANS AREN'T EQUAL

The material your pans are made from and whether their surface is shiny or dull affects the baking time. If you are using glass or nonstick pans, especially those that are dark, lower the oven temperature by 25°F (10°C).

Make Removal Easy

To ensure smooth and easy removal of your baked goods from pans, invest in parchment paper. This baking tool is available in large sheets and rolls or cut to fit round pans. It is heatproof and when used to line them, makes pans and cookie sheets nonstick.

Basic Pans

To prepare the recipes in this book, you will need the following pans:
- 8-inch (2 L) square cake pan
- 9-inch (2.5 L) square cake pan
- two or three 8-inch (1.2 L) round cake pans
- two or three 9-inch (1.5 L) round cake pans
- 10-inch (3 L) Bundt pan
- 10-inch (4 L) tube pan
- 8-inch (20 cm), 9-inch (23 cm) and 10-inch (25 cm) springform pans
- two 8½- by 4½-inch (1.5 L) or 9- by 5-inch (2 L) loaf pans
- six 5¾- by 3¼-inch (500 mL) mini-loaf pans
- two 12-cup muffin (cupcake) pans or one 24-cup muffin pan
- 13- by 9-inch (3.5 L) cake pan
- 15- by 10-inch (2 L) jelly roll pan
- three cookie sheets without sides
- 9-inch (23 cm) pie plate
- 9-inch (23 cm) deep-dish pie plate or quiche pan
- 10-inch (25 cm) pie plate
- 9-inch (23 cm) flan pan with removable side
- 9-inch (23 cm), 10-inch (25 cm) and 11-inch (27 cm) fluted flan pans with removable bottoms
- 7-inch (18 cm) soufflé dish
- 6-cup (1.5 L) baking dish
- 8-cup (2 L) baking dish
- 12-cup (3 L) shallow baking dish
- crêpe pan or nonstick skillet

Pans Matter

Don't use a pan that is a different size from the one recommended in the recipe you are using. If the recipe calls for a 9-inch (2.5 L) square pan and you use one that is 8 inches (2 L) square, the batter will spill over the sides during baking and much of your cake will end up on the floor of your oven. If you are using glass pans, decrease the oven temperature by 25°F (10°C), as glass pans bake more quickly than metal ones. If using nonstick pans, follow the manufacturer's directions. Most recommend decreasing the temperature by 25°F (10°C) since nonstick surfaces, especially those that are dark, bake faster.

To achieve optimum results, we recommend using the pan size specified in the recipe. However, you can substitute a pan that is similar in dimension and volume — just make sure you don't use one that is smaller in volume, as there may not be enough room to accommodate the expansion that takes place during baking. You can also interchange shapes (e.g., round instead of square) if the volume is the same and the pan is not much deeper, shallower, longer or shorter than the one recommended in the recipe.

Bowls

Every kitchen needs a variety of bowls in different sizes for combining and mixing ingredients. Metal or glass bowls are preferable. Plastic does not work well for beating egg whites, as it retains oils, which can affect results. Have a few bowls of each size: small, medium and large.

The bowl needed for an electric mixer is a "mixer bowl." If the recipe doesn't specify a mixer bowl, other bowls will do.

Measuring Cups and Spoons

You will need glass or clear plastic measuring cups for liquid ingredients, a set of graduated dry-ingredient measures and a set of measuring spoons. (See Measure Accurately, page 17.)

Racks

Wire racks are essential for cooling cakes and cookies. Look for racks that have narrow spaces between the steel wires. It's a good idea to have a variety of sizes and shapes (round, square, rectangular) to suit whatever you're making. We recommend stainless-steel racks since they won't rust and have a long life.

Wire Whisks

Even if you use an electric mixer, you should have one medium-size all-purpose whisk for aerating dry ingredients or beating eggs before they are added to batters. If you don't have an electric mixer, a large balloon whisk is essential for jobs such as whipping cream or beating egg whites.

Zester and/or Fine Grater

Some recipes call for the zest of oranges, lemons or limes, which adds indispensable flavor to many dishes. A zester, an inexpensive gadget with tiny teeth, easily strips off the flavorful skin, separating it from the bitter white pith. Depending upon the recipe, it can be used as is or finely chopped. For finely grated zest, use a fine grater, which does the job in a single step.

Tips

If you don't like rack marks on the top of your cake, keep one rack covered with a thick tea towel pinned securely in place. When necessary, remove the towel for washing.

When purchasing wire cooling racks, look for ones that clear the countertop by at least 2 inches (5 cm). The height is necessary to prevent your baked goods from "sweating" on the bottom.

Cookie Cutters

An assortment of cookie cutters in different shapes is both useful and fun. For many round cookies and biscuits, an inverted glass dipped in flour works very well.

Rolling Pin

A rolling pin is essential for making pie crusts and certain kinds of cookies. There are many different rolling pins on the market. Spend some time finding the one that works best for you.

Spatulas

You should have two rubber spatulas for tasks such as folding ingredients and scraping down the side of a mixing bowl. Offset spatulas made from metal are also required for lifting cakes and cookies from pans and racks. An icing spatula is used for applying frostings to cakes.

Pastry Brushes

Pastry brushes are useful for brushing pastry and bread dough with a wash or glaze, or for greasing pans.

Knives

A sharp serrated knife with a blade about 12 inches (30 cm) long makes cutting cakes horizontally a breeze. However, some people prefer to use dental floss for an even slice. Try both methods and pick your favorite. Electric knives are excellent for cutting angel food cakes. A good-quality chef's knife is also essential for chopping ingredients.

Kitchen Shears

These are useful for many tasks, especially snipping herbs, such as chives, or dried fruits, such as apricots.

Pastry Bags and Tips

Although rarely essential, these devices, which can be used to shape batters and icings, give home baking a professional look. If you are writing names or greetings in frosting, a plastic squeeze bottle makes an acceptable substitute.

Mixer

Use an electric countertop mixer or a good-quality hand mixer, not the heavy-duty commercial type, which is too powerful for normal consumer-style baking. If you do a lot of baking, the countertop model is much more efficient and easier to use.

Food Processor

A food processor is a valuable kitchen tool that performs many tasks. It is useful for bakers, as it quickly chops ingredients such as fruits and nuts and purées mixtures. It also prepares an excellent pie crust, quickly cutting the fat into appropriately sized pieces and distributing them evenly throughout the dough.

Baking Tips and Techniques

As mentioned earlier, baking is a science as well as an art, which helps to explain why things can so easily go wrong. Unless you understand the science behind recipes, which is reflected in baking techniques, it's all too easy to produce less-than-ideal results. Baking can get off track right from the get-go, as errors in measuring are one of the most common mistakes novice bakers make. Because so many things can go wrong in baking, it's important to understand the basic techniques and use carefully written, well-tested recipes.

Be Prepared

The first step to baking success is choosing a good recipe and reading it carefully, from beginning to end, before you start to bake. After you've read the recipe, measure all your ingredients and assemble them, along with the necessary equipment, on the counter. Few things are more frustrating than not being able to locate an ingredient when you're in the midst of mixing. You don't want to leave something out or be madly searching for a pan when your cake should be in the oven.

Allow adequate time to soften butter and bring cold ingredients, such as eggs, to room temperature. At least 15 minutes before you plan to bake, preheat your oven, being aware that some brands of ovens take longer to reach the desired temperature. Check your oven racks and adjust them, if necessary.

Prepare pans and baking sheets, if required, by greasing lightly with shortening or a vegetable cooking spray. Don't use butter, margarine or oil, as they are more likely to stick and burn. If the pan needs to be floured as well, sprinkle the flour lightly over the greased surface. Shake the pan to distribute the flour evenly, then shake out the excess. Pans and baking sheets can also be lined with parchment paper, which ensures foolproof removal.

Tip

Most baked goods — cakes, muffins and cookies — are baked on the middle rack. For a well-browned bottom crust, bake yeast breads, pizzas and pies on the lower rack unless otherwise specified.

Tip

To ensure that goods don't overbake, check them early. Also use your nose. When things start to smell delicious, that's an indication that it's almost time to check for doneness.

Why Your Recipe Was Overdone

There is no such thing as an exact baking time in any recipe because so many factors affect the time it takes to produce the desirable "golden brown" result. These include:
- the temperature of the ingredients — remember, unless otherwise specified, room temperature is ideal;
- the material your pans are made of and whether the finish is shiny or dull — if you are using glass or nonstick pans, reduce the temperature by 25°F (10°C);
- the accuracy of your oven setting — use an oven thermometer to get a sense of how much your oven is off; and
- the number of pans in the oven — unless you have a convection oven, your goods will bake unevenly if you are using multiple racks or too many pans, which can prevent the air from circulating properly around them.

Measure Accurately

Inaccurate measuring is one of the most common mistakes in baking. Every kitchen needs a set of graduated measures, both cups and spoons, specifically intended for dry ingredients. These have a straight rim so the ingredient being measured can be leveled off. To measure dry ingredients, spoon them lightly into the cup (you want them to be reasonably airy). Don't tap or pack. Then, using a spatula or the flat side of a knife, level off. Flour, cocoa powder and granulated and icing sugars should all be measured using this method, before sifting unless otherwise specified.

Brown sugar is measured differently from other dry ingredients. It is packed firmly into the measure, then leveled off. If you invert the measure and tap the bottom, brown sugar should unmold in the shape of the cup.

Liquids should be measured in clear glass or plastic liquid measuring cups, and the measurement should be read at eye level.

To accurately measure solid fats, such as butter, margarine or shortening, use the water displacement method. For example, if a recipe calls for $\frac{1}{2}$ cup (125 mL) butter, fill a liquid measuring cup with $\frac{1}{2}$ cup (125 mL) cold water. Add butter until the water level reaches the 1 cup (250 mL) mark. This ensures that you have exactly $\frac{1}{2}$ cup (125 mL) butter.

Use measuring spoons for small amounts of both liquid and dry ingredients. Fill to the top, then level off.

When measuring, pay particular attention to how the instruction is written. *One cup (250 mL) pitted cherries, chopped* is a different quantity than *1 cup (250 mL) chopped pitted cherries*. In the first amount, whole pitted cherries would be measured, then chopped. In the second amount, the chopped pitted cherries would be measured. They fit more tightly in the cup, meaning more cherries in your recipe.

Sift as Required

Some ingredients, such as icing sugar, cocoa powder and cake flour, need to be sifted before being blended with other ingredients. If you don't have a sifter, a fine sieve will do. To ease cleanup, place a piece of waxed paper on the counter. Fill the sieve with the ingredients to be sifted and tap until all have sifted through to the paper. Using the paper as a funnel, transfer the dry ingredients to the rest of the mixture.

MEASURE THEN SIFT

All the recipes in this book specify that dry ingredients such as icing sugar and cocoa powder be measured before being sifted. In the recipe ingredient list, this instruction appears as *$\frac{1}{2}$ cup (125 mL) icing sugar, sifted*. If you are using a recipe from a different source, pay attention to how the sifting instruction reads. If it says *$\frac{1}{2}$ cup (125 mL) sifted icing sugar*, it is telling you to sift before measuring, which results in less sugar.

Tip

If you aren't using a countertop mixer, place your mixing bowl on a folded damp towel to prevent it from slipping.

Tip

Assemble all the utensils you'll need, have your ingredients measured and prepare your pans before you start to mix.

Have Ingredients at the Right Temperature

Ideally, ingredients for baking should be at room temperature unless otherwise specified. Eggs and cold butter (unless cold butter is called for in your recipe) should be removed from the refrigerator about 1 hour before baking. (If you're short on time, place eggs in a bowl of warm water for 5 minutes. You can soften cold butter in the microwave for a few seconds, but watch very carefully, as butter that is too soft will not cream effectively.)

One secret to producing flaky pastry is to ensure that all ingredients, including flour, are cold. (See Perfect Pie Crust and Pastry, page 27.)

Mix Carefully

Attention to mixing is as important to baking success as accurate measuring. For best results:

● Combine dry ingredients, such as flour, baking soda, baking powder and salt in a bowl or on a piece of waxed paper and mix together until they are well blended.

● Cream butter and sugar long enough to ensure that the mixture has achieved appropriate aeration (about 5 minutes on medium speed of an electric mixer if you are baking a cake). If using a mixer, stop it several times and scrape down the beaters and the side of the bowl. Often the mixture looks curdled when the eggs are mixed in, but this will correct itself once the flour is added. If adding liquid along with the dry ingredients, alternate them, making three equal additions of the dry ingredients and adding the liquid in two equal parts. Adding these ingredients in alternate increments helps keep the fat emulsified in the liquid, which produces the desired texture.

● When combining sugar and eggs, beat the mixture until it increases in volume and falls in a ribbon when dropped from a spoon, unless the recipe specifies otherwise. This will usually take about 5 minutes on high speed of an electric mixer.

● Carefully fold lighter ingredients, such as beaten egg whites or whipped cream, into heavier ones to maintain the aeration.

Achieving Volume

Volume in baked goods is achieved in a variety of ways, depending upon the result desired. The most obvious method is the use of chemical leavens, such as yeast, baking powder and baking soda. Stiffly whipped egg whites, which contain trapped air bubbles, are another common volumizer. They give foam cakes, such as angel food or sponge cakes, their airy texture. Less well understood is the role of fats in achieving volume. Because solid fats such as butter or shortening coat the proteins in flour, they prevent it from absorbing water, which helps to build structure in baked goods. When butter and sugar are creamed together, the jagged edges of the sugar crystals create bubbles of air in the fat, which contributes to the aeration of the batter.

Bake Attentively

Attention to baking pans, oven temperature and timing are extremely important to baking success. For best results, keep the following in mind:

- Unless otherwise specified, the recipes in this book were developed using metal pans. Reduce the oven temperature by 25°F (10°C) if using glass pans instead of metal.
- Although most ovens have room for two or more oven racks, for best results, bake on only one rack at a time, unless you have a convection oven. Using multiple racks simultaneously produces unevenly baked goods.
- Always test baked goods to see if they are done 5 to 10 minutes before the end of the recommended baking time. This allows for variances in oven temperature. You can always bake longer if your product isn't done. If it is overcooked, it's too late to fix the mistake.

Convection Baking

One advantage to owning a convection oven is that you can use multiple oven racks simultaneously. Depending upon the model of your oven, you may be able to bake as many as six trays of cookies at the same time. So long as you're cooking at the same temperature, you can also bake casseroles or savory pies at the same time as sweets since the circulating air expels odors, preventing them from transferring to other foods. The recipes in this book have been tested in a conventional oven. If using a convection oven, reduce the temperature by 25°F (10°C).

Making Perfect Cakes

Many people find baking cakes intimidating because they require particularly close attention to detail. More than most other baked goods, cakes depend upon the exact proportion of ingredients and the proper execution of certain techniques to achieve their lift. Still, cakes don't need to be daunting; there are many ways to ensure cake-baking success, from using flour specially intended for cakes to making sure that ingredients are properly aerated.

Cake Types

There are two basic types of cakes: **butter cakes** and **foam cakes.** They are distinguished by their leavens and the method they use to add air to the batter. Butter cakes are based on the creaming technique — beating butter and sugar together long enough to create air bubbles in the mixture. They also employ chemical leavens, such as baking powder and baking soda, which produce carbon dioxide. Foam cakes get their lift from beating air into eggs.

Mixing Perfect Cakes

Butter Cakes: For butter cakes, cream the softened butter and sugar until the mixture is light and fluffy. This takes about 5 minutes on medium speed of an electric mixer. You'll need to stop the process several times and scrape down the beaters and the side of the bowl. **Foam Cakes:** When making foam cakes, beat egg yolks with sugar on high speed of an electric mixer until they form a ribbon. This usually takes about 5 minutes. Pay close attention and follow the recipe instructions for beating egg whites. Overbeating will produce curdled whites and is as much of a problem as underbeating; neither has enough structure to support the cake. Fold beaten whites into the batter as soon as they reach the specified degree of firmness. If left to sit, they will soon disintegrate.

Light and Airy Cakes

To get the maximum volume in your cakes:
- Make sure that all ingredients are at room temperature.
- Follow the mixing instructions carefully.
- When using a chemical leaven, such as baking powder, make sure it is evenly distributed among the dry ingredients before they are added to the creamed mixture. Otherwise, your cake may develop tunnels as it bakes.
- Unless otherwise specified, add dry and liquid ingredients in increments, starting and ending with dry.
- Don't overmix. It's easy to create a tough cake just by overmixing.
- When folding ingredients into a recipe, particularly beaten egg whites, be careful not to overblend.
- Bake a cake as soon as it is mixed, as the leavening will start to work once it is moistened.
A delay in baking after mixing will result in poor volume.

Preparing the Pans

When baking cakes, remember to prepare your pans before you begin to mix your batter. How the pan is greased determines how well the cake will release from the pan, a determinant of success. (You don't want pieces missing from your cake that were left behind in the pan.) How well you prepare your pans can also influence the degree of dome on top of the cake — for the best appearance, you want a flat rather than a domed cake.

When baking **layer cakes**, grease the pan with shortening or vegetable oil spray, then dust lightly with flour, tapping the pan to remove any excess. The flour gives the batter some traction and helps it climb up the side of the pan. For added insurance, place a round of parchment paper in the bottom of the pan. After the cake is cooked, it will peel of easily, leaving a smooth bottom.

Most **foam cakes** — a category that includes angel food, sponge and chiffon cakes, which achieve their volume through beaten eggs — are an exception. The pans are not greased so that the batter can cling to the pan and rise up the sides. In addition, the extra fat would weigh the airy batter down. All the recipes in this book have the appropriate instructions for preparing the pans.

Cake Flour

Cake flour is made from softer wheat than its all-purpose counterpart, and many cooks find that it helps them bake better cakes. Since it is lower in gluten and more finely ground, cake flour produces cakes with a more delicate crumb. Because most people always have a supply of all-purpose flour on hand, all our cake recipes have been written using this ingredient, which also produces a very satisfactory result. If you prefer to use cake flour, you will need to use a little bit more than the recipe calls for. When substituting Robin Hood Best For Cake & Pastry Flour for Robin Hood All-Purpose Flour, replace 1 cup (250 mL) Robin Hood All-Purpose Flour with 1 cup plus 2 tablespoons (280 mL) Robin Hood Best For Cake & Pastry Flour.

Is My Cake a Success?

If you're making a butter cake, look for:
- a level or just slightly rounded top (you don't want a dome);
- a fine-grained crumb; and
- an evenly browned crust.

The best foam cakes are:
- light, airy and moist;
- fine textured and tender; and
- deep golden brown.

Baking for Success

Tip
Before baking, check your oven temperature with an oven thermometer to make sure it is as hot as it needs to be. Otherwise, your cake may not rise as much as you would like.

Incorrect oven temperature is one of the most significant factors affecting the success of cakes. As previously noted, use an oven thermometer to check the accuracy of your oven, preheat the oven for at least 15 minutes before you plan to bake and make sure the oven racks are properly positioned. Here are some additional tips.

● Do not use a pan that is smaller in volume than the size recommended, as the cake may overflow. Slightly larger is usually safe, although the cake will be shallower and require less baking time.

● To eliminate any large air bubbles that may have formed in the batter, bang most cake pans firmly against the countertop before placing them in the oven. Do not do this with angel food cake, sponge cake or cakes containing fruit or nuts.

● Use recommended baking times as guidelines. Always set the timer for 5 minutes before the minimum time given to allow for oven variances. As previously noted, ovens are often hotter than the temperature indicated, and cakes can easily be overbaked, especially those high in sugar or baked in a dark pan. It's much safer to add more time in 5-minute increments if the cake isn't done.

Testing for Doneness

Tip
When testing to see if your cake is done, be as quick and efficient as possible. Don't open the door all the way. The rush of cool air may cause your cake to fall.

When cakes are done, a toothpick, wooden skewer or cake tester inserted in the center of the cake will come out clean. (However, this test won't work for some cakes with "gooey" ingredients.) Another indication that the cake is done is that the top springs back when lightly touched and the cake comes away from the sides of the pan. For lighter cakes, color is also a good indicator — the cake should be a nice golden brown.

Removing Cakes from Pans

Unless the recipe specifies otherwise, after they are taken out of the oven, layer cakes should cool in the pans for 10 minutes.

Deeper cakes, such as tube cakes and loaves, should be left for 20 minutes. After the required time has passed, turn the cake out and cool completely on a wire rack. To remove the cake from the pan, run a knife around the edge (and also the center, if baking in a tube pan), then invert the pan and shake it gently to remove the cake. Most cakes are inverted twice so that they finish cooling in the same position (top side up) as they are baked. Bundt and angel food cakes are the two exceptions: after cooling initially for about 20 minutes in the pan, turn out a Bundt cake and finish cooling, fluted side up. Baked angel food cakes should cool completely in the pans. After removing from the oven, immediately turn the baked cake upside down on a funnel or bottle and let it cool completely.

Glazing and Frosting

Glazes differ from frostings in that they are usually a simpler way to finish a cake (for instance, drizzling with melted chocolate). Frostings are thicker and more complicated to make. Cakes are often glazed while still warm, but frostings aren't applied until cakes have completely cooled. Buttercream, a combination of softened butter, flavoring and icing sugar is the most common frosting used by home cooks. Flavored whipped creams also make easy and delicious frostings for cakes. Dusting cakes with sugar or drizzling them with syrup or melted chocolate are popular ways to finish cakes. We hope the following tips will inspire you to think creatively about how to finish your cakes and help you achieve successful results.

Glazing Tips

● Dusting plain cakes with icing sugar is the simplest and most calorie-conscious way to finish them. Just before serving (otherwise the moisture from the cake will quickly absorb the sugar), place icing sugar in a fine sieve and tap over the surface of the cake. For an elegant or festive look, place a paper doily over the unfrosted cake, then remove carefully after dusting, leaving a lacy decoration.

● When finishing cakes that are brushed with syrup while warm (usually tube and Bundt cakes), place the cake on a rack set over waxed paper to catch the drips.

Frosting Tips

● Frost cakes only after they are completely cool. If desired, place cakes to be frosted in the freezer for about 30 minutes to make them less fragile and easier to frost.

● When frosting, place a bit of frosting on the plate to hold the cake in place. To keep the plate clean, set four strips of waxed paper under the edge of the cake to form a square. Carefully remove the strips when you have finished.

● If you are using a filling that is different from the frosting, leave, a ½-inch (1 cm) margin from the edge to ensure that it doesn't run into and discolor the frosting.

Frosting Layer Cakes

Because layer cakes involve setting one cake on top of another, it may be necessary, if the layers are domed, to slice a bit off the top with a serrated knife to make them level before frosting. If there are burned spots on the cakes, cut them off. You can fill them with frosting. Set four strips of waxed paper on your plate to form a square and place a dab of icing in the middle of the plate to hold the cake in place. Place the first cake layer, top side down, on the plate. Spread ½ to ¾ cup (125 to 175 mL) frosting over the layer using a spatula or table knife. Place the second cake layer, top side up, over the frosting. You now have the two flat surfaces together in the center so the cakes will sit evenly. Spread a very thin layer of frosting over the top and sides of the cake. (This seals in crumbs.) Then cover the cake with a second, thicker layer of frosting. You can smooth the surface with a long spatula or make swirls with a small spatula or the back of a spoon. If necessary, chill the cake to firm up the frosting. Remove the waxed paper strips before serving.

Tip

It's a good idea to have a few plain cake layers in the freezer. Wrap unfrosted cake layers tightly in plastic wrap. You can thaw, fill and frost them in no time and quickly have a fabulous cake to serve to guests. Just be sure to cool unfrosted cakes completely before freezing.

Tip

An angel food cake will be easier to slice if you wrap it tightly and freeze it for 24 hours. Return to room temperature before serving.

Storing Cakes

Properly wrapped, cakes keep very well. If the frosting does not contain eggs or dairy products, most cakes can be stored at room temperature, under a dome or a foil tent, for as long as three days. If storing your cake under a dome, add a slice of apple to help keep it moist. You can refrigerate most cakes for up to a week. Unfrosted layer cakes and foam cakes can be frozen for up to 6 months. Wrap them tightly in plastic wrap or place them in a freezer bag, removing as much air as possible.

To make slicing easy and develop the best flavor, make fruitcakes, particularly those flavored with liquor, at least 4 weeks in advance. Wrap them and store in the refrigerator until you're ready to use them. Use a sharp, thin, nonserrated knife to make the nicest slices.

Thawing Frozen Cakes

When thawing unfrosted cakes, leave them covered for approximately three-quarters of the thawing time, then uncover for the remainder. This allows them to dry out slightly, which makes them easier to frost.

If you are thawing a frosted cake and the frosting contains either eggs or cream, thaw it overnight in the refrigerator. Other cakes may be thawed in this manner, or at room temperature, for about 3 hours.

Cookies, Bars and Squares

Almost everyone loves baking (not to mention eating) cookies, a designation which also includes bar cookies, such as brownies and squares. With their many different shapes, sizes and flavor variations, from crisp biscotti and soft chewy oatmeal cookies to rich blondies and apple squares, cookies are among the most versatile of baked goods. Because they are so easy, quick and delicious, cookies are a great starting place for novice bakers, including kids.

Like most cakes, many cookies use the creaming technique for combining butter and sugar. Since leavening is not as important in cookies as it is in cakes, it is not as necessary to beat volume into the mixture when making cookies. You can use a countertop mixer, a handheld mixer or a wooden spoon. Beat on medium speed, just until smoothly blended (about 2 minutes), scraping down the beaters and the side of the bowl if you are using an electric mixer.

Cookie Types

Cookies are usually identified by how they are shaped and placed on the baking sheet. The following are common types of cookies.

Drop cookies, which are dropped by spoonfuls onto the baking sheet, are probably the easiest cookies to make. When making drop cookies, use a measuring spoon or small ice-cream scoop to ensure that all are equal in size so they will bake evenly.

Rolled and cut cookies are made from relatively firm dough that is rolled and cut into shapes; for instance, sugar cookies.

Sliced or refrigerator cookies are made from dough that is shaped into a roll and refrigerated for up to a week. These are among the most convenient cookies, as the dough can be sliced and baked whenever the mood strikes.

Shortbread, a tradition in many parts of the world, is a delicious combination of butter (a must) and flour worked together.

Biscotti are Italian biscuits that are traditionally used for dunking. Because they are baked twice, they are drier than most other cookies. They are particularly well suited to gift giving, as they keep well.

Bar cookies, the category that includes brownies and blondies as well as more-complex layered bars, can be a timesaving way to make bite-size treats. Instead of shaping each piece individually, they are baked in a pan, then cut into pieces.

COOKIES ARE CONVENIENT

One advantage to making cookies is that they store well, not only after they are baked but also as dough. Most cookie dough can be made ahead and frozen, so you can always be ready to bake cookies to serve to unexpected guests or as after-school treats. They also keep longer than cakes and pies and are not as fragile. So long as they are not decorated, they can be packaged and shipped as gifts.

Crisp or Chewy Cookies?

• If you prefer crisp cookies, press the dough flat with the bottom of a glass dipped in granulated sugar before baking.
• If you want soft, chewy cookies, remove them from the oven about 2 minutes before they are done, as they will continue to bake on the hot sheet. If you want crisp cookies, bake for 2 minutes longer.

If you are not baking cookies within 1 hour of making the dough, refrigerate the batter, as the eggs and/or dairy products are likely to spoil at room temperature.

When making cut and rolled cookies, dip the cookie cutter in flour so it won't stick to the dough. Cut the cookies as close together as possible. Although you can re-roll scraps of dough, the less the dough is handled, the more tender your cookies will be.

Reduce Fat

If you are trying to reduce the amount of fat in your diet, try one or all of these lower-fat alternatives the next time you bake cookies.

● Replace some of the whole eggs with egg whites (two whites for one egg).
● Substitute a fruit purée, such as apple butter, for up to half of the butter in a recipe.
● Use lower-fat dairy products. Do not use fat-free products, which do not perform well in baking.

Bake Great Cookies

Although cookies are among the simplest things to bake, these tips will help make yours even better.

● Use flat cookie sheets without sides for even baking.
● Place cookies about 2 inches (5 cm) apart on the cookie sheet to allow for spreading.
● Use cooking spray or a light coating of shortening to grease cookie sheets. It is not necessary to grease the sheets again, between batches, but use a paper towel to wipe off any sugar or crumbs from the surface before adding the next batch.
● Place the cookie sheet on the middle rack of your oven. Make sure that it is narrower than the oven rack and that it doesn't touch the sides of the oven, so the heat can circulate properly. For best results, bake only one sheet at a time to ensure proper heat circulation.
● Since cookies are usually small and bake quickly, pay particular attention to the baking time, as every extra minute can make a big difference. Always aim to underbake rather than overbake, because cookies continue to bake after they are removed from the oven. Begin checking to see if your cookies are done a few minutes before the minimum time specified in the recipe.

Stop Cookie Spread

Sometimes your cookies can come out of the oven looking like a giant pancake because they have all run together on the baking sheet. Here are some ways to ensure that your cookies don't spread too much.
● Don't substitute butter or margarine in a recipe that calls for shortening. Shortening has a higher melting point than butter or margarine, so it doesn't liquefy as quickly, which means it does a better job of holding the dry ingredients together. Cookies made with butter or margarine will spread out more than those made with shortening.
● Grease cookie sheets only if the recipe specifies this and don't use an excessive amount. Unnecessary grease will cause some cookies to spread too much.
● Make sure your oven is preheated for at least 15 minutes before you bake and is set to the proper temperature. If the oven isn't hot enough, the fat will melt before the other ingredients have time to meld together, causing the cookies to spread.

Storing Cookies

Cool cookies completely before storing. Pack them in single layers in an airtight container, with waxed paper between layers to prevent sticking. Do not store crisp and soft cookies in the same container. To freeze cookies, place them in sealed plastic containers or freezer bags and store for up to 6 months.

Perfect Pie Crust and Pastry

Tips

If you lack the confidence or don't have time to make your own crust, try Robin Hood Flaky or Brodie XXX Pie Crust Mix. The ingredients are pre-measured and blended; all you add is water.

For a more tender crust, substitute vinegar for some of the water in your recipe. Acid ingredients, such as vinegar and lemon juice, help break down the gluten.

While nothing defines excellence in home baking better than a freshly baked pie with a tender, flaky crust, few ventures inspire more trepidation. But making pie crust is not that difficult — it just takes practice. The fundamental ingredients couldn't be more basic: flour, fat and water. Once you understand how these ingredients work together, you'll be able to sense when the dough has the proper balance of flour and fat and the right consistency. Allow yourself a few failures and chalk them up as learning experiences. With a bit of practice, you'll be turning out perfect pies and pastry every time you bake.

Making Dough

Perfect pie crust is both tender and flaky, and achieving this balance is the challenge associated with making crust. Gluten, which is formed when flour comes into contact with moisture, is responsible for the flakiness in pie crust. The problem is, too much gluten makes pastry tough. The best pie crusts have just enough gluten to

Tip

You can enhance a pastry to suit its filling by adding complementary ingredients. For dessert pies, try adding cinnamon, ginger, nutmeg, or lemon or orange zest to the dry ingredients before combining with the fat.

be flaky without losing tenderness. Although it isn't flaky, pastry made with oil is particularly tender because, unlike a solid fat, such as butter or shortening, oil coats the flour, limiting the formation of gluten. Similarly, overblending a solid fat and flour (an easy mistake to make when using a food processor) will produce a crust that lacks flakiness. Ideally, when fat such as butter, shortening or lard, is cut into flour, it should be no smaller than the size of peas. This gives the flour space to bind with the water, thus creating the bit of gluten necessary to hold the crust together. The pieces of fat separate the strands of gluten, creating a flaky crust.

Excellent Results Every Time

The following tips will help you make excellent pastry every time.

- For the flakiest pastry, have all the ingredients, including the flour, well chilled. Freeze butter and/or shortening for 30 minutes before using. Use ice water (as little as possible) to bind the ingredients together. Water contributes to gluten formation, and adding too much liquid will produce a tough crust.
- Use the least amount of flour possible when rolling out the dough. The more flour you use, the tougher your pastry will be. Invest in a pastry cloth and rolling pin covered with stockinette, which help prevent the dough from sticking.
- Handle the dough as little as possible once the water is added. If you are re-rolling extra scraps of dough, do not knead them first. Kneading softens the fat, which creates a mealy crust.
- Chill the dough for at least 30 minutes before you roll it out. This allows the water to seep through the flour and ensures that the fat is firm, which contributes to flakiness.
- Start your pies in a hot oven (425°F/220°C). This generates steam in the pastry, creating air pockets that push up the flakes of fat-coated starch. Flakiness is the result.

Rolling out the Dough

When you're ready to roll out the dough, flour your work surface as lightly as possible. Unwrap one piece of dough and center it on the surface. You're now ready to begin rolling.

- Roll away from you, from the center out, in one direction only.
- Rotate the dough as you roll and use as few strokes as possible, until it is the required size, about 3 to 4 inches (7.5 to 10 cm) larger than the inside size of your pie plate. (Check to ensure that you have rolled the dough to the accurate size by holding the pie plate over the dough.)
- To transfer the rolled dough to the pie plate, carefully roll it onto the rolling pin and lift, positioning it properly over the pie plate. Gently set the crust on the plate, then, using your fingers, push it into the sides of the plate. Trim with scissors or a knife, allowing enough overhang to flute.
- If adding a top crust, fill the pie, roll out the pastry as for the bottom crust and center the crust over the filling. Seal the crusts together using a fork or by fluting.

GLAZES TO ENHANCE A TOP CRUST

- For a shiny, deep golden crust, brush with egg yolk beaten with a little water before baking.
- For a shiny crust, brush with lightly beaten egg white or milk.
- For a sugary, sweet crust, brush lightly with water, then sprinkle with sugar, preferably coarse.

Prevent a Soggy Bottom Crust

- Chill the crust for about 20 minutes before filling.
- Brush the crust with lightly beaten egg white, then chill for 15 minutes before filling.
- Bake on the bottom oven rack. For most pies, bake at a high temperature for 10 to 15 minutes, then continue baking at a lower temperature.
- Sprinkle toasted ground nuts on the pastry. Press lightly into the dough with the back of a spoon before filling. This also adds a nice flavor.

Tip
Fruit pies can be prepared ahead of time and frozen for up to 6 weeks. When you're ready to bake, preheat the oven to 425°F (220°C) and place the frozen pie in the oven. Bake for 15 minutes; lower the temperature to 350°F (180°C) and bake until the crust is golden brown and the filling is bubbly, about 50 minutes.

Storing Dough

Unrolled pastry dough can be stored in the refrigerator for up to 3 days or frozen for up to 6 months. Thaw dough overnight in the refrigerator before rolling it out.

Rolled pastry dough can be kept in the fridge for up to 3 days or frozen for up to 6 months. Wrap tightly in plastic before freezing. It isn't necessary to thaw rolled dough before baking.

Muffins and Biscuits

There is nothing quite like a warm muffin or hot scone in the morning or as a welcome afternoon break with a cup of coffee or tea. These tasty tidbits, which, like quick breads, use baking powder, baking soda or eggs rather than yeast to get their lift, are among the quickest and easiest baked goods to make. Additions such as nuts, chocolate chips and candied fruit, or even cheese and bacon if you're looking for a savory result, make them versatile enough for any occasion.

Making Muffins

There are two ways of preparing muffins. The simplest method combines the liquid and dry ingredients separately, then quickly whisks them together before baking (see Raspberry Muffins, page 112). The second uses the same technique as for butter cake: creaming the butter and sugar, then adding the other ingredients (see Chocolate Zucchini Muffins, page 118). No matter what method you are using, it is important not to overmix the batter once the liquid and dry ingredients are combined. Overmixing encourages the gluten to develop, which produces dense, tough muffins with unappealing holes known as tunnels.

Tip

If you're not using all the cups in your muffin tins, don't grease the empty ones. The fat will burn, creating an unpleasant odor and possibly making a mess of your pan.

Bake Better Muffins

- Mix muffin batter very lightly to avoid dense, tough results. Don't worry about small lumps; they will disappear during baking.
- For fast cleanup, bake muffins in paper cups set in ungreased pans.
- Use an ice-cream scoop with a wire release to scoop batter into the pans. Your muffins will be uniform in size and have a nicely shaped top.
- Always fill the tins at least two-thirds full.
- If you have not used all the cups in your pan, fill the empty ones with water before placing the pan in the oven. This helps the muffins bake more evenly.
- To retain freshness, store muffins in an airtight container. Alternatively, wrap them in plastic wrap and freeze. When thawing, leave the plastic on and bring the muffins to room temperature.

Tip

When baking muffins and biscuits, whisk the dry ingredients together to blend. This aerates the flour and produces a lighter result.

Biscuits

There is nothing quite like a sweet or savory biscuit fresh out of the oven. Savory biscuits are the perfect accompaniment to soup or stew. Among their other uses, sweetened biscuits can be the basis for delicious shortcakes during the summer months.

Better Biscuits

Biscuits are fast and simple to make. They take just 10 to 15 minutes, although getting the best results demands attention to technique. Here are some tips to improve your biscuit-making technique.

- Thoroughly combine the dry ingredients before cutting in the fat.
- Use cake-and-pastry flour for the most tender texture.
- For the best flavor, make your biscuits with butter. If flakiness matters most, use shortening.
- Keep the cold ingredients, such as butter and milk, thoroughly chilled and work quickly with them. This helps to ensure flakiness.
- For flaky biscuits, the fat should be the size of small peas. Any smaller and you'll jeopardize flakiness.
- When combining the liquid and dry ingredients, mix with a light touch just until the dry ingredients are moistened. You want a tender biscuit, so keep gluten development to a minimum. Overmixing develops the gluten, which produces a tough result.
- Use a minimum of flour if you're turning out the dough, and handle it as gently and as little as possible to keep it tender.
- A hot oven is important to the success of biscuits. Make sure you have preheated the oven to the specified temperature.

Quick Breads and Yeast Breads

Quick Breads

Quick breads are the loaf versions of muffins. Unlike yeast breads, quick breads, which are made from a softer dough, are leavened with baking powder and baking soda. They do not require kneading. Most can be completed, start to finish, in not much more than an hour. Quick breads, such as Wheaten Bread (see recipe, page 206) or Date-and-Nut Loaf (see recipe, page 202), are delicious sliced and toasted.

Here are some things to look out for when making quick breads.

- Be quick when mixing the batter. Stir it as little as possible and bake immediately, as the leaven begins to work once it meets the liquid. Your bread will lose oomph if the batter is left to sit.
- If your loaf is soggy and fallen in the middle, the dough may have had too much liquid in proportion to the dry ingredients. If it has a coarse texture, it may have had too much fat.
- It is normal for some quick breads to have a lengthwise crack down the top of the loaf, so don't worry if this happens to you.
- For easy removal, line the bottom and sides with greased aluminum foil or parchment paper. To remove the loaves, just lift them out of the pan. Remove the paper and let cool.

PANCAKES AND CRÊPES

You may be surprised to learn that pancakes and crêpes are forms of quick bread. Pancakes get their little bit of lift from baking powder or baking soda, whereas crêpes are flat, not leavened. Like with other quick breads, one key to success is to avoid overmixing.

Yeast Breads

Homemade bread is one of life's great pleasures. Few things taste quite as good as a crusty loaf fresh from the oven or smell as appetizing as its yeasty aroma wafting through the house. Bread is one of the most versatile foods: it can be eaten on its own, as an accompaniment to a meal, toasted for breakfast or made into a sandwich for lunch. It is also an achievable goal. Making bread isn't complicated or time-consuming. It takes longer from start to finish than other baked goods, but most of that time is devoted to rising, which doesn't require your involvement. It is also very satisfying to make. Many people find the act of kneading dough to be a comforting way of dealing with the frustrations of daily life.

Making Better Bread

Bear the following tips and techniques in mind when you're mixing and working with your dough and you'll improve your results.

- To achieve a supple, more elastic consistency, carefully measure the wet and dry ingredients. If the dough appears too wet, knead in more flour, a little at a time. If the dough appears too dry, knead in 1 tbsp (15 mL) of liquid at a time. If given a choice, start with a soft dough and add flour — it is much easier to knead flour into dough than a liquid.
- Test to see if your dough has enough flour when you are kneading. Slap your open hand against the ball of dough. If your hand comes away clean, the dough has enough flour. Also, if the dough is sticking to the kneading surface, knead in a little more flour, as required.
- To knead dough by hand, turn it out on a lightly floured surface. Kneading is the repetitive process of folding the dough and pushing down on it using the heels of your hands until the appropriate consistency is achieved. When kneading bread, it usually takes about 5 minutes to reach the right consistency.
- Allow dough to rise in a warm place (75 to 85°F/24 to 29°C) and away from drafts that can inhibit rising.
- Several factors can affect the volume of bread. Too much or too little flour or salt will inhibit the gluten's performance, and the dough will not rise to its full potential. To test if it has risen sufficiently on the first rise, insert your fingers into the dough. If an indentation remains, it is ready to punch down. If not, allow more time for the dough to finish rising.
- To prevent bread from sinking in the middle, do not allow the dough to rise too much. (Remember, it will rise more during baking.) Only allow dough to rise until it has doubled in volume. Otherwise, it may collapse in the oven during baking. On the second rising, the center of the dough should be about $1\frac{1}{2}$ inches (4 cm) from the top of the pan.
- When shaping loaves, you can eliminate large air bubbles by rolling out the dough on a floured board. Roll the dough into a rectangle approximately 9 by 12 inches (23 by 30 cm), then, beginning with one shorter side, roll up jelly roll–style, sealing the roll with the heel of your hand after each turn.

KNEADING DOUGH

There are different ways of kneading dough. Dough can be kneaded in a countertop mixer with a dough hook, by hand or by using a combination of these methods. You can also skip this process by using a bread machine, which does all the work for you.

Tips

If you're in a hurry, bake bread on a rainy day. Dough rises faster when the barometric pressure is falling.

Too much flour produces a dry loaf. Don't overflour your hands or work surface when kneading.

Know Your Ingredients

Flour is key when making bread. When combined with water, the protein in wheat flour forms gluten, which, when kneaded, become elastic and supports the rise.

Although you can make excellent bread using Robin Hood All-Purpose Flour, Robin Hood Best For Bread Flour has been specially formulated for baking bread, not only from scratch but also in a bread machine. It will produce breads that are higher in volume with a lighter, more even texture. It is milled from hard wheat and is specially designed for yeast baking. If you prefer, you can replace Robin Hood All-Purpose Flour with an equivalent amount of Robin Hood Best For Bread Flour in any yeast bread recipe.

Yeast is the ingredient that gives bread its voluminous rise. Yeast produces carbon dioxide, which causes dough to rise; alcohol, which produces the wonderful aroma when bread bakes; and acids for flavor. Although working with yeast isn't tricky, it does require attention to detail. Store yeast in a cool, dry place or, for best results, in the freezer, and always check the best-before date prior to using. Using yeast that has passed its peak can limit how much your bread will rise.

Sugar adds flavor to breads and a golden color to the crust. It is also quick food for the yeast. Sugar helps produce the carbon dioxide gas that allows the yeast to activate. However, too much sugar can slow down the yeast action or prevent it from activating. Other sweeteners can be used, if desired. When baking fancy or whole grain breads, you can substitute brown sugar, molasses or honey for granulated sugar if you're feeling like a change. However, you may need to adjust your recipe if you're substituting a liquid for a dry ingredient.

Fats, such as butter, margarine, shortening or oil, help improve the flavor, tenderness and quality of bread. They also have a lubricating effect on the gluten's meshwork. In other words, adding fats will permit your dough to stretch more easily. However, adding too much fat will make your dough crumbly.

Bake for Success

No matter how carefully you've mixed, kneaded and risen your dough, your success can be undermined once it reaches the oven. The following baking tips will improve your results.

- Use shortening to grease your pans. Butter or oil can cause the bread to stick to the pan or burn.
- Make sure you use the pan size recommended in the recipe. Using an incorrectly sized pan can result in a flat loaf.
- Since aluminum pans reflect rather than transmit heat, they can result in a lighter-color loaf. For a darker loaf, try using a baking pan made from something other than aluminum.
- Score the loaf before putting it in the oven. Scoring improves the appearance of the finished loaf and allows the carbon dioxide to escape in a pattern. Otherwise, it will erupt randomly.
- For a different look, try baking loaves free-form on a baking sheet that has been sprinkled with cornmeal or greased. Cornmeal will prevent the bread from sticking and give it an interesting texture.
- Position pans in the oven so that the air can circulate between them and they are evenly exposed to the heat. Bread should be baked on a lower rack in the oven unless otherwise directed. If the crust is becoming too brown, cover the pan loosely with aluminum foil for the duration of the baking time.
- Doughs made with water generally yield a crisper crust than those made with milk. To achieve a crisp crust, spritz the loaf with water during baking. For a darker, richer color, brush with an egg wash before baking or brush finished loaves lightly with butter or margarine and return to the oven for 5 to 10 minutes.
- Too much flour, or too little sugar or fat, can toughen your crust. To soften a crust, brush the loaf with melted butter as soon as it comes out of the oven.

Tips

For nice light loaves, make sure your dough is just a tiny bit sticky. Too much flour in the dough produces bread that is dry and dense.

To know for sure if your loaf is done, insert an instant-read thermometer into the center of the loaf. Regular loaves are done when the temperature reads 190°F (90°C). If you're making a whole grain bread, which is more dense, the temperature should be 210°F (100°C).

Store Breads Appropriately

For a crisp crust, keep bread in a paper bag for up to 2 days. Do not wrap bread in plastic wrap unless you want an especially soft crust. Store bread at room temperature or freeze (refrigeration tends to dry out bread). To freshen bread, heat it, unwrapped, in a 350°F (180°C) oven for 10 to 15 minutes.

If you're planning to freeze your bread, allow it to cool completely first. Frozen bread keeps and freshens well. To freeze, place the cooled loaf in a freezer bag. Remove all of the air from the bag or ice crystals will form during the freezing process. Thaw frozen bread inside the plastic freezer bag so it can absorb the moisture lost during the freezing process. To freshen previously frozen bread, place the thawed loaf on a baking sheet and heat for 10 to 15 minutes in a 350°F (180°C) oven.

Baking at High Altitudes

When baking at altitudes above 3,000 feet (915 m), you may need to adjust baking times and/or temperatures or fine-tune your recipe in other ways. The higher the altitude, the more the leavening gases in breads and cakes expand. Because water and other liquids boil at lower temperatures (which means that the internal heat needed to cook food takes more time to develop because the food is being cooked at a lower temperature), they also evaporate more quickly.

If you are baking at high altitude, you'll want to make sure that your cakes, breads, muffins and cookies are the best they can be, so please read the following tips carefully.

Breads

At high altitudes, the lower air pressure can cause flour to dry out, water takes longer to boil and yeast ferments faster, making dough rise more quickly.

The following tips will show you how to counteract the effects altitude can have on your finished loaf.

Quick Breads: Quick breads vary from muffinlike to cakelike in cell structure. Although the cell structure of biscuits and muffin-type quick breads is firm enough to withstand the increased internal pressure at high altitudes, a bitter or alkaline flavor may result because baking soda or baking powder is not adequately neutralized. In such cases, a slight decrease in the quantity of baking soda or baking powder will usually improve results.

Quick breads with a cakelike texture are more delicately balanced and can usually be improved at high altitudes by following the adjustment recommendations given below for cakes.

Cakes (General)

Most cake recipes perfected at sea level need no modification up to an altitude of 3,000 feet (915 m). Above that, decreased atmospheric pressure may result in excessive rising, which stretches the cell structure of the cake. This makes the texture coarse or breaks the cells, which causes the cake to fall. This can usually be corrected by decreasing the amount of leaven. Also, increasing the baking temperature by 15 to 25°F (5 to 10°C) "sets" the batter before the cells formed by the leavening gas expand too much.

Fast and excessive evaporation of water at high altitudes leads to a higher concentration of sugar, which weakens the cell structure. To counterbalance this problem, sugar is often decreased and liquid is increased.

Only repeated experiments with each recipe can determine the most successful proportions. The accompanying table is a helpful starting point. Try the smaller adjustment first — this may be all that is needed.

Fat, like sugar, weakens the cell structure. Therefore, rich cakes made at high altitudes may also need less fat (1 to 2 tbsp per cup/ 15 to 30 mL per 250 mL) than when made at sea level. On the other hand, because eggs strengthen cell structure, the addition of an egg may help prevent a "too-rich" cake from falling.

Angel Food and Sponge Cakes: These cakes present special problems at high altitudes. Since the leavening gas for these cakes is largely air, it is important not to beat too much air into the eggs. They should be beaten only until they form a peak that falls over, not until they are stiff and dry. Overbeating causes the air cells to expand too much and leads to their collapse. By using less sugar and more flour, and increasing the baking temperature, you will also strengthen the cell structure of foam-type cakes.

Cake Recipe Adjustment Guide for High Altitudes

Oven Temperature: Increase by 75°F (25°C) to compensate for faster rising in the oven and slower heating.

Liquids: Based on altitude, for each cup (250 mL), increase liquids by the amount indicated below.

ALTITUDE	INCREASE LIQUIDS BY
more than 3,000 feet (915 m)	1 tbsp (15 mL)
5,000 feet (1,525 m)	2 to 3 tbsp (30 to 45 mL)
8,000 feet (2,440 m)	3 to 4 tbsp (45 to 60 mL)

Sugar: Based on altitude, for each cup (250 mL), decrease sugar by the amount indicated below.

ALTITUDE	DECREASE SUGAR BY
more than 3,000 feet (915 m)	1 tbsp (15 mL)
5,000 feet (1,525 m)	2 to 3 tbsp (30 to 45 mL)
7,000 to 8,000 feet (2,135 to 2,440 m)	3 to 4 tbsp (45 to 60 mL)

Flour: Based on altitude, for each cup (250 mL), decrease flour by the amount indicated below.

ALTITUDE	DECREASE FLOUR BY
more than 3,000 feet (915 m)	1 tbsp (15 mL)
5,000 feet (1,525 m)	2 tbsp (30 mL)
6,500 feet (1,980 m)	3 tbsp (45 mL)

Baking Powder: Based on altitude, for each teaspoon (5 mL), decrease baking powder by the amount indicated below.

ALTITUDE	DECREASE BAKING POWDER BY
more than 3,000 feet (915 m)	$\frac{1}{8}$ tsp (0.5 mL)
5,000 feet (1,525 m)	$\frac{1}{8}$ to $\frac{1}{4}$ tsp (0.5 to 1 mL)
6,500 feet (1,980 m)	$\frac{1}{4}$ tsp (1 mL)

Cookies

Although many sea-level cookie recipes yield acceptable results at high altitudes, they can often be improved by a slight increase in baking temperature; a slight decrease in baking powder or soda, fat and sugar; and/or a slight increase in liquid ingredients and flour. Many cookie recipes contain a higher proportion of sugar and fat than necessary, even at low altitudes.

Ingredients

Flour, sugar and fat: while not appetizing in themselves, these are the primary ingredients from which delicious baked goods evolve. Add eggs, leavening agents, chocolate, nuts and vanilla and you've opened the door to a cornucopia of mouthwatering delights: crusty bread, tender muffins and luscious cakes.

Flour

Flour is the most fundamental ingredient in baking, and the protein content of the flour you use plays a big role in your baking results. With so many different kinds of flours on the market, it's easy to become confused about what kind to use. The safest strategy is to always have all-purpose flour on hand since it can meet all your baking needs. Robin Hood All-Purpose Flour has a relatively high protein content and is made from a combination of soft and hard wheat. It can be used in any of the recipes in this book — from pastry, breads and crusty rolls to cakes, cookies and muffins — and will consistently produce excellent results.

If you prefer, you can substitute other kinds of flour that are appropriate for specific recipes. You can even mix and match flours if you're so inclined. Try altering the texture of cookies, muffins or quick breads by using half all-purpose flour and half whole wheat in a recipe that calls for all-purpose flour. When making biscuits, cakes, pastry and other more-tender baked goods, feel free to substitute 1 cup plus 2 tbsp (280 mL) of Robin Hood Best For Cake & Pastry Flour for every cup (250 mL) of all-purpose flour. Cake-and-pastry flour has a lower protein content than all-purpose flour, so it will produce lighter biscuits and cakes with a finer crumb. When baking yeast breads, feel free to use 1 cup (250 mL) Robin Hood Best For Bread Flour for every cup (250 mL) of all-purpose flour. The high protein level of this flour encourages the development of gluten, which helps ensure sturdy dough.

Fats

Fats play many roles in baking, from adding flavor and influencing the texture and moistness of baked goods to creating creaminess and the smooth feel on the tongue known as "mouth appeal." They tenderize by coating the flour, preventing it from absorbing water and developing gluten. There are two kinds of fat: those that are solid at room temperature and those that are liquid. The more liquid the fat, the more thoroughly it coats the flour and the more tender the result. When creamed with sugar, solid fats, such as butter, contribute to leavening. Their different melting points and their composition determines how they interact with other ingredients.

Butter is the most popular fat in baking for one simple reason: it has the best flavor. However, from a technical standpoint, it is not

Unless otherwise specified, it is not necessary to sift flour before using it in a recipe. Just spoon it lightly into a dry measuring cup and level it off using the back of a knife. Do not pack the flour down in the cup (see Measure Accurately, page 17).

Tip

Store flour in a clean, airtight container in a cool, dry place. White flour lasts for approximately 1 year, and whole wheat lasts for approximately 6 months. To extend the shelf life of flour, store it in sealed containers in the refrigerator or freezer.

the best fat to use. It is only 80 per cent solid fat and it has a low melting point, which means that all-butter pie crusts will be less flaky than those made with shortening or lard, and cookies made with butter rather than shortening won't hold their shape as well. But they will have better taste.

Margarine is imitation butter made from vegetable oils. Like butter, it is only 80 per cent solid fat. It can be used instead of butter in any recipe, unless flavor is an issue; for instance, in Basic Butter Frosting (see recipe, page 154). When using margarine, be sure not to use brands classified as "spreads," which contain a high percentage of water and do not perform well in baking. To avoid consuming trans fatty acids, check to make sure your margarine isn't hydrogenated.

Vegetable shortening, which is made from vegetable oils, is 100 per cent fat and has a high melting point. This means it is excellent for producing flaky biscuits and pie crusts. The problems with shortening are that it lacks the flavor of butter and contains trans fatty acids.

Lard, too, is 100 per cent fat and has a high melting point. Like shortening, it is a desirable fat to use when flakiness is valued. Because it is derived from meat, it is particularly good for use in savory recipes.

Vegetable oils, which are liquid at room temperature, are 100 per cent fat. They can not be used in recipes that are based on creaming and do not contribute to leavening. Because they are liquid at room temperature, they thoroughly coat the flour when blended, which prevents gluten development. The results are tender but not flaky. Vegetable oil is often used in quick breads and muffins, and occasionally in pie crust, where it produces a tender but not flaky crust.

Sweeteners

Sweeteners, such as sugars and honey, give baked goods much of their appeal. Although they don't have many nutrients, sweeteners contribute energy in the form of calories.

White granulated sugar is the most commonly used sugar in baking. It has a mild flavor, is free-flowing and doesn't require sifting. It works well for every baking need.

Icing sugar, also known as confectioner's sugar, is a powdered white sugar with added cornstarch, which prevents it from lumping and crystallizing. Icing sugar is used primarily in frostings and glazes. It dissolves almost instantly in liquids, which makes it wonderful for sweetening whipping cream.

Because of its tendency to clump, icing sugar should always be sifted before it is added to a recipe. When using, spoon it into a dry measure, level it off, then sift. All the recipes in this book have been based on this method rather than the reverse (sifting then measuring).

Although there are a few unrefined **brown sugars** on the market, such as Demerara, turbinado and sugar in the raw, traditional brown sugar is refined granulated sugar with added molasses. The darker the color, the more molasses and moisture refined brown sugar contains and, therefore, the stronger its flavor. In cooking, refined light and dark brown sugars and unrefined brown are interchangeable. Brown sugar is often used for toppings, streusels and some frostings. It isn't used much in tender cake batters because it makes them heavier and too moist. However, brown sugar works well in many recipes for cookies and bars, which benefit from its denser texture and caramel flavor.

Other sweeteners, such as molasses, honey, corn syrup and maple syrup, are effective, depending on the recipe used. Molasses, a by-product of refined sugar, is rich and dark and adds flavor and moisture to recipes. It has a strong flavor; if it is not to your liking, you can substitute an equivalent amount of honey, corn syrup or maple syrup in recipes. When making the recipes in this book, don't substitute liquid sweeteners for granulated or brown sugars, as they lack the texture and flavor of sugar and may break down when heated.

Eggs

Eggs are indispensable in baking and play many different roles in recipes. Eggs contribute to leavening, texture, color, flavor, volume and richness in baked goods. They also add nutritional value and act as an emulsifier, binding ingredients together.

Store eggs in their container in the refrigerator (not on the door, which is not cold enough). One hour before baking, remove the quantity you need from the refrigerator to allow them to come to room temperature. Temperature plays an important role in baking, as it changes the properties of many ingredients; for

Tip

All the recipes in this book have been tested using large eggs. When baking, always use this size, as recipes are traditionally tested with large eggs. If you need to substitute, assume that 1½ medium eggs can be substituted for one large. To substitute for half an egg, beat a medium egg and measure out 2 tbsp (25 mL).

instance, adding cold eggs to a creamed mixture will solidify the butter you've worked so hard to make light and fluffy. This decreases the volumizing potential of the mixture and increases the likelihood of producing a flat, dense cake.

Separating Eggs

If you need to separate eggs for a recipe, do this as soon as you take them from the refrigerator, since eggs separate better when they are cold. After separating the yolks from the whites, cover them tightly with plastic wrap to keep them from drying out and leave them at room temperature for an hour. This also helps ensure that you achieve maximum volume after beating the whites. For food safety reasons, do not leave eggs at room temperature for longer than an hour.

Replacing Eggs

Egg replacement products can replace whole eggs in many recipes. Before using, check package information to make sure the product is appropriate for your use. If you are concerned about cholesterol — a large egg yolk contains about 5.6 g of fat and 274 mg of cholesterol — you can substitute 1½ egg whites for one of the eggs in any recipe. We don't recommend eliminating the egg yolks entirely, as they contribute to tenderness.

Leavening Agents

Leavens are the ingredients that cause baked goods to rise. Some ingredients, such as eggs, contain leavening agents, but baked goods usually rely on biological or chemical leavens, such as yeast, baking powder or baking soda for their lift. Cream of tartar is another common leaven, which is most often used to stabilize meringue.

Yeast

Yeast is the leavening agent that gives bread its voluminous rise (see page 34 for more on yeast). In these recipes, we have used active dry yeast and quick-rise instant yeast.

    Active dry yeast is the most common form of yeast available in supermarkets, likely because in addition to being one of the first yeasts made for consumers, it is easy to store and has a relatively long shelf life. Active dry yeast needs to be "proofed," which means it is brought to life when mixed with lukewarm water. To test the vitality of active dry yeast, dissolve 1 tsp (5 mL) sugar in ¼ cup (50 mL) lukewarm water. Sprinkle in yeast and allow to stand for 10 minutes. This is known as "proofing yeast." If the yeast does not bubble within 10 minutes, it is no longer active.

    Quick-rise instant yeast does not require proofing. It is simply mixed with the other dry ingredients. It also takes less time to rise than active dry yeast, so the traditional first rising is replaced by a 15-minute resting period.

Tip

One package (¼ oz/8 g) of active dry yeast is equivalent to 2¼ tsp (11 mL).

BREAD MACHINE YEAST

This form of yeast is specifically designed for use in bread machines. It is instant dry yeast and can be used in all your bread baking. Mix it directly into the dry ingredients.

Baking Soda

Baking soda is the chemical sodium bicarbonate. When combined with acids, such as yogurt, buttermilk, fruit juice or even chocolate, baking soda creates bubbles of carbon dioxide that cause batter and dough to rise. Batters that contain baking soda should be baked as soon as they are mixed because it starts to act as soon as it comes into contact with an acid. If left to sit, its leavening power will have exhausted itself by the time the batter reaches the oven.

Baking Powder

Baking powder is baking soda combined with an acid, so it works better as a leaven in batters that are low in acidity. Keep baking powder tightly covered in a cool, dry place and replace it every 6 months to ensure it maintains its potency.

Dairy Products

The recipes in this book were tested using 2% **milk,** the most commonly used dairy product. You can also use whole milk (homogenized), low-fat (1%) and nonfat (skim) milk, although your results will vary slightly because of the different fat contents. If you're lactose intolerant, substitute an equal amount of lactose-reduced milk.

Buttermilk, which is made from low-fat milk and a bacterial culture, is particularly useful in batters that require a bit of acidity,

Tip
Check your baking powder and baking soda regularly to make sure they are still active. Stir 1 tsp (5 mL) of baking powder into ½ cup (125 mL) hot water. If it does not bubble immediately, throw it out. To test baking soda, stir 1 tsp (5 mL) into 2 tbsp (25 mL) white vinegar. If it does not bubble, discard it.

which helps to produce a tender crumb. You can find buttermilk in the dairy case of your supermarket or you can make your own. For 1 cup (250 mL) buttermilk, mix 1 tbsp (15 mL) vinegar or lemon juice with enough milk to make 1 cup (250 mL); let stand for 5 minutes, then stir.

Two kinds of **cream** also appear in some of the recipes in this book: half-and-half cream, which has a 10% milk fat (M.F.) content, and whipping cream, which has 35% M.F. and is also called heavy cream. Table cream, which has 18% M.F., can be used in recipes that call for half-and-half or light cream, but it should not be substituted in recipes that call for whipping cream.

Evaporated milk is a canned product made by evaporating milk to half its volume. It has a mild caramel taste and comes in whole or low-fat versions. Mixed with an equal amount of water, evaporated milk can be substituted for milk.

Sweetened condensed milk is evaporated milk that has been reduced further and sweetened. It is available in whole and low-fat versions. All the recipes in this book were tested using the whole (or regular) version.

Regular **sour cream** is about 14% M.F., and all the recipes in this book have been tested using 14% M.F. sour cream. Sour cream is also available in low-fat and nonfat versions. Use regular or low-fat sour cream for baking. We don't recommend the nonfat variety, as it can sometimes result in poor texture and quality of baked goods.

Some of the recipes call for **yogurt**, which is available in plain and flavored varieties, with a range of fat contents. As with sour cream, don't use the nonfat type for baking.

Cream cheese is often used in baking, most commonly for cheesecake. These recipes have been tested using full-fat cream cheese. However, you can usually substitute a lower-fat version, if desired. For smooth blending, use blocks of cream cheese that have been softened to room temperature. Do not use tubs of soft, spreadable cream cheese unless specified in the recipe.

Chocolate

Chocolate is one of the most popular ingredients in baking. In fact, it is second only to vanilla as a flavoring and is a must-have ingredient that no baker should ever be without. Because it is so popular, consumers can now choose from a wide variety of chocolate products, which can make it difficult to know what to buy.

Basically, the quality of chocolate is determined by the blend of cocoa beans used to make it, the roasting and processing methods, and the percentage of chocolate liquor (not alcohol) it contains. The best varieties contain at least 70 per cent chocolate liquor. Chocolate varies dramatically in flavor and texture. Taste it to determine the brand that suits you best. Some cooks use different brands of chocolate for different products — one for cakes, another for cookies, a third for puddings and custards, and so on.

Always keep a supply of semi-sweet, bittersweet and unsweetened squares on hand for chopping, grating or melting in recipes. Chocolate chips, which are formulated to soften but hold their shape during baking, should also be a pantry staple. In general, chocolate chips are used in and on top of cakes and cookies, while squares are used for melting.

White chocolate, a blend of sugar, cocoa butter, milk solids and vanilla, is not really chocolate but has become a popular ingredient in baking. It is available in squares and chips.

Cocoa Powder

Cocoa powder is a dry unsweetened powder made from chocolate liquor with most of the cocoa butter removed. There are several kinds of cocoa on the market. When baking, use natural cocoa or Dutch-process cocoa, not one of the sweetened versions, which are made for drinking. Because cocoa tends to clump during storage, it should be measured then sifted before using. If you run out of unsweetened chocolate, 1 oz (28 g) of unsweetened chocolate can be replaced with 3 tbsp (45 mL) cocoa powder plus 1 tbsp (15 mL) butter, margarine or shortening.

Melting Chocolate

Chocolate is fussy about how it is melted, and if it isn't treated appropriately, it will "seize," leaving you with an unusable glob. However, as long as you follow instructions and ensure that the chocolate does not come into contact with water in the process of melting, you should be successful. (It's OK to melt chocolate in a liquid such as cream as long as the hard chocolate is placed in the liquid before the melting process begins.)

Basically, chocolate can be melted three different ways. In all cases, coarsely chop the chocolate before heating. The safest (and slowest) way is to melt the pieces in the top of a double boiler or a bowl set over hot (not boiling) water, stirring frequently, until the chocolate is smooth and melted. Or you can place the pieces in a small saucepan and melt them over low heat, stirring constantly, until the mixture is smooth. Many cooks find a microwave oven useful for this job. Place the chopped chocolate in a microwaveable bowl and heat at Medium (50%) until almost melted, about 1 minute per ounce (28 g). (Times will vary with microwave power.) Remove from microwave and stir until the chunks are completely melted. Be sure not to cover chocolate when melting, as this will create steam, which will cause the chocolate to seize.

STORING CHOCOLATE

Unsweetened, semi-sweet and bittersweet chocolates will keep for up to 2 years in a cool place. White chocolate, which contains dairy solids, should be used more quickly than that. Store chocolate in the refrigerator only as a last resort.

Tip

To make chocolate curls, heat a chocolate square in the microwave for 10 seconds, just until it's warm but not melted. Using a vegetable peeler, shave to make curls.

Nuts

Nuts add flavor and texture to many baked goods. However, because they are high in fat, they spoil quickly. Consequently, we recommend you store them in the freezer to keep them fresh. When you're ready to use them, let them thaw and use as directed — or, for optimum flavor, toast before using in a recipe.

To toast nuts: Spread nuts in a single layer on a baking sheet. Bake at 350°F (180°C) for 5 to 10 minutes, stirring often, until golden and fragrant. Chopped nuts will take less time to toast than whole nuts. For hazelnuts, rub off skins in a tea towel while warm. The weight equivalent of 1 cup (250 mL) lightly toasted nuts is approximately 3.8 oz (100 g).

Tip
Because nuts spoil so quickly, always purchase them from a source with rapid turnover such as a natural or bulk foods store. To ensure freshness, make a point of tasting before you buy.

Measuring Nuts

When indicating quantities of nuts to be used, the recipes in this book specify that the nuts are chopped first, then measured. This means the ingredient reads: *½ cup (125 mL) finely chopped almonds,* not *½ cup (125 mL) almonds, finely chopped.* In the second notation, the nuts would be measured, then chopped. "Finely chopped" means the nuts should be chopped to a uniform size of less than ⅛ inch (3 mm) in diameter.

Coconut

Like nuts, coconut should be stored in the freezer, and its flavor improves when it is toasted. Flaked or shredded coconut both work well in baking. Whether you use sweetened or unsweetened is a matter of choice — they are interchangeable in recipes.
To toast coconut: Spread in a single layer on a cookie sheet. Bake at 350°F (180°C) for about 5 minutes, stirring often, until it begins to brown. Watch carefully, as coconut burns quickly.

Flavorings

The two most common flavorings used in baking are vanilla and almond extract. Although they are more expensive, we recommend the use of pure extracts, which produce much better results than their artificial counterparts. Extracts should be at room temperature when they are added to ingredients.

Spices

Spices are essential to the success of many recipes, and you should always have a good selection on hand. To make the recipes in this book, you'll need allspice, cinnamon, cloves, nutmeg and ginger. For the savories, make sure you have black pepper, oregano, paprika, rosemary, thyme and savory. Store your spices in tightly sealed glass containers in a cool dark place. Once spices are ground, they lose their potency quite quickly. Consequently, we recommend you buy them in small amounts and replace them within 6 to 9 months.

Fruit

Fruit is a great addition to many recipes. Fresh fruit in season is usually the ideal, but if it is unavailable, canned or frozen fruit can usually be substituted.

Keep a supply of the common types of **canned fruit**, such as pineapple (crushed, chunks and rings), apricots, peaches and mandarins, in your pantry. When using canned fruit, be aware that the proportion of solid fruit to liquid will vary from brand to brand, as will the size of fruit pieces, and this may affect the quantity required.

Frozen fruit, such as rhubarb and berries, can be purchased as needed. Cranberries are a great addition to many breads and desserts but they can be hard to find during the summer. As a result, we recommend that you keep a few bags in your freezer.

Keep **dried fruit**, such as raisins, apricots, cranberries and dates on hand for general baking and buy specialty items, such as candied fruit, for holiday baking or as needed.

Tip
Because the flavor of freshly ground black pepper is so superior to the pre-ground variety, we recommend that you buy whole peppercorns and invest in a good pepper mill.

Tip
To extend the shelf life of dried fruit, store it in an airtight container in the refrigerator.

Tip

Fruits may sink in a batter if it is not stiff enough. Chopping fruits finely and tossing them in flour to coat will help keep them suspended in batters.

Fresh Fruit Yields

Often recipes call for a quantity such as 1 tsp (5 mL) lemon zest or 1 cup (250 mL) mashed bananas. To make your baking easier, we've provided some measured yields for fresh fruits commonly used in baking.

Lemons: One medium lemon yields about $1/4$ cup (50 mL) juice and 2 tsp (10 mL) grated zest.

Oranges: Two or three medium oranges yield about 1 cup (250 mL) juice and 3 tbsp (45 mL) grated zest.

Apples: One pound (500 g) or three medium apples yield about 2 cups (500 mL) chopped cored apples.

Bananas: One pound or two or three large bananas yield about 1 cup (250 mL) mashed bananas.

Strawberries or raspberries: One pound (500 g) contains about 4 cups (1 L) whole, 3 cups (750 mL) sliced or 2 cups (500 mL) crushed berries.

Emergency Substitution Tables

Whenever possible, use ingredients that the recipe calls for. But in a pinch, here are some substitutions you can use to avoid a last-minute trip to the store.

Leavens

1 tsp (5 mL) baking powder =
¼ tsp (1 mL) baking soda *plus*
½ tsp (2 mL) cream of tartar

1 tsp (5 mL) double-acting baking powder =
1½ tsp (7 mL) single-acting baking powder
(phosphate or tartrate)

Flour

1 cup (250 mL) all-purpose flour, without sifting =
1 cup (250 mL) plus 2 tbsp (30 mL)
cake-and-pastry flour, without sifting

1 cup (250 mL) cake-and-pastry flour, without sifting =
1 cup (250 mL) minus 2 tbsp (30 mL) all-purpose
flour, without sifting

1 cup (250 mL) self-rising flour, without sifting =
1 cup (250 mL) all-purpose flour *plus* 1½ tsp (7 mL)
baking powder *plus* ½ tsp (2 mL) salt

1 cup (250 mL) whole wheat flour =
1 cup (250 mL) all-purpose flour

Sweeteners

1 cup (250 mL) granulated sugar =
1 cup (250 mL) firmly packed brown sugar

corn syrup =
equal amount of maple syrup

1 cup (250 mL) honey =
1¼ cups (300 mL) granulated sugar
plus ¼ cup (50 mL) liquid

Chocolate

1 square (1 oz/28 g) unsweetened chocolate =
3 tbsp (45 mL) cocoa powder *plus* 1 tbsp (15 mL)
shortening, butter or margarine

Dairy Products

1 cup (250 mL) butter =
1 cup (250 mL) firm margarine
OR
1 cup (250 mL) shortening plus 2 tbsp (30 mL) water

1 cup (250 mL) buttermilk or soured milk =
1 tbsp (15 mL) lemon juice or vinegar *plus* whole
milk to make 1 cup (250 mL)
(let stand for 5 minutes before using)

1 cup (250 mL) whole milk =
½ cup (125 mL) evaporated milk *plus*
½ cup (125 mL) water
OR
1 cup (250 mL) skim milk *plus* 2 tbsp (30 mL) butter

1 cup (250 mL) buttermilk =
1 cup (250 mL) plain yogurt

1 cup (250 mL) sour cream =
⅞ cup (225 mL) buttermilk or plain yogurt *plus*
3 tbsp (45 mL) butter

1 cup (250 mL) whipping (35%) cream
(for use in cooking, not for whipping) =
¾ cup (175 mL) whole milk *plus*
⅓ cup (75 mL) butter

Cereals and Grains

1 cup (250 mL) fine dry bread crumbs =
¾ cup (175 mL) cracker crumbs

¼ cup (50 mL) dry bread crumbs =
1 slice of bread

½ cup (125 mL) soft bread crumbs =
1 slice of bread

¼ cup (50 mL) dry bread crumbs (for mixing
with ground meats) =
¾ cup (175 mL) rolled oats

Egg

1 whole egg =
2 egg whites

Tomato Products

4 medium tomatoes, chopped =
2¼ cups (550 mL) canned tomatoes, including juice

1⅓ cups (325 mL) chopped fresh tomatoes, lightly simmered =
1 cup (250 mL) canned tomatoes

1 cup (250 mL) tomato juice =
½ cup (125 mL) tomato sauce *plus*
½ cup (125 mL) water

2 cups (500 mL) tomato sauce =
¾ cup (175 mL) tomato paste *plus*
1 cup (250 mL) water

1 cup (250 mL) ketchup or chili sauce =
1 cup (250 mL) tomato sauce *plus* ¼ cup (50 mL) sugar *plus* 2 tbsp (30 mL) vinegar

1 tbsp (15 mL) tomato paste =
1 tbsp (15 mL) ketchup

Seasonings

1 medium onion =
1 tbsp (15 mL) minced dried onion
OR
1 tsp (5 mL) onion powder

1 clove garlic =
⅛ tsp (0.5 mL) garlic powder
OR
1 tsp (5 mL) garlic salt (reduce salt in recipe by ½ tsp/2 mL)

1 tbsp (15 mL) fresh herbs =
1 tsp (5 mL) crushed dried herbs

1 tbsp (15 mL) chopped fresh chives =
1 tbsp (15 mL) chopped green onion tops

1 tsp (5 mL) lemon juice =
½ tsp (2 mL) vinegar

1 tbsp (15 mL) prepared mustard =
1 tsp (5 mL) dry mustard

1 drop hot pepper sauce =
pinch cayenne or red pepper

2 tbsp (30 mL) soy sauce =
1 tbsp (15 mL) Worcestershire sauce
plus 2 tsp (10 mL) water

1½ tsp (7 mL) Worcestershire sauce =
1 tbsp (15 mL) soy sauce *plus* dash hot pepper sauce

1 tsp (5 mL) allspice =
½ tsp (2 mL) cinnamon *plus* pinch ground cloves

1 tbsp (15 mL) chopped gingerroot =
1 tsp (5 mL) dried ginger
OR
1 tbsp (15 mL) candied ginger with sugar washed off

Miscellaneous

1 tbsp (15 mL) cornstarch, for thickening =
2 tbsp (30 mL) all-purpose flour in sauces and gravies

½ cup (125 mL) raisins =
½ cup (125 mL) dried cranberries OR plumped pitted prunes OR dates, chopped

2¼ tsp (11 mL) active dry yeast =
1 package active dry yeast
OR
1 compressed yeast cake

COOKIES

◄ *Triple Chocolate Cookies and Chocolate Almond Macaroon Logs*

Triple Chocolate Cookies

**MAKES ABOUT
4 DOZEN COOKIES**

Preparation: 20 minutes
Baking: 10 minutes
Freezing: excellent

Three chocolates in one cookie! Try these cookies warm, then again, after they have cooled — if there are any left.

Tips

Chocolate chips can develop a whitish coating when stored. Don't worry — it disappears with baking.

Use cooking spray or a light coating of shortening to grease cookie sheets. Do not use butter, as it will burn. You don't have to regrease sheets between batches, but do wipe off any crumbs or sugar with a paper towel.

- *Preheat oven to 375°F (190°C)*
- *Cookie sheet, greased*

1 cup	butter, softened	250 mL
¾ cup	packed brown sugar	175 mL
½ cup	granulated sugar	125 mL
1	egg	1
2 tsp	vanilla	10 mL
1⅔ cups	Robin Hood All-Purpose Flour	400 mL
⅓ cup	unsweetened cocoa powder, sifted	75 mL
1 tsp	baking soda	5 mL
½ tsp	salt	2 mL
1 cup	semi-sweet chocolate chips	250 mL
1 cup	milk chocolate chips	250 mL
1 cup	coarsely chopped pecans	250 mL

1. Cream butter in a large bowl on medium speed of electric mixer until light. Gradually beat in brown and granulated sugars, egg and vanilla until smooth. Combine flour, cocoa powder, baking soda and salt. Gradually add to creamed mixture, beating on low speed until blended. Stir in semi-sweet and milk chocolate chips and pecans.

2. Drop dough by tablespoonfuls (15 mL), about 2 inches (5 cm) apart, on prepared cookie sheet. Bake for 8 to 10 minutes or until set. Cool for 5 minutes on sheet, then transfer to rack and cool completely.

Variation

Vary the kind of chips and nuts to suit your taste.

Chocolate Almond Macaroon Logs

If you like coconut, you'll love these cookies, which have the texture and taste of a mini candy bar.

Tips

Use flaked or shredded coconut for the best texture.

Store coconut in the freezer to keep it fresh. It tends to dry out quickly.

Don't be surprised: the egg whites are not beaten until stiff as they are in many macaroon recipes.

- *Preheat oven to 350°F (180°C)*
- *Cookie sheet, lined with parchment paper*

3 cups	flaked coconut	750 mL
½ cup	granulated sugar	125 mL
6 tbsp	Robin Hood All-Purpose Flour	90 mL
4	egg whites	4
1 tsp	vanilla	5 mL
½ cup	finely chopped almonds	125 mL
2	squares (each 1 oz/28 g) semi-sweet chocolate, melted	2

1. Combine coconut, sugar and flour in a large bowl. Add egg whites and vanilla. Mix well. Stir in almonds.
2. Shape heaping tablespoonfuls (20 mL) of mixture into logs and place on prepared cookie sheet.
3. Bake for 8 to 12 minutes or until golden around edges. Cool cookies completely on sheets, then remove from pan.
4. Dip ends of cooled cookies in melted chocolate. Place on waxed paper. Chill until chocolate is set, about 5 minutes.

Variation

Omit chocolate or dip one end of each cookie in white chocolate and the other in semi-sweet.

Chocolate Eclipse Cookies

**MAKES ABOUT
5 DOZEN COOKIES**

Preparation: 20 minutes
Baking: 12 minutes
Freezing: excellent

*The blend of light and dark
dough gives these cookies
tremendous eye appeal.
They taste good, too.*

Tips

If you prefer a chewy texture,
underbake these cookies by
about 2 minutes. They will
become quite crisp if you
extend the baking time
by about 2 minutes.

Don't forget to leave room
on the cookie sheet for
spreading. Cookies,
particularly those made
with butter, flatten and
spread during baking.

Don't improvise when
trying a new recipe. Read it
through carefully and follow
the instructions to the letter.
You can make it your own
next time.

- *Preheat oven to 375°F (190°C)*
- *Cookie sheet, ungreased*

1 cup	butter, softened	250 mL
1 cup	granulated sugar	250 mL
1 cup	packed brown sugar	250 mL
2	eggs	2
1 tsp	vanilla	5 mL
2½ cups	Robin Hood All-Purpose Flour	625 mL
1 tsp	baking soda	5 mL
¼ tsp	salt	1 mL
¾ cup	semi-sweet chocolate chips, melted	175 mL
1 cup	semi-sweet chocolate chips	250 mL
1 cup	white chocolate chips	250 mL

1. Beat butter, sugars, eggs and vanilla until light and creamy.

2. Combine flour, baking soda and salt. Gradually add to creamed mixture, beating until blended. Divide dough in half. Stir melted chocolate and semi-sweet chocolate chips into one portion of dough. Stir white chocolate chips into the other.

3. To shape, take small spoonful of each dough and roll together into a 1-inch (2.5 cm) ball. Place about 2 inches (5 cm) apart on cookie sheet.

4. Bake for 8 to12 minutes or until set. Cool for 5 minutes on sheet, then transfer to rack and cool completely.

Variations

Add 1 tsp (5 mL) grated orange zest to one portion of dough.

Add ½ cup (125 mL) chopped nuts to one portion of dough.

Chocolate Butterscotch Almond Crisps

*This crispy, crunchy cookie
has a great butterscotch taste.
What more could you want?*

Tips

Crisp rice cereal, such as
Rice Krispies, works well in
cookies. It stays crisp during
baking and adds an
appealing crunch to every
bite. Crushed cornflakes
produce a similar result.

Be sure to use fresh chips.
They melt much more easily
than stale ones.

Cool cookies completely
before storing, and pack
similar cookies together.
You don't want to mix moist
and dry cookies, as dry
cookies will absorb moisture
and become soft, and you
don't want strong flavors
like ginger to mix with
subtle, buttery shortbread.

- *Preheat oven to 375°F (190°C)*
- *Cookie sheet, ungreased*

½ cup	milk chocolate chips	125 mL
½ cup	butter, softened	125 mL
⅔ cup	packed brown sugar	150 mL
1	egg	1
1 tsp	vanilla	5 mL
1⅓ cups	Robin Hood All-Purpose Flour	325 mL
1 tsp	baking soda	5 mL
¼ tsp	salt	1 mL
1½ cups	crisp rice cereal	375 mL
1 cup	butterscotch chips	250 mL
½ cup	slivered almonds	125 mL

1. Heat milk chocolate chips in small saucepan over low heat, stirring constantly, until smooth and melted.

2. Beat butter, brown sugar, egg and vanilla until thoroughly blended. Stir in melted chocolate.

3. Combine flour, baking soda and salt. Gradually add to butter mixture, mixing until smooth. Stir in cereal, butterscotch chips and almonds. Mix well.

4. Shape dough into 1-inch (2.5 cm) balls. Place on cookie sheet, about 2 inches (5 cm) apart. Flatten slightly with a fork dipped in sugar. Bake for 10 to 14 minutes or until light golden. Cool for 5 minutes on sheet, then transfer to rack and cool completely.

Variation

Use butterscotch chips in place of the milk chocolate chips for a stronger butterscotch flavor.

Chunky Chocolate Almond Cookies

These chunky, nutty cookies are a delightful treat. Don't count on them lasting too long.

Tips

Bake cookies in the center of the oven to ensure that the tops and bottoms are evenly browned. If the cookies at the back of the oven are browning more quickly than those in front, your oven bakes unevenly. Turn the sheet around halfway through baking.

To store cookies, cool completely, then pack in single layers in an airtight container, spreading waxed paper between each layer to prevent sticking.

- *Preheat oven to 375°F (190°C)*
- *Cookie sheet, ungreased*

1 cup	butter, softened	250 mL
¾ cup	packed brown sugar	175 mL
½ cup	granulated sugar	125 mL
1	egg	1
1 tsp	vanilla	5 mL
2 cups	Robin Hood All-Purpose Flour	500 mL
1 tsp	baking soda	5 mL
¼ tsp	salt	1 mL
10	squares (each 1 oz/28 g) semi-sweet chocolate, chopped	10
¾ cup	slivered almonds	175 mL

1. Beat butter, sugars, egg and vanilla in a large bowl on medium speed of electric mixer until light and creamy.

2. Combine flour, baking soda and salt. Add to creamed mixture, beating on low speed until blended. Stir in chocolate and almonds.

3. Drop dough by heaping tablespoonfuls (20 mL), about 2 inches (5 cm) apart, onto prepared cookie sheet. Bake for 10 to 12 minutes or until light golden. Cool for 5 minutes on sheet, then transfer to rack and cool completely.

Variations

Replace chopped chocolate with 2 cups (500 mL) chocolate chips.

Replace almonds with pecans or walnuts.

Hazelnut Biscotti

**MAKES ABOUT
30 BISCOTTI**

Preparation: 20 minutes
Baking: 50 minutes
Freezing: excellent

*Enjoy biscotti dipped in a
steaming cup of cappuccino
or hot chocolate for a great
treat any time of the day.*

Tips

If using ground nuts in a
dough or batter, grind them
with a small amount of the
flour called for in the recipe.
This helps keep them
from clumping together.

The hard texture of biscotti
makes them ideal for storage,
which means you can bake
them ahead for convenience.

Be sure to bake biscotti
thoroughly to achieve the
right hard, dry texture.
Otherwise, they will soften
and become slightly chewy
when stored.

Biscotti make a wonderful
hostess gift. Pack them
standing up in a large mug
or glass jar tied with a
colorful ribbon.

For added taste and
presentation flair, dip both
ends of the biscotti in
melted chocolate.

- *Preheat oven to 350°F (180°C)*
- *Cookie sheet, greased*

2	eggs	2
¾ cup	granulated sugar	175 mL
½ cup	vegetable oil	125 mL
1 tbsp	grated lemon zest	15 mL
1 tsp	vanilla	5 mL
2 cups	Robin Hood All-Purpose Flour	500 mL
⅓ cup	ground hazelnuts	75 mL
1¼ tsp	baking powder	6 mL
¼ tsp	salt	1 mL
1 cup	coarsely chopped hazelnuts	250 mL

1. Beat eggs, sugar, oil, lemon zest and vanilla until smooth and blended.

2. Combine flour, ground hazelnuts, baking powder and salt. Add to egg mixture, stirring until blended. Add chopped nuts. Knead until dough is smooth and holds together. (There are a lot of nuts, so work them in well with your hands. The dough comes together quite easily.)

3. Divide dough in half. Shape each half into a log about 6 inches (15 cm) long. Place about 4 inches (10 cm) apart on prepared cookie sheet. Flatten logs until they are 3 inches (7.5 cm) wide, leaving top slightly rounded.

4. Bake for 30 minutes or until light golden. Remove from oven. Cool on rack for 15 minutes. Transfer to a cutting board. Cut into ½-inch (1 cm) thick slices. Arrange cut side up on cookie sheet and bake for 10 minutes longer. Turn slices over and bake for 5 to 10 minutes longer or until golden and crisp. Cool for 5 minutes on sheet, then transfer to rack and cool completely. Store in an airtight container for up to 2 weeks.

Variation

Replace hazelnuts with almonds, and vanilla with ½ tsp (2 mL) almond extract.

Chocoholic's Dream Cookies

The next time you need a gift for a chocolate lover, bake a batch of these mouthwatering cookies instead of buying a box of chocolates.

Tips

Be careful not to overbake these cookies. They will firm up as they cool.

Toasting nuts before baking improves their flavor. Spread nuts out in a single layer on a baking sheet and bake at 350°F (180°C) for 10 minutes, or less if using chopped nuts, watching carefully and stirring often. Cool before using.

Pack completely cooled cookies in single layers in an airtight container with a sheet of parchment or waxed paper between each layer.

- *Preheat oven to 325°F (160°C)*
- *Cookie sheet, ungreased*

6	squares (each 1 oz/28 g) semi-sweet chocolate, chopped	6
4	squares (each 1 oz/28 g) unsweetened chocolate, chopped	4
6 tbsp	butter	90 mL
1¼ cups	granulated sugar	300 mL
3	eggs	3
1 tsp	vanilla	5 mL
1 cup	Robin Hood All-Purpose Flour	250 mL
1 tsp	baking powder	5 mL
¼ tsp	salt	1 mL
2 cups	coarsely chopped nuts	500 mL

1. Heat semi-sweet chocolate, unsweetened chocolate and butter in a medium saucepan over low heat, stirring until smooth. Remove from heat. Stir in sugar. Add eggs, one at a time, beating after each addition. Stir in vanilla.

2. Combine flour, baking powder and salt. Gradually add to chocolate mixture, mixing until blended. Stir in nuts.

3. Drop dough by tablespoonfuls (15 mL), about 2 inches (5 cm) apart, onto cookie sheet. Bake for 12 to 14 minutes or until set. Cool for 5 minutes on sheet, then transfer to rack and cool completely.

Variations

Any nuts work well in this recipe.

Omit nuts if desired, but remember you'll end up with fewer cookies.

Peanut Butter Cookies

**MAKES ABOUT
5 DOZEN COOKIES**

Preparation: 25 minutes
Baking: 15 minutes
Freezing: excellent

*No cookbook is complete
without this old-fashioned
favorite.*

Tips

Use smooth, creamy peanut
butter for baking cookies.
If you prefer a nutty texture,
add chopped peanuts
(see Variation).

For a change, use a potato
masher to make an attractive
design on top of the cookies,
instead of the traditional
crisscross fork pattern.

Top each cookie with a
peanut before baking.

Make cookie sandwiches by
spreading raspberry jam or
Peanut Butter Frosting (see
recipe, right) on the bottom
of one cookie and placing
a second cookie on top,
bottom side down.

If you have leftover frosting,
store it in the refrigerator
for up to 2 weeks. Bring
to room temperature
before using.

If you're using this frosting
on a cake, sprinkle chopped
peanuts on the top and/or
sides of the cake for
added crunch.

* *Preheat oven to 375°F (190°C)*
* *Cookie sheet, ungreased*

1 cup	butter, softened	250 mL
1 cup	smooth peanut butter	250 mL
1 cup	granulated sugar	250 mL
1 cup	packed brown sugar	250 mL
2	eggs	2
2½ cups	Robin Hood All-Purpose Flour	625 mL
2 tsp	baking soda	10 mL
¼ tsp	salt	1 mL

1. Cream butter, peanut butter and sugars until light and creamy. Beat in eggs, one at a time, mixing well after each addition.

2. Combine flour, baking soda and salt. Add to creamed mixture, beating until blended. Shape dough into 1-inch (2.5 cm) balls. Place on cookie sheet. Press flat with a fork dipped in sugar or flour.

3. Bake for 12 to 15 minutes or until set and golden. Cool for 5 minutes on sheet, then transfer to rack and cool completely.

Variation

Stir ½ cup (125 mL) finely chopped peanuts into the dough after the dry ingredients have been added.

Peanut Butter Frosting

* *Makes about 3 cups (750 mL) frosting*
* *Enough to fill and frost a 9-inch (23 cm) 2-layer cake*

⅔ cup	creamy peanut butter	150 mL
3½ cups	icing sugar, sifted	875 mL
½ to ⅔ cup	milk	125 to 150 mL

1. In a large mixer bowl, on medium speed of electric mixer, beat peanut butter until creamy. Gradually add icing sugar alternately with milk, beating until smooth and creamy.

Nice 'n' Nutty Refrigerator Cookies

With a roll or two of this dough in your fridge, you'll be able to bake delicious cookies at a moment's notice.

Tips

Small plastic-wrap boxes work well for shaping square cookies. Line the box with plastic wrap and pack the dough firmly into it.

For perfectly round cookies, wash and dry frozen juice containers and fill with dough. When you're ready to bake, remove the bottom of the container, push the chilled dough out and slice.

If nut allergies are a problem, replace the nuts in this recipe with candied fruit or mini chocolate chips.

Dark and nonstick cookie sheets bake faster. Always set your timer for the minimum time. You can return the cookies to the oven if they are underbaked.

Store rolls of dough in the refrigerator for up to 3 months or the freezer for up to 6 months.

- *Preheat oven to 375°F (190°C)*
- *Cookie sheet, ungreased*

1 cup	butter, softened	250 mL
1 cup	granulated sugar	250 mL
2	eggs	2
1½ tsp	vanilla	7 mL
2½ cups	Robin Hood All-Purpose Flour	625 mL
1 tsp	baking powder	5 mL
½ tsp	baking soda	2 mL
¼ tsp	salt	1 mL
½ cup	each chopped almonds, pecans and hazelnuts	125 mL

1. Beat butter, sugar, eggs and vanilla until light and creamy. Combine flour, baking powder, baking soda and salt. Add to creamed mixture gradually, mixing until smooth. Stir in nuts.

2. Shape dough into two rolls, each about 1½ inches (4 cm) in diameter. Wrap in waxed paper or plastic wrap and chill overnight.

3. Cut roll into ¼-inch (5 mm) slices. Place 2 inches (5 cm) apart on cookie sheet. Bake for 8 to 12 minutes or until light golden. Cool for 5 minutes on sheet, then transfer to rack and cool completely.

Variation

Any nut works well in this recipe. Use your favorites, keeping the total amount at 1½ cups (375 mL).

Peanut Butter Oatmeal Cookies

*An abundance of nuts makes
these cookies a healthy choice
for children's snacks.*

Tips

To add more fiber, substitute
Robin Hood Whole Wheat
Flour for the all-purpose.

For an even more nutritious
cookie, substitute dried fruit,
such as raisins or cranberries,
for the chips.

Choose light-color cookie
sheets with low or no sides
for even baking. Dark ones
absorb more heat and may
cause cookies to overbrown
on the bottom.

• *Preheat oven to 375°F (190°C)*
• *Cookie sheet, ungreased*

¾ cup	butter, softened	175 mL
½ cup	creamy peanut butter	125 mL
1 cup	granulated sugar	250 mL
½ cup	packed brown sugar	125 mL
2	eggs	2
1 tsp	vanilla	5 mL
1¼ cups	Robin Hood All-Purpose Flour	300 mL
1 tsp	baking powder	5 mL
½ tsp	baking soda	2 mL
2 cups	Robin Hood or Old Mill Oats	500 mL
1 cup	semi-sweet chocolate chips	250 mL
1 cup	coarsely chopped pecans	250 mL

1. Beat butter, peanut butter, sugars, eggs and vanilla until thoroughly blended.

2. Combine flour, baking powder and baking soda. Add to butter mixture gradually, beating until blended. Stir in oats, chocolate chips and pecans. Mix well.

3. Drop dough by heaping tablespoonfuls (20 mL), about 2 inches (5 cm) apart, onto cookie sheet. Bake for 10 to 12 minutes or until golden. Cool for 5 minutes on sheet, then transfer to rack and cool completely.

Variations

Replace semi-sweet chocolate chips with butterscotch or peanut butter chips.

Replace pecans with peanuts.

Super Chunky Peanut Butter Chocolate Cookies

Here's a cookie that looks and tastes just great. The mild peanut butter flavor is enhanced with an abundance of peanuts and chocolate.

Tips

Buy good-quality chocolate to chop for cookies. Cookies are only as good as the ingredients you use to make them.

Bittersweet chocolate has a more intense flavor than semi-sweet, but the two can be used interchangeably.

If you're using nonstick bakeware, be sure to use a spatula that won't scratch the surface, such as one made of plastic, when you remove the cookies.

- *Preheat oven to 350°F (180°C)*
- *Cookie sheet, greased*

1/2 cup	butter, softened	125 mL
1/3 cup	smooth peanut butter	75 mL
3/4 cup	packed brown sugar	175 mL
1/4 cup	granulated sugar	50 mL
1	egg	1
1 tsp	vanilla	5 mL
1 cup	Robin Hood All-Purpose Flour	250 mL
1/2 tsp	baking soda	2 mL
1/4 tsp	salt	1 mL
2 cups	coarsely chopped semi-sweet chocolate (12 oz/375 g)	500 mL
1 cup	coarsely chopped peanuts	250 mL

1. Beat butter, peanut butter, sugars, egg and vanilla until thoroughly blended.

2. Combine flour, baking soda and salt. Gradually add to butter mixture, mixing until smooth. Stir in chocolate and peanuts.

3. Drop dough by heaping tablespoonfuls (20 mL), about 2 inches (5 cm) apart, onto prepared cookie sheet. Bake for 10 to 12 minutes or until golden. Cool for 5 minutes on sheet, then transfer to rack and cool completely.

Variation

Use dark brown sugar rather than golden for a more intense butterscotch taste.

Chewy Peanut Butter Chocolate Chip Cookies

The combination of peanut butter and chocolate is always hard to resist.

Tips

Honey-roasted peanuts give great flavor to cookies.

Cool cookies completely on a wire rack or they will soften when stored.

For a crisper cookie, increase the baking time by 2 minutes.

If you accidentally overbake a batch of cookies but haven't burned them, crumble them and sprinkle over fruit, ice cream or yogurt.

- *Preheat oven to 350°F (180°C)*
- *Cookie sheet, ungreased*

½ cup	butter, softened	125 mL
½ cup	smooth peanut butter	125 mL
½ cup	granulated sugar	125 mL
½ cup	packed brown sugar	125 mL
1	egg	1
1 tsp	vanilla	5 mL
¾ cup	Robin Hood All-Purpose Flour	175 mL
½ tsp	baking soda	2 mL
½ cup	coarsely chopped peanuts	125 mL
½ cup	chocolate chips	125 mL

1. Beat butter, peanut butter, sugars, egg and vanilla until thoroughly blended.

2. Combine flour and baking soda. Add to butter mixture, beating until thoroughly blended. Stir in peanuts and chocolate chips.

3. Drop dough by heaping tablespoonfuls (20 mL), about 2 inches (5 cm) apart, on cookie sheet. If desired, press down lightly with a fork dipped in flour for a patterned look. Bake for 10 to 12 minutes or until golden. Cool for 5 minutes on sheet, then transfer to rack and cool completely.

Variation

For an extra hit of peanut, use peanut butter chips.

White Chocolate Macadamia Nut Cookies

Crisp or chewy, these cookies are every bit as delectable as their photo on page 67 suggests.

Tips

Store flour in the freezer if you don't use it often. At room temperature, the shelf life of all-purpose flour is 1 year. Whole wheat flour stays fresh for only 3 months.

Baked cookies can be frozen for up to 6 months.

- *Preheat oven to 375°F (190°C)*
- *Cookie sheet, greased*

1½ cups	butter, softened	375 mL
1½ cups	packed brown sugar	375 mL
1 cup	granulated sugar	250 mL
2	eggs	2
1 tsp	vanilla	5 mL
3¼ cups	Robin Hood All-Purpose Flour	800 mL
1 tsp	baking soda	5 mL
1 tsp	salt	5 mL
12	squares (each 1 oz/28 g) white chocolate, chopped	12
2 cups	coarsely chopped macadamia nuts	500 mL

1. Beat butter, sugars, eggs and vanilla until thoroughly blended. Combine flour, baking soda and salt. Add to butter mixture, mixing until thoroughly blended. Stir in chocolate and nuts.

2. Drop dough by heaping tablespoonfuls (20 mL), about 2 inches (5 cm) apart, on prepared cookie sheet. Bake for 8 to 12 minutes or until light golden. Cool for 5 minutes on sheet, then transfer to rack and cool completely.

Variation

Use any of your favorite nuts in this recipe. If nut allergies are a problem, omit the nuts completely and add more chocolate (about 1 cup/250 mL, or 5 squares, each 1 oz/28 g, coarsely chopped).

Crisp Butterscotch Oatmeal Cookies

These cookies are ideal for the cookie jar. They stay crisp and make a nutritious treat the whole family can enjoy.

Tips

If you prefer, use Robin Hood Unbleached or Whole Wheat Flour in cookie recipes in the same quantity as all-purpose flour. If you have never used whole wheat flour, you may want to begin by blending it with an equal amount of all-purpose flour. Whole wheat flour gives baked goods a pleasant nutty flavour and a slightly coarse and drier texture.

Crisp cookies are good for shipping. They travel well and stay fresh longer than soft ones. A gift of homemade cookies is always welcome.

There is no egg in this recipe, making these cookies a good choice for people with egg allergies.

- *Preheat oven to 350°F (180°C)*
- *Cookie sheet, greased*

1 cup	butter, softened	250 mL
1 cup	packed brown sugar	250 mL
1/4 cup	water or milk	50 mL
1 tsp	vanilla	5 mL
1 3/4 cups	Robin Hood All-Purpose Flour	425 mL
1/2 tsp	baking soda	2 mL
1/4 tsp	salt	1 mL
2 cups	Robin Hood or Old Mill Oats	500 mL
1 1/2 cups	butterscotch chips	375 mL
1/2 cup	flaked coconut	125 mL

1. Beat butter, brown sugar, water and vanilla in large bowl on medium speed of electric mixer until thoroughly blended.

2. Combine flour, baking soda and salt. Gradually add to butter mixture, beating on low speed until blended. Stir in oats, butterscotch chips and coconut.

3. Drop dough by tablespoonfuls (15 mL), about 2 inches (5 cm) apart, onto prepared cookie sheet. Press flat with fork dipped in sugar or flour. Bake for 15 to 20 minutes or until crisp and golden. Cool for 5 minutes on sheet, then transfer to rack and cool completely.

Variation

Replace butterscotch chips with semi-sweet chocolate chips, dried cranberries or raisins.

Year-Round Shortbread

**MAKES ABOUT
3 DOZEN COOKIES**

Preparation: 25 minutes
Baking: 25 minutes
Freezing:
not recommended

*Although shortbread is
a holiday tradition, it
is delicious any time of
the year.*

Tips

Shortbread is best stored in a cool place or the refrigerator for up to 1 month. Freezing alters its texture.

Always use butter when making shortbread. Margarine just doesn't have the flavor.

Don't make shortbread just at Christmas. Use a variety of cutters to suit different holidays, such as bunnies for Easter and hearts for Valentine's Day.

For best results when making shortbread, use superfine or fruit sugar instead of granulated.

- *Preheat oven to 300°F (150°C)*
- *Cookie sheet, ungreased*

1 cup	butter, softened	250 mL
$\frac{1}{2}$ cup	granulated sugar	125 mL
2 cups	Robin Hood All-Purpose Flour	500 mL
2 tbsp	cornstarch	30 mL

1. Cream butter and sugar in a mixing bowl until light and creamy. Stir in flour and cornstarch. Mix well, then knead with hands, blending in flour thoroughly to form a smooth dough.

2. Roll out dough on lightly floured surface to $\frac{1}{4}$-inch (5 mm) thickness. Cut into desired shapes using cookie cutter dipped in flour. Place on cookie sheet. Sprinkle with colored sugar or decorate as desired with cherries and nuts.

3. Bake for 15 to 25 minutes or until cookies just start to brown around edges. (The time will depend on the size of the cookies.) Cool for 5 minutes on sheet, then transfer to rack and cool completely.

Variation

Add $\frac{1}{2}$ cup (125 mL) finely chopped nuts to the dough.

Candied Ginger Rounds

Preparation: 20 minutes
Chilling: 1 hour
Baking: 12 minutes
Freezing: excellent

*If you like ginger, this is the
cookie for you.*

Tips

Buy crystallized ginger when
you are ready to use it, as
it hardens quickly. Candied
ginger is best when it is
slightly soft and has a strong
ginger flavor. It's usually sold
in the baking section with
other candied fruit.

Use room-temperature butter
for baking. It mixes easily
and will make smoother,
lighter doughs.

Coarse sugar adds a nice
flavour, texture and
appearance to cookie tops.

Bake these cookies until they
are golden all over, not just
around the edges.

If you are concerned about
dietary cholesterol, replace
1 egg with 2 egg whites in
this recipe.

- *Preheat oven to 375°F (190°C)*
- *Cookie sheet, ungreased*

1 cup	butter, softened	250 mL
¾ cup	granulated sugar	175 mL
¾ cup	packed brown sugar	175 mL
2	eggs	2
2¾ cups	Robin Hood All-Purpose Flour	675 mL
1 tsp	baking soda	5 mL
1 tsp	cream of tartar	5 mL
½ tsp	ground ginger	2 mL
¼ tsp	salt	1 mL
½ cup	finely chopped crystallized ginger	125 mL
	Granulated sugar	

1. Cream butter and ¾ cup (175 mL) granulated sugar and brown
   sugar until light and creamy. Add eggs, one at a time, beating
   after each addition.

2. Combine flour, baking soda, cream of tartar, ground ginger and
   salt. Add to creamed mixture gradually, beating until blended.
   Stir in crystallized ginger. Cover and chill dough for 1 hour for
   easy shaping.

3. Shape dough into 1-inch (2.5 cm) balls. Roll in granulated
   sugar. Place on cookie sheet, about 2 inches (5 cm) apart. Bake
   for 8 to 12 minutes or until golden. Cool for 5 minutes on
   sheet, then transfer to rack and cool completely.

Variation

Add ½ cup (125 mL) finely chopped almonds for extra crunch.

Apricot Oat Chews

**MAKES ABOUT
4 DOZEN COOKIES**

Preparation: 20 minutes
Baking: 12 minutes
Freezing: excellent

*This chewy apricot version
of oatmeal cookies is
simply yummy.*

Tips

Oatmeal cookies tend to dry
out when they are stored.
Freeze extras for up to
3 months to keep them fresh.

Use scissors to cut apricots
easily. Spray blades with
cooking spray so the fruit
doesn't stick.

Soluble fiber, found in
foods such as oats and
apples, helps lower levels
of blood cholesterol.

- *Preheat oven to 375°F (190°C)*
- *Cookie sheet, ungreased*

1 cup	butter, softened	250 mL
¾ cup	packed brown sugar	175 mL
½ cup	granulated sugar	125 mL
1	egg	1
½ tsp	almond extract	2 mL
2½ cups	Robin Hood or Old Mill Oats	625 mL
1 cup	Robin Hood All-Purpose Flour	250 mL
1 tsp	baking soda	5 mL
1 cup	chopped dried apricots	250 mL

1. Beat butter, sugars, egg and almond extract until thoroughly blended.
2. Combine oats, flour and baking soda. Add to butter mixture gradually, beating until well blended. Stir in apricots.
3. Drop dough by heaping tablespoonfuls (20 mL), about 2 inches (5 cm) apart, onto cookie sheet. Bake for 8 to 12 minutes or until golden. Cool for 5 minutes on sheet, then transfer to rack and cool completely.

Variation

Add a drizzle of icing for an attractive presentation. Leave these cookies plain for everyday eating or if you're planning to store them.

Oats 'n' Seeds Cookies

Preparation: 20 minutes
Baking: 12 minutes
Freezing: excellent

These nutritious cookies taste as good as they look, making them a healthy choice for the entire family.

Tips

Store wheat germ and whole wheat flour in the freezer to keep the flavor fresh.

Use large-flake oats for a more wholesome look and taste.

Honey makes a softer cookie than one made with granulated sugar. It also has great flavor and keeps well.

Flaxseeds are a great source of soluble fiber and omega-3 fatty acids, both of which may reduce the risk of heart disease. They also contain phytochemicals called lignins, which act as antioxidants and may reduce the risk of cancer.

- *Preheat oven to 375°F (190°C)*
- *Cookie sheet, greased*

1 cup	butter, softened	250 mL
1 cup	packed brown sugar	250 mL
½ cup	liquid honey	125 mL
2	eggs	2
1 tsp	vanilla	5 mL
1½ cups	Robin Hood Whole Wheat Flour	375 mL
½ cup	wheat germ	125 mL
1 tsp	baking soda	5 mL
½ tsp	salt	2 mL
1½ cups	Robin Hood or Old Mill Oats	375 mL
1½ cups	raisins	375 mL
1 cup	chopped walnuts	250 mL
¾ cup	sunflower seeds	175 mL
¼ cup	flaxseeds	50 mL
¼ cup	sesame seeds	50 mL

1. Beat butter, brown sugar, honey, eggs and vanilla until thoroughly blended.

2. Combine flour, wheat germ, baking soda and salt. Add to butter mixture gradually, beating until blended. Stir in oats, raisins, walnuts, sunflower seeds, flaxseeds and sesame seeds. Mix well.

3. Drop dough by heaping tablespoonfuls (20 mL), about 2 inches (5 cm) apart, onto prepared cookie sheet. Bake for 8 to 12 minutes or until golden. Cool for 5 minutes on sheet, then transfer to rack and cool completely.

Variation

Replace raisins with chocolate chips for a more decadent treat.

Cranberry Cereal Crisps

*If you find it difficult to
imagine a cookie that is
delicate enough to melt in
your mouth but chunky and
chewy at the same time, try
these delectable fruit crisps
which are pictured on page 75.*

Tips

You can use either unsalted
or salted butter when baking
cookies and achieve the taste
you are accustomed to. The
advantage to using unsalted
butter is that it allows you to
control the amount of salt
in the recipe.

This recipe makes a big batch
of cookies. They keep well, so
enjoy some now and keep the
rest to satisfy cravings later.

Emphasize cereals, breads
and other grain products, as
well as vegetables and fruits,
in your diet. These foods
contain dietary fiber, vitamins
and minerals — important
nutrients that help you to
be healthy.

- *Preheat oven to 325°F (160°C)*
- *Cookie sheet, ungreased*

1 cup	butter, softened	250 mL
1 cup	granulated sugar	250 mL
1 cup	packed brown sugar	250 mL
1	egg	1
1 cup	vegetable oil	250 mL
1 tsp	vanilla	5 mL
3½ cups	Robin Hood All-Purpose Flour	875 mL
1 tsp	baking soda	5 mL
½ tsp	salt	2 mL
1 cup	Robin Hood or Old Mill Oats	250 mL
2 cups	crisp rice cereal	500 mL
1 cup	dried cranberries	250 mL

1. Beat butter, sugars and egg on medium speed of electric mixer until light and creamy. Stir in oil and vanilla.

2. Combine flour, baking soda and salt. Add to creamed mixture along with oats, mixing on low speed until blended. Stir in cereal and cranberries.

3. Drop dough by heaping tablespoonfuls (20 mL), about 2 inches (5 cm) apart, onto cookie sheet. Bake for 13 to 18 minutes or until golden. Cool for 5 minutes on sheet, then transfer to rack and cool completely.

Variation

Substitute chopped dried apricots for the cranberries.

Breakfast Cereal Crunchies

The goodness of oats and raisins, with the crunch of crisp cereal, makes these cookies a particularly appetizing morning snack.

Tips

When baking cookies, to ensure perfect results, test-bake two cookies. If they spread out too much, stir in a little more flour, about 1 tbsp (15 mL) at a time. If they are dry and crumbly, a little water stirred into the dough, about 1 tbsp (15 mL) at a time, will do the trick.

After opening a package of raisins, put leftovers in a jar with a few pieces of orange or lemon peel. Close the lid tightly and refrigerate. The raisins will stay moist and absorb the pleasant citrus flavor, too.

- *Preheat oven to 350°F (180°C)*
- *Cookie sheet, greased*

¾ cup	butter, softened	175 mL
1¼ cups	packed brown sugar	300 mL
1	egg	1
1 tsp	vanilla	5 mL
1½ cups	Robin Hood All-Purpose Flour	375 mL
½ tsp	baking soda	2 mL
¼ tsp	salt	1 mL
1½ cups	Robin Hood or Old Mill Oats	375 mL
1 cup	raisins	250 mL
¾ cup	crisp rice cereal	175 mL

1. Beat butter, brown sugar, egg and vanilla in a large bowl on medium speed of electric mixer until light and creamy.

2. Combine flour, baking soda and salt. Add to butter mixture gradually, beating on low speed until blended. Stir in oats, raisins and cereal.

3. Drop dough by heaping tablespoonfuls (20 mL), about 2 inches (5 cm) apart, on prepared cookie sheet. Flatten slightly with a fork dipped in flour. Bake for 12 to 15 minutes or until golden. Cool for 5 minutes on sheet, then transfer to rack and cool completely.

Variation

Replace raisins with your favorite dried fruit or a combination of several kinds.

Chunky Chocolate Oatmeal Cookies

*Sweet oatmeal dough loaded
with chunks of chocolate
produces a wholesome yet
decadent cookie.*

Tips

Large-flake oats look and
taste wonderful in these
cookies. They give them
a great homemade
appearance that brings back
childhood memories.

When baking a lot of cookies,
it's helpful to have cookie
sheets without sides and a
supply of parchment paper.
You can line the sheets with
parchment paper, then slip
the paper and cookies off
once the cookies have
finished baking. While one
batch is baking, you can be
preparing the next on a sheet
of parchment spread on the
counter. Slip it onto the first
available cookie sheet
and bake.

- *Preheat oven to 350°F (180°C)*
- *Cookie sheet, greased*

½ cup	butter, softened	125 mL
½ cup	packed brown sugar	125 mL
½ cup	granulated sugar	125 mL
1	egg	1
1 tsp	vanilla	5 mL
1 cup	Robin Hood or Old Mill Oats	250 mL
¾ cup	Robin Hood All-Purpose Flour	175 mL
½ tsp	baking soda	2 mL
¼ tsp	salt	1 mL
2 cups	coarsely chopped semi-sweet chocolate (10 squares, each 1 oz/28 g)	500 mL
1 cup	coarsely chopped pecans	250 mL

1. Beat butter, sugars, egg and vanilla until thoroughly blended.

2. Combine oats, flour, baking soda and salt. Gradually add to butter mixture, mixing until smooth. Stir in chocolate and pecans. Mix well.

3. Drop dough by heaping tablespoonfuls (20 mL), about 2 inches (5 cm) apart, onto prepared cookie sheet. Bake for 10 to 12 minutes or until golden. Cool for 5 minutes on sheet, then transfer to rack and cool completely.

Variations

Replace some or all of the chocolate with dried cranberries.

Almonds, walnuts and hazelnuts are nice alternatives to the pecans.

BARS AND SQUARES

◄ *Chunky Caramel Nut Squares and Chewy Chocolate Brownies*

Chunky Caramel Nut Squares

If you can bear to part with them, these chewy squares, which are chock-full of nuts, make a perfect gift.

Tips

The look and taste of these squares depends entirely on the nuts you use. You can buy mixed nuts, with or without peanuts, or you can make your own mix.

Be sure your butterscotch chips are fresh for easy melting.

- *Preheat oven to 350°F (180°C)*
- *13- by 9-inch (3.5 L) cake pan, greased*

Crust

2 cups	Robin Hood All-Purpose Flour	500 mL
1 cup	packed brown sugar	250 mL
¼ tsp	salt	1 mL
1 cup	butter, softened	250 mL
1	egg yolk	1

Topping

1½ cups	butterscotch chips	375 mL
¾ cup	corn syrup	175 mL
3 tbsp	butter	45 mL
2½ cups	salted mixed nuts (12 oz/375 g)	625 mL

1. *Crust:* Combine flour, brown sugar and salt. Using two knives, a pastry blender or your fingers, cut in butter until mixture resembles coarse crumbs. Stir in egg yolk. Press into prepared pan.

2. Bake for 20 to 25 minutes or until golden. Cool.

3. *Topping:* Combine butterscotch chips, corn syrup and butter in a small saucepan. Cook over low heat, stirring occasionally, until smooth and melted. Cool slightly. Spread over cooled crust and sprinkle with nuts; press nuts gently into topping. Refrigerate until topping is firm, about 1 hour. Cut into squares.

Variation

Chocoholics may prefer semi-sweet chocolate chips in place of the butterscotch.

Chewy Chocolate Brownies

*A dense, moist brownie with
a rich chocolate taste is
every chocoholic's dream.
For a great dessert, cut into
larger squares and serve
slightly warm, topped with
ice cream, and chocolate or
caramel sauce.*

Tips

Use the pan size called for in
the recipe when making bars
and squares. If the pan is too
large, the bars will be thin
and dry. If the pan is too
small, they will not bake
through properly.

Add a chocolate frosting
(see recipes, page 154) for
an indulgent treat. Spread it
on after the brownies have
cooled but before you cut
them into squares.

- *Preheat oven to 350°F (180°C)*
- *9-inch (2.5 L) square cake pan, greased*

½ cup	butter	125 mL
3	squares (each 1 oz/28 g) unsweetened chocolate	3
1¼ cups	granulated sugar	300 mL
1 tsp	vanilla	5 mL
3	eggs	3
⅔ cup	Robin Hood All-Purpose Flour	150 mL
½ tsp	baking powder	2 mL
½ tsp	salt	2 mL
½ cup	chopped pecans or walnuts, optional	125 mL

1. Melt butter and chocolate over low heat in a medium saucepan, stirring until smooth. Remove from heat. Add sugar and vanilla and beat well. Add eggs, one at a time, beating lightly after each addition.

2. Combine flour, baking powder and salt. Add to chocolate mixture, stirring until well blended. Stir in nuts, if using. Spread in prepared pan.

3. Bake for 25 to 30 minutes or until set. Cool completely in pan on rack, then frost, if desired, and cut into squares.

Variation

If you prefer a more cake like brownie, add an extra egg to the batter.

Marbled Cream Cheese Brownies

A creamy white filling marbled through a decadent chocolate brownie makes these squares an extra-special treat.

Tips

The top layer of brownie batter won't completely cover the filling. Don't worry — after marbling and baking, it will be beautiful.

The frosting is more like a chocolate glaze than an icing. You can omit it entirely if time is of the essence or if you're counting calories.

- *Preheat oven to 350°F (180°C)*
- *9-inch (2.5 L) square cake pan, greased*

Filling

4 oz	cream cheese, softened	125 g
2 tbsp	butter, softened	30 mL
¼ cup	granulated sugar	50 mL
1 tbsp	Robin Hood All-Purpose Flour	15 mL
1	egg	1
1 tsp	vanilla	5 mL

Brownie

4	squares (each 1 oz/28 g) semi-sweet chocolate	4
3 tbsp	butter	45 mL
¾ cup	granulated sugar	175 mL
2	eggs	2
½ cup	Robin Hood All-Purpose Flour	125 mL
½ cup	chopped nuts, optional	125 mL
1 tsp	baking powder	5 mL
1 tsp	vanilla	5 mL
¼ tsp	salt	1 mL

Frosting, optional

1 cup	icing sugar	250 mL
1 tbsp	unsweetened cocoa powder	15 mL
2 tbsp	half-and-half or light (10% or 18%) cream	30 mL
1 tbsp	butter, softened	15 mL

1. *Filling:* Beat cream cheese, butter and sugar in a small bowl on low speed of electric mixer until smooth and blended. Add flour, egg and vanilla, beating until blended. Set aside.

2. *Brownie:* Heat chocolate and butter in a small saucepan over low heat, stirring until melted. Remove from heat. Stir in sugar and eggs. Mix thoroughly. Add flour, nuts (if using), baking powder, vanilla and salt, stirring to blend. Spread half of batter in prepared pan. Spread filling on top. Cover evenly with spoonfuls of remaining batter. Swirl mixtures with the tip of a knife just enough to marble.

3. Bake for 35 to 40 minutes or until set. Cool in pan on rack for 20 minutes.

4. *Frosting:* Sift icing sugar and cocoa into a small saucepan. Add cream and butter. Cook over medium-high heat just until mixture starts to boil around the edge of the pan. Remove from heat. Beat with a wooden spoon until mixture starts to dull and is a thin, spreadable consistency. (It will harden when cool.) Spread evenly over warm brownies. Cool completely, then cut into squares.

Cranberry Apricot Almond Squares

Although delicious any time of the year, these tasty squares are particularly nice to have on hand during the holiday season, when they can make a colorful addition to a cookie tray.

Tips

Since ovens are often not accurate in their temperature, a good oven thermometer is a worthwhile investment. Just leave it in the oven, check the temperature and adjust the temperature control accordingly.

When baking, set the timer for the minimum time recommended in a recipe. You can always bake longer but you can't fix items that are overbaked.

If using a glass pan, decrease the oven temperature by 25°F (10°C).

- *Preheat oven to 325°F (160°C)*
- *9-inch (2.5 L) square cake pan, greased*

Crust

½ cup	butter, softened	125 mL
¼ cup	granulated sugar	50 mL
1 cup	Robin Hood All-Purpose Flour	250 mL

Topping

½ cup	dried cranberries	125 mL
½ cup	chopped dried apricots	125 mL
	Water	
2	eggs	2
1 cup	packed brown sugar	250 mL
⅓ cup	Robin Hood All-Purpose Flour	75 mL
½ tsp	baking powder	2 mL
1 tsp	vanilla	5 mL
½ cup	chopped almonds	25 mL

1. *Crust:* Cream butter and granulated sugar until light and creamy. Add flour; mix well. Press into prepared pan.

2. Bake for 15 to 20 minutes or until light golden.

3. *Topping:* Combine cranberries, apricots and enough water to cover in small saucepan. Bring to a boil over low heat and simmer for 10 minutes. Drain well; set aside.

4. Beat eggs and brown sugar until smoothly blended. Stir in flour, baking powder and vanilla. Mix well. Stir in almonds and cranberry-apricot mixture. Spread over warm crust.

5. Bake for 30 to 35 minutes longer. Cool completely in pan on rack, then cut into squares.

Variations

Replace almonds with hazelnuts.

If you prefer an all-apricot version, replace cranberries with apricots.

Apple Squares

Preparation: 25 minutes
Baking: 50 minutes
Freezing:
not recommended

Here's a versatile square that meets many needs. Cut small squares for a cookie tray or larger ones for a pastry tray, or serve warm with ice cream for a great dessert.

Tips

These squares are best enjoyed the same day they are baked. When stored, the moisture comes out of the apples, making the pastry soggy.

Slice apples thinly for even cooking.

If you're a cinnamon fan, increase the amount.

Sprinkle coarse sugar on top before baking or dust with icing sugar after baking for a decorative touch.

For a dessert, top these squares with cinnamon ice cream. To make cinnamon ice cream, stir ground cinnamon into slightly softened vanilla ice cream, then refreeze.

- *Preheat oven to 350°F (180°C)*
- *13- by 9-inch (3.5 L) cake pan, greased*

Crust

1 cup	butter, softened	250 mL
¾ cup	granulated sugar	175 mL
1	egg, beaten	1
1 tsp	vanilla	5 mL
2½ cups	Robin Hood All-Purpose Flour	625 mL
1½ tsp	baking powder	7 mL

Filling

6 cups	thinly sliced peeled apples	1.5 L
¼ cup	granulated sugar	50 mL
1 tsp	ground cinnamon	5 mL

1. *Crust:* Cream butter, sugar, egg and vanilla in large bowl until smooth and creamy. Gradually add flour and baking powder, mixing until blended. Knead lightly to form a smooth dough. Press half of the dough into prepared pan.

2. *Filling:* Combine apples, sugar and cinnamon, tossing to coat apples evenly with cinnamon and sugar. Spread evenly over dough.

3. Divide remaining dough into 10 equal portions and roll into pencil-like strips. Crisscross diagonally over the filling to form a lattice.

4. Bake for 45 to 50 minutes or until apples are tender and crust is firm and golden. Cool completely in pan on rack, then cut into squares.

Variations

Add a touch of nutmeg to the apples to enhance their flavor.

Fruits such as peaches, plums and cherries also work well in this recipe.

Caramel Macadamia Nut Squares

**MAKES ABOUT
2 DOZEN SQUARES**

Preparation: 20 minutes
Cooking: 3 minutes
Baking: 50 minutes
Freezing: excellent

What could be more appetizing than a layer of whole macadamia nuts stuck together with caramel on a shortbread crust? These squares are amazing to look at and even better to eat.

Tips

Use salted macadamia nuts in this recipe. The combination of sweet and salty is fantastic!

For best results, when you are baking, have all the ingredients at room temperature. This makes them easier to mix, as well.

Unless you line the pan completely with parchment paper or well-greased aluminum foil, you will have trouble cutting these bars, because the caramel will stick to the pan.

- *Preheat oven to 350°F (180°C)*
- *8-inch (2 L) square cake pan, lined with parchment paper or greased aluminum foil*

Crust

2/3 cup	butter, softened	150 mL
1/3 cup	granulated sugar	75 mL
1 1/4 cups	Robin Hood All-Purpose Flour	300 mL

Topping

6 tbsp	butter	90 mL
1/4 cup	packed brown sugar	50 mL
1/4 cup	liquid honey	50 mL
1 3/4 cups	salted whole macadamia nuts	425 mL
2 tbsp	whipping (35%) cream	30 mL

1. *Crust:* Cream butter and sugar until smooth and creamy. Gradually add flour, mixing until smooth. Knead lightly, if necessary, to make a smooth dough. Press evenly into prepared pan.

2. Bake for 20 to 25 minutes or until light golden.

3. *Topping:* Combine butter, brown sugar and honey in a medium saucepan. Cook over medium-high heat, stirring constantly, until mixture comes to a full rolling boil. Cook, without stirring, for 1 minute or until slightly thickened and bubbles are large. Remove from heat. Immediately stir in nuts and cream. Mix well. Spread over crust.

4. Bake for 20 to 25 minutes longer or until set and caramel is bubbly. Cool completely in pan on rack, then cut into squares.

Variation

Replace macadamia nuts with cashews, pecans, pine nuts or a mixture of nuts.

White Chocolate Raspberry Squares

Preparation: 20 minutes
Baking: 65 minutes
Freezing: excellent

The combination of white chocolate, raspberry and crunchy almonds is a knockout that's guaranteed to receive compliments.

Tips

White chocolate can be tricky to melt. The temperature must be low, and it needs to be stirred constantly.

Use butter, not margarine, for the best flavor in this creamy delight.

In this recipe, sliced almonds with the skins on are preferable to blanched almonds, as the contrast between the dark and light colors has more eye appeal.

Drizzle some white chocolate over the top to dress these up.

Cut into triangles for a different look. Different shapes add interest and variety to an assorted cookie tray.

Be sure to grease the sides of the pan well, as the jam tends to stick during baking.

- *Preheat oven to 325°F (160°C)*
- *9-inch (2.5 L) square cake pan, greased*

1 cup	white chocolate chips	250 mL
½ cup	butter	125 mL
2	eggs	2
½ cup	granulated sugar	125 mL
1 cup	Robin Hood All-Purpose Flour	250 mL
1 tsp	vanilla	5 mL
¾ cup	raspberry jam	175 mL
1 cup	white chocolate chips	250 mL
¼ cup	sliced almonds	50 mL

1. Heat 1 cup (250 mL) white chocolate chips and butter in a small saucepan over low heat, stirring until melted and smooth; set aside.

2. Beat eggs and sugar in small bowl on high speed of electric mixer until thick and light, about 5 minutes. Stir in melted chocolate mixture, flour and vanilla. Mix on low speed until well blended. Spread half of the batter in prepared pan.

3. Bake for 20 to 25 minutes or until light golden. Cool for 5 minutes. Spread jam on top. Stir 1 cup (250 mL) white chocolate chips into remaining batter. Drop by small spoonfuls evenly over jam. Spread out gently. Sprinkle with almonds.

4. Bake for 40 minutes longer or until set. Cool completely in pan on rack, then cut into squares.

Variation

Replace the raspberry jam with apricot and the almonds with hazelnuts.

Raspberry Coconut Dream Bars

*These chewy bars are a
favorite with kids. They are
a bit on the gooey side, but
that's part of the appeal.*

Tips

When making bars, line pans
with parchment paper or
greased aluminum foil. After
cooling, chill bars until firm,
remove them from the pan
and peel off paper. Place on
a board for easy cutting.

Mix crust in a food processor
for convenience.

Stir jam before using. This
makes it easier to spread
over the crust.

Buy a good-quality jam.
Cheaper jams have more
pectin, which makes them
stiffer and less flavorful.
Remember, baked goods
are only as good as the
ingredients you use to
make them.

- *Preheat oven to 425°F (220°C)*
- *9-inch (2.5 L) square cake pan, greased*

Crust

1 1/3 cups	Robin Hood All-Purpose Flour	325 mL
1/3 cup	granulated sugar	75 mL
1/2 tsp	baking powder	2 mL
1/2 cup	butter	125 mL
1	egg, beaten	1
1/3 cup	raspberry jam	75 mL

Topping

1 cup	packed brown sugar	250 mL
3/4 cup	chopped walnuts	175 mL
3/4 cup	shredded coconut	175 mL
2 tbsp	Robin Hood All-Purpose Flour	30 mL
1 tbsp	lemon juice	15 mL
1 tsp	baking powder	5 mL
2	eggs, beaten	2

1. *Crust:* Combine flour, sugar and baking powder in a mixing bowl. Using two knives, a pastry blender or your fingers, cut in butter until mixture resembles coarse crumbs. Add egg; mix thoroughly. Press mixture evenly into prepared pan.

2. Bake for 10 minutes. Reduce heat to 350°F (180°C). Spread jam over partially baked crust.

3. *Topping:* Combine brown sugar, walnuts, coconut, flour, lemon juice, baking powder and eggs in a bowl. Mix well. Spread evenly over jam.

4. Bake for 20 to 25 minutes longer or until set and golden. Cool completely in pan on rack, then cut into bars.

Variation

If you prefer, substitute strawberry, peach or pineapple jam for the raspberry.

Raspberry Lattice Bars

**MAKES ABOUT
30 BARS**

Preparation: 20 minutes
Baking: 30 minutes
Freezing: excellent

*These dainty bars are
attractive to look at and
wonderful to eat!*

Tips

The strength and flavor
of almond extract varies
considerably among brands.
It's best to use a smaller
amount the first time you
bake with an extract, then
gradually increase the
quantity to suit your taste.

Both salted and unsalted
butter work well in baking.
In most cases, they are
interchangeable — it just
depends on what you are
accustomed to.

Choose a jam that is thick
for this recipe. Seedless jam
tends to be thinner and
darker in color.

Using a fork, rather than
a spoon, to mix the dough
helps keep it crumbly. If you
use a spoon, it is tempting
to make it smooth, which
you don't want.

- Preheat oven to 375°F (190°C)
- 9-inch (2.5 L) square cake pan, greased

1½ cups + 2 tbsp	Robin Hood All-Purpose Flour, divided	405 mL
½ cup	packed brown sugar	125 mL
¼ cup	granulated sugar	50 mL
½ tsp	baking powder	2 mL
½ tsp	salt	2 mL
½ tsp	ground cinnamon	2 mL
½ cup	butter	125 mL
1	egg, beaten	1
1 tsp	almond extract	5 mL
4 tsp	water, divided	20 mL
1 cup	raspberry jam	250 mL
2 tbsp	Robin Hood All-Purpose Flour	30 mL
1	egg yolk	1

1. Combine 1½ cups (375 mL) flour, sugars, baking powder, salt and cinnamon in mixing bowl. Mix well. Using two knives, a pastry blender or your fingers, cut in butter until mixture resembles coarse crumbs. Add egg and extract. Mix with a fork. Transfer ½ cup (125 mL) of mixture to a small bowl and set aside. Press remaining mixture into prepared pan. Spread jam evenly over top.

2. Add 2 tbsp (30 mL) flour to reserved mixture and stir to blend. Stir in water (about 1 tbsp/15 mL) until the dough holds together. (It will resemble pastry dough.) Divide dough into 12 portions and roll into pencil-like strips. Crisscross strips diagonally over jam to form a lattice. Mix egg yolk and 1 tsp (5 mL) water in a small bowl. Brush over lattice.

3. Bake for 25 to 30 minutes or until golden. Cool completely in pan on rack, then cut into bars.

Variation

Substitute raspberry jam with apricot. It's not as attractive as raspberry, but the flavor is great.

Oatmeal Date Squares

Preparation: 20 minutes
Cooking: 10 minutes
Baking: 30 minutes
Freezing: excellent

The whole family loves this old-fashioned favorite, which is often called "Matrimonial Squares."

Tips

Loaded with dates and oats, these tasty squares are a great choice for a healthy snack. For even more fiber, use Robin Hood Whole Wheat Flour instead of all-purpose.

Dates are very sweet. Balancing them with a little lemon or orange juice cuts the sweetness while adding flavor.

Dried fruits, such as dates, raisins, figs and apricots, are packed with vitamins and fiber.

- *Preheat oven to 375°F (190°C)*
- *13- by 9-inch (3.5 L) cake pan, greased*

Filling

3 cups	chopped pitted dates	750 mL
1 tbsp	grated orange zest	15 mL
1¼ cups	orange juice	300 mL
½ cup	granulated sugar	125 mL

Base & Topping

1¾ cups	Robin Hood or Old Mill Oats	425 mL
1⅓ cups	Robin Hood All-Purpose Flour	325 mL
1 cup	packed brown sugar	250 mL
1 tsp	baking soda	5 mL
¾ cup	butter	175 mL

1. *Filling:* Combine dates, orange zest and juice, and sugar in a saucepan. Cook over medium heat, stirring often, until thick and smooth, about 10 minutes. Remove from heat and cool.

2. *Base & Topping:* Combine oats, flour, brown sugar and baking soda in a large bowl. Using two knives, a pastry blender or your fingers, cut in butter until mixture resembles coarse crumbs. Press half of the mixture (2½ cups/625 mL) into prepared pan. Spread filling over base. Sprinkle remaining oat mixture on top. Pat down lightly.

3. Bake for 25 to 30 minutes or until light golden. Cool completely in pan on rack, then cut into squares.

Variation

Replace the orange zest with lemon. Replace the orange juice with ¼ cup (50 mL) lemon juice plus 1 cup (250 mL) water.

Ginger Date Bars

Preparation: 20 minutes
Baking: 30 minutes
Freezing: excellent

If you like lots of gingery flavor, try these cakelike bars.

Tips

Candied ginger should be slightly soft. If yours has hardened, don't use it — invest in fresh.

Honey dates are wonderful for baking. They have great flavor and a soft, buttery texture, which makes them easy to chop.

Store dates in a tightly covered airtight container. If they are exposed to air, they become dry and sugary.

To make it easier to remove these — and many other — bars from the pan, line it completely with parchment paper or greased aluminum foil.

- *Preheat oven to 350°F (180°C)*
- *8-inch (2 L) square cake pan, lined with parchment paper or greased aluminum foil*

¾ cup	chopped pitted dates	175 mL
½ cup	boiling water	125 mL
⅓ cup	chopped candied ginger	75 mL
⅓ cup	butter, softened	75 mL
½ cup	granulated sugar	125 mL
1	egg	1
1 cup	Robin Hood All-Purpose Flour	250 mL
1½ tsp	baking powder	7 mL
1 tsp	ground cinnamon	5 mL
¼ tsp	salt	1 mL

1. Combine dates, water and candied ginger in a small bowl; set aside to soften for 10 minutes.

2. Beat butter, sugar and egg in a large bowl until light and creamy. Stir in date mixture.

3. Combine flour, baking powder, cinnamon and salt. Stir into date mixture. Mix well. Spread batter evenly in prepared pan.

4. Bake for 25 to 30 minutes or until set and golden. Cool completely in pan on rack, then cut into bars.

Variations

A mixture of icing sugar and cinnamon sprinkled over these bars just before serving adds a nice finishing touch.

For a change, try finishing these bars with Lemon Glaze (see recipe, page 157).

Butter Tart Squares

*Here's a simplified version
of the all-time Canadian
favorite. It bakes in one pan
and eliminates fussing
with pastry.*

Tips

A food processor works well
for shortbread-like crusts,
but you can also make them
by hand, in which case the
butter should be at room
temperature. Combine flour
and icing sugar in a bowl.
Using two knives, a pastry
blender or your fingers, cut in
butter until mixture resembles
coarse crumbs. Then press
into pan as directed.

These squares are foolproof
compared to tarts, which
have a tendency to overflow.
They are a great choice for
novice bakers.

If your raisins have become
dry during storage, plump
them in boiling water for a
few minutes, then pat dry.

These bars are delicious
served warm with ice cream.

• *Preheat oven to 350°F (180°C)*
• *9-inch (2.5 L) square cake pan, greased*

Crust

1 cup	Robin Hood All-Purpose Flour	250 mL
2 tbsp	icing sugar, sifted	30 mL
1/3 cup	cold butter, cut in chunks	75 mL

Topping

2	eggs	2
1 1/3 cups	lightly packed brown sugar	325 mL
1/4 cup	butter, melted	50 mL
1 tbsp	vinegar	15 mL
1 tsp	vanilla	5 mL
1 cup	raisins	250 mL

1. *Crust:* Combine flour, icing sugar and butter in a food processor fitted with a metal blade and process until crumbly, about 20 seconds. Press into prepared pan. Bake for 10 minutes or until light golden.

2. *Topping:* Combine eggs, brown sugar, butter, vinegar and vanilla in a mixing bowl. Beat just until blended. Stir in raisins. Pour over crust. Bake for 25 to 30 minutes longer or until set and browned. Cool completely in pan on rack, then cut into squares.

Variations

Replace all or half of the raisins with dried cranberries or chopped dried apricots.

Replace 1/4 cup (50 mL) raisins with chopped nuts.

Pecan Cheesecake Squares

**MAKES ABOUT
3 DOZEN SQUARES**

Preparation: 20 minutes
Baking: 40 minutes
Chilling: 2 hours
Freezing:
not recommended

*Who could resist this yummy
pecan cheesecake cut in
bite-size squares?*

Tips

To ensure a smooth texture,
make sure your cream cheese
is at room temperature.

To cut butter into a dry
mixture, you can use your
fingers, a food processor,
a pastry blender, two knives
or a fork. Cold butter is
necessary if you're using
a food processor.

Use real vanilla extract in
all your baking. The flavor
is far better than that of
artificial vanilla.

If you're trying to reduce fat
and calories in your baking,
light cream cheese works
well in these squares. You
can also decrease the nuts
to 2 tbsp (30 mL).

- *Preheat oven to 350°F (180°C)*
- *8-inch (2 L) square cake pan, greased*

Crust

1 cup	Robin Hood All-Purpose Flour	250 mL
¼ cup	packed brown sugar	50 mL
⅓ cup	butter	75 mL

Topping

1	package (8 oz/250 g) cream cheese, softened	1
⅓ cup	packed brown sugar	75 mL
1	egg	1
2 tsp	milk	10 mL
1 tsp	vanilla	5 mL
⅓ cup	finely chopped pecans	75 mL

1. *Crust:* Combine flour and brown sugar. Using two knives, a pastry blender or your fingers, cut in butter until mixture resembles coarse crumbs. Press firmly into prepared pan.

2. Bake for 10 minutes or until light golden.

3. *Topping:* Beat cream cheese in a small bowl on medium speed of electric mixer until creamy. Add brown sugar, egg, milk and vanilla, beating until smooth, about 2 minutes. Spread evenly over crust. Sprinkle with pecans. Bake for 25 to 30 minutes longer, or until the edges are lightly browned. Cool completely in pan on rack, then refrigerate for at least 2 hours before cutting into bite-size squares.

Variation

Replace pecans with finely chopped hazelnuts.

Chocolate Caramel Pecan Squares

*Rich, sweet, gooey, these
squares are worth every
sinful bite. You can always
diet tomorrow.*

Tips

Choose caramel sauce
carefully for use in this
recipe. If it seems thin,
you may need to add a little
more flour.

Because the caramel sauce
will stick, the pan should be
lined completely with
aluminum foil or baking
parchment and the sides
well greased. After the
squares are completely cool,
you can remove them from
the pan and cut them easily.

If your brown sugar gets
lumpy, add a slice of apple,
seal tightly and leave for a
few days to soften. For
instant softening, put brown
sugar in a covered bowl with
an apple slice and microwave
on High for 20 seconds.

- *Preheat oven to 350°F (180°C)*
- *9-inch (2.5 L) square cake pan, greased*

¾ cup	Robin Hood All-Purpose Flour	175 mL
½ cup	Robin Hood or Old Mill Oats	125 mL
⅓ cup	packed brown sugar	75 mL
½ tsp	baking soda	2 mL
⅓ cup	butter, melted	75 mL
1 cup	caramel sauce	250 mL
¼ cup	Robin Hood All-Purpose Flour	50 mL
1 cup	semi-sweet chocolate chips	250 mL
¾ cup	chopped pecans	175 mL

1. Combine ¾ cup (175 mL) flour, oats, brown sugar and baking soda; stir well to blend. Add melted butter; mix well. Press evenly into prepared pan. Bake for 10 minutes.

2. Combine caramel sauce and ¼ cup (50 mL) flour, mixing until smooth. Sprinkle chocolate chips and chopped pecans over warm crust. Drizzle caramel mixture evenly over top. Bake for 20 to 25 minutes longer or until bubbly and browned. Cool completely in pan on rack, then cut into squares.

Variations

For an extra caramel taste, replace chocolate chips with butterscotch chips.

Replace chocolate chips and pecans with peanut butter chips and peanuts, and caramel sauce with chocolate sauce.

Lickety-Split Lemon Bars

Preparation: 15 minutes
Baking: 50 minutes
Freezing: excellent

*If you like the flavor of lemon,
you'll love the hint of tartness
in these luscious bars.*

Tips

Bars are cookies that are
particularly easy to make,
as they are baked in one
pan, then cut into pieces.

Most bars freeze well.

Use fresh lemon juice for
the best flavor.

To obtain almost twice as
much juice from a lemon,
submerge it in hot water for
15 seconds before squeezing.

When grating the zest, try to
use only the yellow part. The
white pith has a bitter taste.

Add a dusting of icing sugar
just before serving for a
finishing touch.

- *Preheat oven to 350°F (180°C)*
- *8-inch (2 L) square cake pan, greased*

Crust

1 cup	Robin Hood All-Purpose Flour	250 mL
1/4 cup	granulated sugar	50 mL
1/2 cup	butter	125 mL

Topping

1 cup	granulated sugar	250 mL
3 tbsp	Robin Hood All-Purpose Flour	45 mL
3	eggs	3
1 1/2 tsp	grated lemon zest	7 mL
1/2 cup	fresh lemon juice	125 mL

1. *Crust:* Combine flour and sugar. Using two knives, a pastry blender or your fingers, cut in butter until mixture resembles coarse crumbs. Press into prepared pan. Bake for 15 to 20 minutes or until light golden.

2. *Topping:* Beat sugar, flour, eggs, and lemon zest and juice in a small bowl just until smooth. Don't overbeat. Pour over warm crust. Bake for 25 to 30 minutes longer or until set. Cool completely in pan on rack, then cut into bars.

Variation

Replace 1/4 cup (50 mL) of the flour in the crust with 1/2 cup (125 mL) ground almonds.

Apple Nut Bars

**MAKES ABOUT
2 DOZEN BARS**

Preparation: 15 minutes
Cooking: 5 minutes
Baking: 35 minutes
Freezing: excellent

Moist, chewy and nutty, these flavorful bars are like a thin apple cake that needs no icing.

Tips

Use crisp tart apples for the best flavor. Granny Smiths, Northern Spys and Spartans are good choices.

Grate apples on a coarse grater just before using to prevent browning.

Nuts go rancid quickly. Store them in the freezer.

To enhance their flavor, toast the nuts on a baking sheet in a 350°F (180°C) oven for 5 to 10 minutes, stirring often.

If apples are very wet, increase the baking time by 5 to 10 minutes.

To turn these bars into a dessert, add a thin layer of Basic Cream Cheese Frosting (see recipe, page 146). You'll need about 1½ cups (375 mL), or half the recipe.

- Preheat oven to 350°F (180°C)
- 9-inch (2.5 L) square cake pan, greased

6 tbsp	butter	90 mL
1 cup	packed brown sugar	250 mL
2	eggs	2
1 cup	Robin Hood All-Purpose Flour	250 mL
1 tsp	baking powder	5 mL
1 tsp	ground cinnamon	5 mL
¼ tsp	salt	1 mL
¼ tsp	ground nutmeg	1 mL
1 cup	chopped walnuts	250 mL
1	medium apple, peeled, cored and coarsely grated	1

1. Melt butter in a large saucepan. Stir in brown sugar. Bring mixture to a boil over medium heat, stirring often. Remove from heat; cool.

2. Beat eggs, one at a time, into cooled sugar mixture.

3. Combine flour, baking powder, cinnamon, salt and nutmeg. Add to saucepan, mixing until smooth. Stir in walnuts and apple. Mix well. Spread in prepared pan. Bake for 25 to 35 minutes or until toothpick inserted in center comes out clean. Cool completely in pan on rack, then cut into bars.

Variations

For a change, try using pears in this recipe. Their flavor is not as tart as apples.

Add dried cranberries or raisins to the batter.

Chocolate Almond Bars

These bars are delicious yet especially easy to make.

Tips

You can substitute hard margarine, not soft margarine, for butter in most baking. However, in some baking, such as shortbread, you really need the flavor of butter — no substitute will do.

Use golden corn syrup, not white, for baking. White syrup is usually used in candy making.

If using a glass pan, decrease the oven temperature by 25°F (10°C).

- *Preheat oven to 350°F (180°C)*
- *9-inch (2.5 L) square cake pan, greased*

Crust

1 cup	Robin Hood All-Purpose Flour	250 mL
¼ cup	granulated sugar	50 mL
⅓ cup	butter	75 mL

Topping

2	eggs	2
½ cup	granulated sugar	125 mL
½ cup	corn syrup	125 mL
2 tbsp	butter, melted	30 mL
1 cup	semi-sweet chocolate chips	250 mL
¾ cup	slivered almonds	175 mL

1. *Crust:* Combine flour and sugar. Using two knives, a pastry blender or your fingers, cut in butter until mixture resembles coarse crumbs. Press into prepared pan. Bake for 12 to 15 minutes or until light golden.

2. *Topping:* Beat eggs, sugar, corn syrup and melted butter until blended. Stir in chocolate chips and almonds. Pour evenly over warm crust. Bake for 25 to 30 minutes longer or until set and golden. Cool completely in pan on rack, then cut into bars.

Variation

Vary the kind of chips and nuts to suit your taste.

Blondies

Blondies are blond brownies. They have a similar moist, slightly chewy texture but are flavored with butterscotch rather than chocolate.

Tips

Most bars and squares freeze well, which makes them ideal to have on hand for unexpected guests.

To freeze blondies, cool completely and cut into squares. Wrap individual servings in plastic wrap and freeze. When preparing to serve, remove the quantity required and let thaw. Cut in individual pieces, they thaw quickly, and you can remove just one for yourself or several for company. They actually taste great frozen, too.

These will rise during baking then collapse as they cool.

- *Preheat oven to 325°F (160°C)*
- *8-inch (2 L) square cake pan, greased*

½ cup	butter, softened	125 mL
1¼ cups	packed brown sugar	300 mL
1	egg	1
1 tsp	vanilla	5 mL
1 cup	Robin Hood All-Purpose Flour	250 mL
1 tsp	baking powder	5 mL
¾ cup	white chocolate chips	175 mL
¾ cup	chopped hazelnuts	175 mL

1. Cream butter and brown sugar in a medium bowl until smooth and creamy. Add egg and vanilla, beating until smooth.

2. Combine flour and baking powder. Add to creamed mixture. Mix well. Stir in chips and nuts. Spread evenly in prepared pan.

3. Bake for 40 to 45 minutes or until just set and golden. Cool completely in pan on rack, then cut into squares.

Variation

Blondies are quite versatile. Make them with your favorite additions, such as nuts, chips, coconut, raisins or chopped dried apricots.

Decadent Chocolate Macaroon Bars

**MAKES ABOUT
4 DOZEN BARS**

Preparation: 25 minutes
Baking: 40 minutes
Chilling: 30 minutes
Freezing: excellent

Proceed with caution when sampling these bars. The soft, chewy coconut filling sandwiched between layers of chocolate and crowned with a rich chocolate topping is addictive.

Tips

Because these bars are so rich, one pan goes a long way. Cut the bars small. People can always come back for more.

Sweetened condensed milk should not be confused with evaporated milk. It is considerably sweeter and much thicker in consistency.

The recipes in this book were tested with whole, or regular, sweetened condensed milk. Lower-fat versions are also available and make a satisfactory substitute.

Bittersweet chocolate can be substituted for semi-sweet in baking.

Drop the filling on the top layer of chocolate batter by small spoonfuls to ensure that it spreads evenly.

- *Preheat oven to 350°F (180°C)*
- *13- by 9-inch (3.5 L) cake pan, greased*

Base

4	squares (each 1 oz/28 g) unsweetened chocolate	4
1 cup	butter	250 mL
2 cups	granulated sugar	500 mL
3	eggs	3
1¼ cups	Robin Hood All-Purpose Flour	300 mL

Filling

3 cups	flaked coconut	750 mL
1	can (10 oz/300 mL) sweetened condensed milk	1
1 tsp	vanilla	5 mL

Topping

1½ cups	semi-sweet chocolate chips, melted	375 mL
½ cup	finely chopped nuts, optional	125 mL

1. *Base:* Heat chocolate and butter in a medium saucepan over low heat, stirring until smooth and melted. Remove from heat. Stir in sugar until blended. Add eggs, one at a time, mixing lightly after each addition. Add flour; mix well. Spread half of the batter in prepared pan.

2. *Filling:* Combine coconut, condensed milk and vanilla in a medium bowl. Mix well. Drop by small spoonfuls over base. Carefully spread remaining chocolate batter over filling. Bake for 35 to 40 minutes or until set. Cool completely in pan on rack.

3. *Topping:* Spread melted chocolate chips evenly over baked bar. Sprinkle nuts on top, if using. Chill until chocolate is set, about 30 minutes, then cut into bars.

Variation

The nut garnish is a matter of preference. Use your favorite nut or omit it completely.

Downright Decadent Truffle Brownies

Every sinful bite of these mouthwatering brownies is worth the calories. Each piece is like a truffle and will satisfy any chocolate craving.

Tips

Bittersweet chocolate can be substituted for semi-sweet in baking. The flavor will be slightly richer and more intense.

People have been known to enjoy rich chocolate brownies straight from the freezer. Stash a few away and give it a try. It's easier to eat just one when they are stored out of sight!

- Preheat oven to 350°F (180°C)
- 9-inch (2.5 L) square cake pan, greased

Brownie

6	squares (each 1 oz/28 g) semi-sweet chocolate	6
¾ cup	butter	175 mL
4	eggs	4
1 cup	granulated sugar	250 mL
1½ tsp	vanilla	7 mL
¾ cup	chopped walnuts	175 mL
½ cup	Robin Hood All-Purpose Flour	125 mL
½ tsp	ground cinnamon, optional	2 mL
¼ tsp	salt	1 mL

Ganache Topping

6	squares (each 1 oz/28 g) semi-sweet chocolate	6
2 tbsp	butter	30 mL
2 tbsp	whipping (35%) cream	30 mL

1. *Brownie:* Heat chocolate and butter in a small saucepan over low heat, stirring until smooth and melted. Remove from heat; set aside.

2. Beat eggs and sugar in a small bowl on high speed of electric mixer until thick, about 5 minutes. Stir in reserved chocolate mixture and vanilla. Add walnuts, flour, cinnamon (if using), and salt, stirring just until combined. Spread evenly in prepared pan. Bake for 30 to 35 minutes or until set. Cool completely in pan on rack, then chill for 1 hour.

3. *Ganache:* Combine chocolate, butter and whipping cream in a small saucepan. Heat over low heat, stirring often, until smooth and melted. Pour over chilled brownie. Chill until ganache is set, about 2 hours. Cut into squares.

Variation

If you're concerned about calories, omit the ganache. You'll still have a delicious brownie, although this compromise won't have such exceptional taste.

MUFFINS AND BISCUITS

 Cranberry Orange Muffins (on plate)

Cranberry Orange Muffins

*Tart cranberries combine
with orange in this refreshing
muffin that is not too sweet.*

Tips

In addition to adding unique flavor to baked goods, honey keeps them moist.

Use liquid honey rather than the creamed variety in these muffins.

For easy cleanup, measure the melted butter before the honey. The slippery butter will coat the cup, and the honey won't stick to the sides.

When fresh cranberries aren't available, use partially thawed frozen ones. Don't thaw them completely or the batter will be pink.

- *Preheat oven to 400°F (200°C)*
- *12-cup muffin pan, greased or lined with paper liners*

Muffins

1	egg	1
1¼ cups	milk	300 mL
⅓ cup	butter, melted	75 mL
⅓ cup	liquid honey	75 mL
1 tbsp	grated orange zest	15 mL
2½ cups	Robin Hood All-Purpose Flour	625 mL
1 tbsp	baking powder	15 mL
½ tsp	salt	2 mL
1½ cups	fresh or frozen cranberries	375 mL

Topping

2 tbsp	granulated sugar	30 mL

1. *Muffins:* Beat egg, milk, butter, honey and orange zest in a large bowl until thoroughly blended.
2. Combine flour, baking powder and salt. Add to liquid ingredients all at once and stir just until moistened. Fold in cranberries. Spoon batter into prepared muffin pan.
3. *Topping:* Sprinkle sugar over top of muffins.
4. Bake for 20 to 25 minutes or until tops spring back when lightly touched.

Variation

Replace the orange zest with lemon zest and the cranberries with blueberries.

Blueberry Orange Muffins

**MAKES
1 DOZEN MUFFINS**

Preparation: 20 minutes
Baking: 23 minutes
Freezing: excellent

Although these muffins are especially delicious made with fresh blueberries, in season, you can enjoy them year-round made with frozen fruit.

Tips

Make these with wild blueberries, if available. The flavor is intense and, because they are smaller, there is more luscious fruit in every bite.

Frozen berries will bleed into the white batter.

Sprinkle coarse sugar over the top just before baking for a glistening top.

- *Preheat oven to 400°F (200°C)*
- *12-cup muffin pan, greased or lined with paper liners*

½ cup	butter, softened	125 mL
1 cup	granulated sugar	250 mL
2	eggs	2
½ cup	sour cream	125 mL
1 tbsp	grated orange zest	15 mL
½ cup	orange juice	125 mL
2 cups	Robin Hood All-Purpose Flour	500 mL
1 tsp	baking powder	5 mL
½ tsp	baking soda	2 mL
¼ tsp	salt	1 mL
1 cup	blueberries	250 mL

1. Cream butter and sugar in a large bowl until light and creamy. Add eggs, one at a time, beating lightly after each addition. Add sour cream, and orange zest and juice. Mix well.

2. Combine flour, baking powder, baking soda and salt. Stir into creamed mixture just until blended. Gently fold in berries. Spoon batter into prepared muffin pan.

3. Bake for 18 to 23 minutes or until tops spring back when lightly touched.

Variation

Replace blueberries with cranberries.

Raspberry Muffins

**MAKES 10 LARGE OR
12 MEDIUM MUFFINS**

Preparation: 15 minutes
Baking: 25 minutes
Freezing: excellent

*These sweet, fruit-filled
muffins are not typical
breakfast fare. Enjoy them
as a treat with coffee or as
a simple dessert.*

Tips

If using frozen raspberries,
don't thaw them before
adding to the batter. They
won't hold their shape and
will color the batter pink.

If you're making 10 large
muffins, fill the empty muffin
cups with water to ensure
uniform baking.

- *Preheat oven to 400°F (200°C)*
- *12-cup muffin pan, greased or lined with paper liners*

Muffins

1 cup	milk	250 mL
½ cup	butter, melted	125 mL
1	egg	1
2 cups	Robin Hood All-Purpose Flour	500 mL
⅓ cup	granulated sugar	75 mL
1 tbsp	baking powder	15 mL
½ tsp	salt	2 mL
1 cup	fresh or frozen raspberries	250 mL

Topping

2 tbsp	granulated sugar	30 mL

1. *Muffins:* Beat milk, melted butter and egg thoroughly in a large mixing bowl.
2. Combine flour, sugar, baking powder and salt. Stir into liquid ingredients just until combined. Fold in raspberries. Spoon into prepared muffin pan.
3. *Topping:* Sprinkle sugar over top of muffins.
4. Bake for 20 to 25 minutes or until tops spring back when lightly touched.

Variation

For a decadent touch, stir ⅔ cup (150 mL) white or semi-sweet chocolate chips into the batter. After the muffins have baked, drizzle tops with the same kind of melted chocolate.

Apple Cranberry Muffins

*Apples and cranberries are
in season at the same time
for a reason: they make a
delectable combination.*

Tips

These muffins are as good
for breakfast as they
are for dessert.

Grease the tops of the pans,
as well as the bottoms and
sides, so the topping won't
stick and the muffins will
be easy to remove.

Moist muffins freeze very
well. It's nice to have extras
on hand for days when
there's no time to bake.

- *Preheat oven to 325°F (160°C)*
- *Two 12-cup muffin pans, greased or lined with paper liners*

Topping

1/3 cup	granulated sugar	75 mL
1/2 tsp	ground cinnamon	2 mL
1 tbsp	butter, softened	15 mL

Muffins

1 1/3 cups	packed brown sugar	325 mL
2/3 cup	vegetable oil	150 mL
1	egg	1
1 cup	buttermilk	250 mL
2 1/2 cups	Robin Hood All-Purpose Flour	625 mL
1 tsp	baking soda	5 mL
3/4 tsp	salt	3 mL
1/2 tsp	ground cinnamon	2 mL
1 1/2 cups	finely chopped peeled cored apple	375 mL
3/4 cup	fresh or frozen cranberries	175 mL

1. *Topping:* Combine sugar, cinnamon and butter, mixing with a fork until crumbly. Set aside.

2. *Muffins:* Beat brown sugar, oil, egg and buttermilk in a large bowl until thoroughly blended.

3. Combine flour, baking soda, salt and cinnamon. Add to liquid ingredients, stirring just until blended. Fold in apple and cranberries. Spoon into prepared muffin pans.

4. Bake for 25 to 30 minutes or until tops spring back when lightly touched.

Variation

Replace cranberries with the same quantity of fresh blueberries or dried cranberries.

Apple Spice Muffins

A spicy crumble tops these healthy oat-apple muffins. Freeze some to have on hand for a quick breakfast when you're on the run.

Tips

Grated apple adds moistness and flavor to muffins.

Grate the apple just before using to avoid browning.

Choose firm tart apples, such as Granny Smith.

This batter will be very stiff. The moisture is released from the apples during baking.

Buy spices in small amounts and store them in a cool place to keep them fresh.

- *Preheat oven to 400°F (200°C)*
- *12-cup muffin pan, greased or lined with paper liners*

2 cups	Robin Hood All-Purpose Flour	500 mL
1 cup	Robin Hood or Old Mill Oats	250 mL
¾ cup	packed brown sugar	175 mL
1 tbsp	baking powder	15 mL
½ tsp	salt	2 mL
½ cup	butter	125 mL
1 tsp	ground cinnamon	5 mL
¼ tsp	ground nutmeg	1 mL
2	eggs	2
1 cup	milk	250 mL
1 cup	grated peeled cored apple (about 2)	250 mL

1. Combine flour, oats, brown sugar, baking powder and salt in a mixing bowl. Using two knives, a pastry blender or your fingers, cut in butter until mixture resembles coarse crumbs. Set aside ½ cup (125 mL) for topping; stir cinnamon and nutmeg into reserved topping.

2. Beat eggs, milk and apple in a small bowl. Add to dry ingredients all at once, stirring just until moistened. Spoon batter into prepared muffin pan. Sprinkle topping evenly over batter; pat down gently.

3. Bake for 20 to 25 minutes or until tops spring back when lightly touched.

Variation

Replace apple with the same quantity of grated zucchini.

Spicy Carrot Muffins

Preparation: 15 minutes
Baking: 27 minutes
Freezing: excellent

*These flavorful muffins are
nutritious as well as delicious.*

Tips

For added fiber, use Robin
Hood Whole Wheat Flour
in place of all or part of the
all-purpose flour.

Be sure to peel the carrots.
The reaction of the peel in
the batter to the leavening
can form green specks.

If you're making large
muffins, grease the top of
the pan. Cut the parts of the
tops that have overflowed
and run into each other into
squares, then remove from
the pan.

- *Preheat oven to 350°F (180°C)*
- *One or two 12-cup muffin pans, greased or lined with paper liners*

2 cups	Robin Hood All-Purpose Flour	500 mL
1¼ cups	granulated sugar	300 mL
¾ cup	raisins	175 mL
½ cup	chopped walnuts	125 mL
2 tsp	baking soda	10 mL
1½ tsp	ground cinnamon	7 mL
½ tsp	ground nutmeg	2 mL
½ tsp	salt	2 mL
2½ cups	grated peeled carrots	625 mL
3	eggs	3
¾ cup	vegetable oil	175 mL

1. Combine flour, sugar, raisins, walnuts, baking soda, cinnamon, nutmeg, salt in a large bowl. Stir well.

2. Beat carrots, eggs and oil. Add to dry ingredients all at once, stirring just until moistened. Spoon batter into prepared muffin pans, filling three-quarters full for regular-size or full for large-size muffins.

3. Bake for 20 minutes for regular muffins or 27 minutes for large muffins or until tops spring back when lightly touched.

Variations

Omit nuts, if desired.

Replace the carrots with shredded zucchini.

Replace raisins with dried cranberries or dried cherries.

Chocolate Zucchini Muffins

Chocolate fans will especially appreciate these moist, tasty muffins.

Tips

Don't peel the zucchini before shredding. The green flecks add color and texture.

Shred zucchini just before using. Let stand, it releases a fair amount of moisture.

Add healthy fiber to your diet by replacing half of the all-purpose flour with Robin Hood Whole Wheat Flour.

Because cocoa tends to clump when stored, it needs to be sifted before it is added to a recipe. Measure, then sift before using.

- *Preheat oven to 375°F (190°C)*
- *Two 12-cup muffin pans, greased or lined with paper liners*

¾ cup	butter, softened	175 mL
2 cups	granulated sugar	500 mL
3	eggs	3
2½ cups	Robin Hood All-Purpose Flour	625 mL
½ cup	unsweetened cocoa powder, sifted	125 mL
2½ tsp	baking powder	12 mL
1½ tsp	baking soda	7 mL
½ tsp	salt	2 mL
½ tsp	ground cinnamon	2 mL
2 cups	shredded zucchini	500 mL
½ cup	milk	125 mL
1 cup	semi-sweet chocolate chips	250 mL

1. Cream butter and sugar in a large bowl until light and creamy. Add eggs, one at a time, beating lightly after each addition.

2. Combine flour, cocoa, baking powder, baking soda, salt and cinnamon. Add to creamed mixture alternately with zucchini and milk, making two additions of each. Mix well. Fold in chocolate chips. Spoon batter into prepared muffin pan.

3. Bake for 20 to 25 minutes or until tops spring back when lightly touched.

Variations

Replace chocolate chips with any kind of nut.

Replace zucchini with shredded peeled carrot.

Best-Ever Banana Muffins

MAKES
1 DOZEN MUFFINS

Preparation: 20 minutes
Baking: 25 minutes
Freezing: excellent

Once you've tried this recipe, you'll always want to have ripe bananas on hand so you can whip up a batch of these delicious muffins.

Tips

The riper the bananas, the better the flavor.

One large banana should yield about 1/2 cup (125 mL) mashed banana.

To measure flour and other dry ingredients, spoon lightly into a dry measuring cup and level off with a spatula or the back of a knife.

The large quantity of bananas makes these muffins particularly flavourful and moist.

If you're concerned about fat, decrease the butter to 1/3 cup (75 mL).

- *Preheat oven to 375°F (190°C)*
- *12-cup muffin pan, greased or lined with paper liners*

1	egg	1
1 1/2 cups	mashed banana (3 or 4 large)	375 mL
1/2 cup	butter, melted	125 mL
1 1/2 cups	Robin Hood All-Purpose Flour	375 mL
3/4 cup	granulated sugar	175 mL
1 tsp	baking powder	5 mL
1 tsp	baking soda	5 mL
1/2 tsp	salt	2 mL

1. Beat egg, mashed banana and melted butter in a large bowl until thoroughly blended.

2. Combine flour, sugar, baking powder, baking soda and salt. Add to banana mixture and stir just until moistened. Spoon batter into prepared muffin pan.

3. Bake for 20 to 25 minutes or until tops spring back when lightly touched.

Variations

Add 1 cup (250 mL) fresh or frozen cranberries or blueberries to the batter.

Add 3/4 cup (175 mL) semi-sweet chocolate chips to the batter.

Cheddar, Bacon and Corn Muffins

Enjoy traditional breakfast foods all in one savory muffin.

Tips

Savory muffins are at their most flavorful when served warm. Enjoy these with soup or a salad for lunch or with a hearty stew or chili for dinner.

For another taste sensation, try splitting baked muffins and grilling them under the broiler or on the barbecue.

Cook bacon until very crisp. Cool, then crumble. If you are cooking it ahead of time, and the reserved bacon drippings have solidified, be sure to melt them before adding to the batter.

Use a good brand of creamed corn; the better the brand, the higher the percentage of kernels to sauce.

- *Preheat oven to 375°F (190°C)*
- *12-cup muffin pan, greased or lined with paper liners*

8	slices bacon	8
1 cup	Robin Hood All-Purpose Flour	250 mL
1 cup	cornmeal	250 mL
2 tbsp	granulated sugar	30 mL
1 tbsp	baking powder	15 mL
¼ tsp	salt	1 mL
1	egg, beaten	1
1	can (10 oz/284 mL) creamed corn	1
1 cup	grated Cheddar cheese	250 mL
½ cup	milk	125 mL
¼ cup	bacon drippings	50 mL

1. Cook bacon in a skillet over medium heat until very crisp. Drain on paper towels. Crumble and set aside. Reserve ¼ cup (50 mL) of the drippings.

2. Combine flour, cornmeal, sugar, baking powder, salt and bacon in a mixing bowl. In a separate bowl, beat egg, corn, cheese, milk and reserved bacon drippings until thoroughly blended. Add all at once to dry ingredients. Stir just until moistened. Spoon batter into prepared muffin pan.

3. Bake for 15 to 20 minutes or until tops spring back when lightly touched. Serve warm.

Variation

You can replace the bacon drippings with vegetable oil or melted butter, but the muffins will not be as flavorful.

Luscious Date Bran Muffins

High in flavor and fiber but low in fat, these muffins are a healthy choice.

Tips

Because the dates are cooked to a purée, they add flavor and moistness throughout the muffin. The use of a fruit purée also reduces the quantity of fat required in the recipe.

For use in this recipe, be sure to buy natural bran, which should not be confused with cold-cereal bran products. Natural bran, which is also found in the cereal section of the supermarket, is small dry flakes that look like wheat germ.

- *Preheat oven to 375°F (190°C)*
- *12-cup muffin pan, greased or lined with paper liners*

Filling

1 cup	chopped pitted dates	250 mL
1 cup	hot water	250 mL
½ cup	packed brown sugar	125 mL
1 tbsp	lemon juice	15 mL

Muffins

1½ cups	natural bran	375 mL
1 cup	Robin Hood All-Purpose Flour	250 mL
1 tsp	baking soda	5 mL
1 tsp	salt	5 mL
½ tsp	baking powder	2 mL
1	egg	1
1 cup	buttermilk	250 mL
½ cup	packed brown sugar	125 mL
1 tbsp	vegetable oil	15 mL

1. *Filling:* Mix dates, water, brown sugar and lemon juice in a saucepan. Simmer over medium heat until thickened. Set aside to cool.
2. *Muffins:* Combine bran, flour, baking soda, salt and baking powder in a mixing bowl.
3. In a separate bowl, beat egg, buttermilk, brown sugar and oil until thoroughly blended. Add all at once to dry ingredients. Stir just until moistened. Stir in date filling. Mix well. Spoon batter into prepared muffin pan.
4. Bake for 20 to 25 minutes or until tops spring back when lightly touched.

Variation

Add 1 tbsp (15 mL) grated orange zest to the filling.

Date 'n' Orange Muffins

**MAKES
1 DOZEN MUFFINS**

Preparation: 20 minutes
Baking: 20 minutes
Freezing: excellent
(without topping)

A double hit of orange combined with soft, sweet dates make these muffins a real delight. Enjoy them plain, with a drizzle of honey or spread with cream cheese.

Tips

Be sure to use soft dates in this recipe. Dates dry out as they age. If yours are dry, cover them with boiling water to soften before using. Drain off the water before using.

When cutting dates, spray your knife or scissors with cooking spray or brush lightly with oil to prevent them from sticking.

Use freshly squeezed juice for optimum flavor.

Use a soft toothbrush to clean a citrus grater easily.

- *Preheat oven to 375°F (190°C)*
- *12-cup muffin pan, greased or lined with paper liners*

Muffins

2 cups	Robin Hood All-Purpose Flour	500 mL
1/2 cup	granulated sugar	125 mL
1 tbsp	grated orange zest	15 mL
2 tsp	baking powder	10 mL
1 tsp	baking soda	5 mL
1/2 tsp	salt	2 mL
1	egg	1
1 cup	chopped pitted dates	250 mL
1/2 cup	orange juice	125 mL
1/2 cup	milk	125 mL
1/4 cup	vegetable oil	50 mL

Topping, optional

1/4 cup	granulated sugar	50 mL
1 tbsp	grated orange zest	15 mL

1. *Muffins:* Combine flour, sugar, orange zest, baking powder, baking soda and salt in a large bowl.

2. Beat egg, dates, orange juice, milk and oil in a small bowl. Add to dry ingredients, stirring just until moistened. Spoon into prepared muffin pan.

3. *Topping:* Mix sugar with orange zest. Sprinkle 1 tsp (5 mL) over each muffin.

4. Bake for 15 to 20 minutes or until tops spring back when lightly touched.

Variation

Replace dates with raisins or dried cranberries.

Buttermilk Biscuits

MAKES ABOUT
12 BISCUITS

Preparation: 15 minutes
Baking: 15 minutes
Freezing: excellent

This versatile favorite will always be a winner. Enjoy these homey biscuits warm with butter and homemade preserves. In season, sweeten them up and use as a base for individual shortcakes, topped with fresh berries and whipped cream. Or serve them with dinner for a down-home treat.

Tips

To simplify last-minute preparation, prepare the dry mixture, cut in the shortening and chill until needed. When ready to serve, preheat the oven while you are mixing and shaping the biscuits. Then pop them in the oven to bake.

A sour milk product, such as buttermilk, yogurt or sour cream, is used in doughs that contain baking soda. Plain milk is usually used when baking powder is the only leavening.

Biscuits made with shortening have a light, tender texture. With butter, they are slightly moister and more compact. Both are delicious; the choice is yours.

Place biscuits close together for soft-sided biscuits or about 1 inch (2.5 cm) apart for crusty-sided biscuits.

- *Preheat oven to 425°F (220°C)*
- *Baking sheet, ungreased*

2 cups	Robin Hood All-Purpose Flour	500 mL
2½ tsp	baking powder	12 mL
1 tsp	salt	5 mL
½ tsp	baking soda	2 mL
½ cup	shortening or butter	125 mL
1 cup	buttermilk	250 mL

1. Combine flour, baking powder, salt and baking soda in a mixing bowl. Using two knives, a pastry blender or your fingers, cut in shortening until mixture resembles coarse crumbs.

2. Add buttermilk all at once to dry ingredients and stir with a fork until a soft dough forms. Turn dough out onto a lightly floured surface and knead gently eight to 10 times. Roll or pat to ¾-inch (2 cm) thickness. Cut with a 1¾-inch (4.5 cm) round cutter dipped in flour. Place on baking sheet.

3. Bake for 12 to 15 minutes or until light golden. Serve warm.

Variations

Brush tops with melted butter and sprinkle with sugar for a finishing touch.

Stir in about 1 cup (250 mL) shredded Cheddar cheese for a savory biscuit.

Add 2 tbsp (30 mL) sugar to the dough for a sweet biscuit that you can use as a base for shortcake.

124   Muffins and Biscuits

Cheesy Drop Biscuits

These easy-to-make biscuits are like tea biscuits that don't require kneading, rolling and cutting.

Tips

Prepare more of these biscuits than you think you'll need. They will vanish quickly.

Be sure your baking powder is fresh. As it ages, it loses its leavening power. If you don't bake often, purchase it in small amounts.

Bake the biscuits as soon as they are mixed. Once the liquid combines with the baking powder, the leavening starts to work.

Use old Cheddar cheese. A five- or six-year-old Cheddar has a flavorful nip that works well in these biscuits.

Expect the dough to be slightly sticky — that's what makes the biscuits moist and tender.

The shape will vary with each biscuit. Their unique appearance gives the biscuits homemade appeal.

- *Preheat oven to 400°F (200°C)*
- *Baking sheet, greased*

2 cups	Robin Hood All-Purpose Flour	500 mL
1 tbsp	baking powder	15 mL
¾ tsp	salt	3 mL
⅓ cup	butter	75 mL
1½ cups	shredded old Cheddar cheese	375 mL
1	green onion, chopped	1
1¼ cups	milk	300 mL

1. Combine flour, baking powder and salt in a large bowl. Using two knives, a pastry blender or your fingers, cut in butter until mixture resembles coarse crumbs. Stir in cheese and green onion.

2. Add milk all at once, stirring to make a soft, sticky dough. Divide dough into 12 portions, about ⅓ cup (75 mL) each. Drop onto prepared baking sheet.

3. Bake for 18 to 20 minutes or until edges are golden. Serve warm or cool.

Variations

Replace Cheddar with Swiss cheese.

Add some diced cooked bacon or ham (about ½ cup/125 mL) to the dough, along with the cheese.

Use chives in place of the green onion.

Cornbread

**MAKES ABOUT
12 SERVINGS**

Preparation: 15 minutes
Baking: 25 minutes
Freezing: excellent

Warm cornbread is a quite a delicacy in the American South. This tasty version has extra corn and peppers to make it particularly appetizing.

Tips

Peaches-and-cream corn has a pleasant mild flavor and tender texture. Yellow corn is a bit firmer and slightly stronger in taste. Use whatever variety you prefer.

Fresh, canned or thawed frozen corn kernels work well in this recipe.

Use old Cheddar cheese for a strong cheese flavor or medium for a more mellow taste.

For individual servings, spoon batter into 12 greased muffin cups and bake for about 18 minutes.

- *Preheat oven to 400°F (200°C)*
- *8-inch (2 L) square cake pan, greased*

2	eggs	2
1 cup	buttermilk	250 mL
1/4 cup	butter, melted	50 mL
1 cup	fresh, canned or thawed frozen corn kernels	250 mL
1 cup	shredded Cheddar cheese (see Tips, left)	250 mL
1/4 cup	finely chopped sweet red pepper	50 mL
1 cup	Robin Hood All-Purpose Flour	250 mL
1 cup	cornmeal	250 mL
1 tbsp	granulated sugar	15 mL
1 tbsp	baking powder	15 mL
1 tsp	salt	5 mL
1/2 tsp	baking soda	2 mL

1. Whisk eggs, buttermilk and melted butter in a large bowl. Stir in corn, cheese and pepper.

2. Combine flour, cornmeal, sugar, baking powder, salt and baking soda. Add to liquid ingredients all at once, stirring just until moistened. Spread batter in prepared pan.

3. Bake for 20 to 25 minutes or until toothpick inserted in center comes out clean. Cut into squares and serve warm or cool.

Variations

Replace peppers with green or black olives.

Add minced jalapeño pepper to taste for added zip.

Butterscotch Pecan Rolls

MAKES 12 ROLLS

Preparation: 25 minutes
Baking: 23 minutes
Freezing: excellent

Warm from the oven, these sticky buns made with tender biscuit dough and covered in crunchy, sugary nuts are impossible to resist.

Tips

Biscuit dough should be soft. You can always add a little more flour if it's too sticky, but a soft dough is much more tender than one that is too stiff.

Store nuts in the freezer to keep them fresh.

- Preheat oven to 425°F (220°C)
- 9-inch (2.5 L) square cake pan, greased

Topping

½ cup	corn syrup	125 mL
⅓ cup	packed brown sugar	75 mL
3 tbsp	butter	45 mL
1 tbsp	water	15 mL
½ cup	chopped pecans	125 mL

Dough

2 cups	Robin Hood All-Purpose Flour	500 mL
4 tsp	baking powder	20 mL
1 tsp	salt	5 mL
½ cup	shortening	125 mL
1 cup	milk	250 mL

Filling

2 tbsp	packed brown sugar	30 mL
1 tbsp	butter, softened	15 mL
1 tsp	ground cinnamon	5 mL

1. *Topping:* Mix syrup, brown sugar, butter and water in cake pan. Cook on top of stove over medium heat until sugar is dissolved. Sprinkle with pecans. Set aside.

2. *Dough:* Combine flour, baking powder and salt in a mixing bowl. Using two forks, a pastry blender or your fingers, cut in shortening until mixture resembles coarse crumbs. Add milk all at once and stir with a fork until ingredients are moistened and a soft dough forms. Turn out onto a floured surface. Form into a ball and knead gently about 10 times. Roll out or pat dough to a 9-inch (23 cm) square.

3. *Filling:* Mix brown sugar, softened butter and cinnamon until well combined. Spread evenly over dough. Roll up jelly-roll fashion. Cut into nine 1-inch (2.5 cm) slices with a sharp knife. Place over topping in prepared pan.

4. Bake for 18 to 23 minutes or until golden brown and the center of each biscuit is firm. Invert pan onto serving plate immediately. Let stand for 5 minutes, then remove pan. Serve warm.

Variation

Use your favorite nut. Walnuts and hazelnuts also work well in this recipe.

CAKES AND FROSTINGS

◄ *Chocolate Raspberry Torte*

Chocolate Raspberry Torte

The combination of chocolate, fresh raspberries and whipped cream is always a winner. You can also make this using strawberry jam and fresh strawberries.

Tips

To make chocolate curls, use milk chocolate bars at room temperature. Draw a vegetable peeler across the bar. For smaller curls, use the narrow edge of the bar; for large curls, use the wide side.

When spreading a cream filling between cake layers, leave a small border around the edge so the cream doesn't spread into the frosting on the side of the cake.

Because it is soft, the chocolate–sour cream frosting spreads beautifully. It firms up as it cools.

Seedless raspberry jam or homemade versions have more flavor than regular store-bought.

- *Preheat oven to 350°F (180°C)*
- *Two 9-inch (1.5 L) round cake pans, greased and floured*

Cake

2 cups	Robin Hood All-Purpose Flour	500 mL
2 cups	granulated sugar	500 mL
3/4 cup	unsweetened cocoa powder	175 mL
1 1/2 tsp	baking powder	7 mL
1 1/2 tsp	baking soda	7 mL
1 tsp	salt	5 mL
2	eggs	2
1 cup	milk	250 mL
1/2 cup	vegetable oil	125 mL
2 tsp	vanilla	10 mL
1 cup	boiling water	250 mL

Filling

2 cups	whipping (35%) cream	500 mL
1/4 cup	icing sugar, sifted	50 mL
1 cup	raspberry jam	250 mL

Frosting

1 1/2 cups	semi-sweet chocolate chips	375 mL
3/4 cup	sour cream	175 mL
	Chocolate curls, optional (see Tips, left)	
	Fresh raspberries, optional	

1. *Cake:* Sift flour, sugar, cocoa, baking powder, baking soda and salt into a large mixer bowl. Add eggs, milk, oil and vanilla. Beat on medium speed of electric mixer for 2 minutes. Stir in boiling water until smooth. (Batter will be thin.) Pour into prepared pans.

2. Bake for 35 to 40 minutes or until a toothpick inserted in center comes out clean. Cool for 10 minutes in pans on rack, then remove layers and cool completely. Cut each in half horizontally to make four layers.

3. *Filling:* Beat whipping cream and icing sugar until stiff peaks form.

4. *Frosting:* In a small saucepan over low heat, melt chocolate chips (or microwave on Medium (50 %) for 2 minutes). Stir until smooth. Stir in sour cream.

5. *Assembly:* Place one halved cake layer cut-side up on serving plate. Spread with 1/3 cup (75 mL) jam and one-third of the cream mixture. Repeat layering, ending with top cake layer cut-side down. Frost top and sides of cake with frosting. Decorate with chocolate curls and fresh raspberries, if using. Chill until ready to serve and chocolate has set, about 30 minutes.

Rhubarb Cake

Fresh, rosy rhubarb adds its refreshing flavor to this delicious cake — a wonderful way to use up any surplus rhubarb from the garden.

Tips

Use only fresh rhubarb in this recipe. The cake is very moist, and frozen rhubarb would make the texture too soggy. Choose stalks of uniform thickness and cut into similarly sized pieces to ensure that they cook evenly.

Stalks that are fairly thin and pink to red, rather than green, are the most flavorful and tender.

One stalk should give you about ½ cup (125 mL) chopped rhubarb.

Baked goods containing rhubarb go well with custard sauce, vanilla ice cream or whipped cream.

When you're trying to watch your calorie intake, especially over the holidays, don't do without. Cut down on portion sizes, eat slowly and increase your activity level.

- *Preheat oven to 350°F (180°C)*
- *9-inch (2.5 L) square cake pan, greased*

Cake

½ cup	butter, softened	125 mL
1⅓ cups	packed brown sugar	325 mL
1	egg	1
1 tsp	vanilla	5 mL
1 cup	buttermilk	250 mL
2 cups	Robin Hood All-Purpose Flour	500 mL
1 tsp	baking soda	5 mL
½ tsp	salt	2 mL
2 cups	chopped fresh rhubarb	500 mL

Topping

⅓ cup	packed brown sugar	75 mL
1 tsp	ground cinnamon	5 mL

1. *Cake:* Beat butter, brown sugar, egg and vanilla in a large mixer bowl on medium speed of electric mixer until smooth and blended. Add buttermilk; mix well.

2. Combine flour, baking soda and salt. Add to buttermilk mixture, beating just until smooth. Fold in rhubarb. Spread batter evenly in prepared pan.

3. *Topping:* Combine brown sugar and cinnamon. Sprinkle evenly over batter.

4. Bake for 45 to 50 minutes or until toothpick inserted in center comes out clean. Cool in pan on rack.

Variation

Replace half of the rhubarb with strawberries or raspberries.

Pineapple Upside-Down Cake

**MAKES ABOUT
9 SERVINGS**

Preparation: 20 minutes
Baking: 75 minutes
Freezing:
not recommended

Though simple to make, this dessert always looks and tastes fabulous. Keep a can of pineapple rings in your pantry so you'll be able to prepare this anytime.

Tips

To add color and eye appeal, place a maraschino cherry in the center of each pineapple ring. Candied cherries also work well.

A 19 oz (540 mL) can of pineapple rings will give you the right number of rings. There may be one left over for the cook to eat.

You can prepare the brown-sugar topping right in the pan, so there won't be an extra pan to clean. To melt the butter, place the pan, with the butter, in the preheated oven or on the stove top over low heat.

- Preheat oven to 350°F (180°C)
- 9-inch (2.5 L) square cake pan, ungreased

Topping

1/3 cup	butter	75 mL
1 cup	packed brown sugar	250 mL
9	slices canned pineapple, drained	9
9	maraschino cherries, drained, optional	9

Cake

1/2 cup	butter, softened	125 mL
1 cup	granulated sugar	250 mL
2	eggs	2
1 tsp	vanilla	5 mL
1 3/4 cups	Robin Hood All-Purpose Flour	425 mL
1 tbsp	baking powder	15 mL
1/2 tsp	salt	2 mL
3/4 cup	milk	175 mL

1. *Topping:* Melt butter in cake pan (see Tips, left). Stir in brown sugar; mix well and spread evenly over bottom of pan. Place pineapple on top and a cherry in the center of each ring, if using. Set aside.

2. *Cake:* Cream butter, sugar, eggs and vanilla in a large bowl on medium speed of electric mixer until light and creamy. Combine flour, baking powder and salt. Add to creamed mixture alternately with milk, making three dry and two liquid additions and beating lightly after each addition. Spread batter evenly over pineapple.

3. Bake for 65 to 75 minutes or until toothpick inserted in center comes out clean. Cool for 10 minutes in pan on rack, then loosen cake around edges and invert onto a serving plate. Serve warm or cool.

Variation

Replace pineapple with enough peach slices to cover the bottom of the pan in a single layer. If using canned, drain first.

Jelly Roll

Preparation: 25 minutes
Baking: 15 minutes
Freezing: excellent

*Try this once and you'll
realize that making a jelly roll
is not as hard as it looks. The
hard part is choosing a filling,
because there are so many
tasty options.*

Tips

A jelly roll pan is a cookie sheet
with 1/2-inch (1 cm) sides.
Although 15- by 10 1/2-inch
(2 L) is the most common size,
they also come in a larger
version. All our recipes have
been made in the smaller pan.
Check to make sure you have
the right size or your cake will
not cook properly.

Although it uses extra dishes,
it is important to beat both
the egg whites and the yolks
in separate small bowls to get
the necessary volume.

An endless variety of fillings
work well in a plain jelly roll.
You can use jam or jelly, pie
filling, frosting, ice cream, or
plain or flavored whipped
cream, among others.

Complete the roll with a
dusting of icing sugar,
whipped cream or a frosting
that suits the filling.

The decorations are up to
you. Chopped nuts, shaved
chocolate and small candies
are just a start. Add a row of
candles for a birthday.

- *Preheat oven to 375°F (190°C)*
- *15- by 10 1/2-inch (2 L) jelly roll pan, greased and lined with waxed paper*

4	eggs, separated	4
1/3 cup	granulated sugar	75 mL
1/2 cup	granulated sugar	125 mL
1 tsp	vanilla	5 mL
3/4 cup	Robin Hood All-Purpose Flour	175 mL
1 tsp	baking powder	5 mL
1/2 tsp	salt	2 mL
2/3 cup	icing sugar	150 mL
1 1/2 cups	jam	375 mL

1. Beat egg whites in a small bowl on high speed of electric mixer until soft peaks form. Gradually add 1/3 cup (75 mL) sugar, beating until stiff peaks form. Set aside.

2. Beat egg yolks in a separate small bowl on high speed of electric mixer until creamy. Gradually add 1/2 cup (125 mL) sugar and vanilla, beating on high speed until thick, about 5 minutes. Transfer to a large bowl.

3. Combine flour, baking powder and salt. Sprinkle over egg yolk mixture. Add beaten egg white mixture and gently fold to blend thoroughly. Spread batter evenly in prepared pan.

4. Bake for 12 to 15 minutes or until the top is golden and springs back when lightly touched.

5. Sprinkle a large tea towel with 1/3 cup (75 mL) of the icing sugar. Immediately invert hot cake onto towel. Carefully remove waxed paper. Trim any crisp cake edges, if necessary. Roll warm cake up in towel, starting from one narrow end. Cool cake completely in towel on rack.

6. Unroll cake and spread with jam. Reroll tightly without towel. Sprinkle with remaining 1/3 cup (75 mL) icing sugar.

Glazed Apple Pinwheel Cake

**MAKES ABOUT
16 SERVINGS**

Preparation: 25 minutes
Baking: 55 minutes
Freezing:
not recommended

This showstopper fruit cake looks much harder to make than it actually is. It's an easy way to impress your guests.

Tips

Use firm apples, such as Golden Delicious, which will hold their shape during baking.

Select apples that are the same size.

Look for apricot jam that doesn't have a lot of chunks of fruit in it. It will be easier to strain to make a smooth glaze.

Brush cut fruit such as apples, pears, peaches and bananas with lemon juice to prevent it from turning brown.

Heat jam or jelly slightly to soften, if necessary.

- *Preheat oven to 350°F (180°C)*
- *10-inch (25 cm) springform pan, greased*

4 or 5	Golden Delicious apples, peeled, cored and quartered	4 or 5
1 tbsp	lemon juice	15 mL
½ cup	butter, softened	125 mL
¾ cup	granulated sugar	175 mL
2	eggs	2
1 tsp	lemon extract	5 mL
1¾ cups	Robin Hood All-Purpose Flour	425 mL
1½ tsp	baking powder	7 mL
½ tsp	salt	2 mL
½ cup	milk	125 mL
¾ cup	strained apricot jam	175 mL

1. Cut several deep slashes lengthwise in each apple quarter. Brush cut apples with lemon juice; set aside.
2. Beat butter, sugar, eggs and lemon extract in a large bowl on medium speed of electric mixer until light and creamy.
3. Combine flour, baking powder and salt. Add to creamed mixture alternately with milk, making three dry and two liquid additions on low speed, mixing well. Spread batter in prepared pan. Arrange apple quarters, slashed side up, on top of batter.
4. Bake for 50 to 55 minutes or until toothpick inserted in center comes out clean. Cool completely in pan on rack. Brush apricot jam over cooled cake.

Variation

Use apple jelly instead of apricot jam to glaze this cake. It works well for many cakes. If you're using red fruits, use red currant jelly.

Raspberry Streusel Coffee Cake

*Enjoy this luscious cake warm
for breakfast or brunch.*

Tips

This cake freezes well, so take advantage of fresh raspberries in season and make a few extra.

Thawed frozen raspberries work well in this recipe, although they are more likely to bleed into the batter.

For easy snacking and packing in lunch boxes, cut, wrap and freeze individual pieces of this cake. Simply remove the number required and let them thaw in their wrappers.

- *Preheat oven to 375°F (190°C)*
- *9-inch (2.5 L) square cake pan, greased*

Topping

⅓ cup	Robin Hood All-Purpose Flour	75 mL
⅓ cup	lightly packed brown sugar	75 mL
¼ cup	butter, softened	50 mL
1 tsp	ground cinnamon	5 mL

Cake

¾ cup	granulated sugar	175 mL
¼ cup	butter, softened	50 mL
1	egg	1
1 tsp	vanilla	5 mL
¾ cup	milk	175 mL
1¾ cups	Robin Hood All-Purpose Flour	425 mL
1 tbsp	baking powder	15 mL
½ tsp	salt	2 mL
1½ cups	fresh or frozen raspberries, thawed and drained	375 mL

1. *Topping:* Combine flour, sugar, butter and cinnamon, mixing until crumbly. Set aside.

2. *Cake:* Cream sugar, butter, egg and vanilla until thoroughly blended. Add milk, blending well. Combine flour, baking powder and salt; stir well. Add to creamed mixture all at once and stir just until moistened. Spread half of the batter in prepared pan. Spoon raspberries over batter. Spread remaining batter over berries.

3. Sprinkle topping evenly over batter. Press in lightly.

4. Bake for 40 to 45 minutes or until toothpick inserted in center comes out clean. Serve warm.

Variation

Replace raspberries with blueberries.

Sour Cream Coffee Cake

*This not-too-sweet cake is a
coffee-time favorite.*

Tips

Always have your ingredients
at room temperature before
you start to bake.

Don't substitute margarine
for butter — the flavor just
won't be the same.

When adding dry
ingredients to sour cream,
beat just enough to blend.
Overbeating at this stage will
toughen the cake and give
it a coarser texture.

Press nuts lightly into batter
on top of cake before baking
to help them stick.

- *Preheat oven to 350°F (180°C)*
- *8-inch (20 cm) springform pan, greased*

Cake

1 cup	sour cream	250 mL
1 tsp	baking soda	5 mL
½ cup	butter, softened	125 mL
1 cup	granulated sugar	250 mL
2	eggs	2
1 tsp	vanilla	5 mL
1¾ cups	Robin Hood All-Purpose Flour	425 mL
1 tsp	baking powder	5 mL
½ tsp	salt	2 mL

Topping

½ cup	packed brown sugar	125 mL
¼ cup	chopped pecans	50 mL
1 tsp	ground cinnamon	5 mL

1. *Cake:* Combine sour cream and baking soda in a small bowl; set aside.

2. Cream butter and sugar in a large mixer bowl on medium speed of electric mixer until light and fluffy. Add eggs, one at a time, beating thoroughly after each addition. Stir in vanilla.

3. Combine flour, baking powder and salt. Add to creamed mixture alternately with sour cream mixture, making three dry and two liquid additions on low speed, mixing lightly after each addition. Spread half of the batter in prepared pan.

4. *Topping:* Combine brown sugar, pecans and cinnamon. Sprinkle half over batter. Cover with remaining batter, then remaining topping. Press topping lightly into batter.

5. Bake for 50 to 60 minutes or until toothpick inserted in center comes out clean. Cover with aluminum foil if top is browning too quickly. Cool completely in pan on rack. Loosen edge of cake with a knife, then remove pan rim.

Variation

Replace pecans with walnuts, almonds, hazelnuts or cashews.

Queen Elizabeth Cake

**MAKES ABOUT
12 SERVINGS**

Preparation: 25 minutes
Baking: 45 minutes
Cooking: 3 minutes
Broiling: 3 minutes
Freezing: excellent

*A broiled topping works well
on almost any cake, and on
this moist, old-fashioned date
cake, it's a real winner.*

Tips

Broiled toppings brown very
quickly. Place them about
6 inches (15 cm) below the
element and watch carefully.

In this recipe, flaked coconut
works better than shredded,
which tends to burn under
the broiler.

The dates in this cake are
so subtle you can hardly
tell they are there. If
you're serving it to people
who think they don't like
dates, don't tell them —
they'll love the moist cake
without knowing the
secret ingredient.

- Preheat oven to 350°F (180°C)
- 9-inch (2.5 L) square cake pan, greased

Cake

1 cup	boiling water	250 mL
1 cup	chopped pitted dates	250 mL
1 tsp	baking soda	5 mL
¼ cup	butter, softened	50 mL
1 cup	granulated sugar	250 mL
1	egg	1
1 tsp	vanilla	5 mL
1½ cups	Robin Hood All-Purpose Flour	375 mL
1 tsp	baking powder	5 mL
½ tsp	salt	2 mL

Topping

1 cup	flaked coconut	250 mL
½ cup	packed brown sugar	125 mL
¼ cup	butter	50 mL
¼ cup	half-and-half (10%) cream	50 mL

1. *Cake:* Pour boiling water over dates and baking soda in a small bowl; mix and let stand until lukewarm.

2. Cream butter and sugar in a medium bowl until light and creamy. Beat in egg and vanilla. Combine flour, baking powder and salt. Add to creamed mixture alternately with date mixture, making three dry and two liquid additions. Mix well. Spread evenly in prepared pan.

3. Bake for 40 to 45 minutes or until toothpick inserted in center comes out clean.

4. *Topping:* While cake is baking, combine flaked coconut, brown sugar, butter and cream in a saucepan. Bring to a boil over medium heat and boil for 1 minute, stirring often. Spread over cake as soon as it comes out of the oven.

5. Broil 6 inches (15 cm) from element for 2 to 3 minutes or until bubbly and golden. Cool completely in pan on rack.

Variation

Substitute chopped nuts for half of the coconut in the topping.

Best-Ever Banana Cake

Light, moist and big on banana flavor — make this your next birthday cake.

Tips

This cake can also be prepared in a 13- by 9-inch (3.5 L) cake pan — just increase the baking time by 5 minutes.

If you don't have buttermilk, put 1½ tsp (7 mL) vinegar or lemon juice in a measuring cup and fill with milk to make ½ cup (125 mL). Let stand for 5 minutes, then stir.

The riper the bananas, the better the flavor. Ripe bananas also give a nice texture and appearance to baked goods. The dark flecks scattered throughout are very attractive.

This is an easy-to-make, one-bowl cake in which everything is beaten together. The conventional method adds liquid and dry ingredients alternately, in stages.

Try garnishing this cake with dried banana chips.

- Preheat oven to 350°F (180°C)
- Two 8-inch (1.2 L) round cake pans, greased and floured

2 cups	Robin Hood All-Purpose Flour	500 mL
1¾ tsp	baking powder	8 mL
1 tsp	baking soda	5 mL
½ tsp	salt	2 mL
1¼ cups	granulated sugar	300 mL
1 cup	mashed ripe banana (2 large)	250 mL
½ cup	butter, softened	125 mL
½ cup	buttermilk	125 mL
2	eggs	2
1 tsp	vanilla	5 mL

1. Combine flour, baking powder, baking soda and salt in a large mixer bowl. Add sugar, banana, butter and buttermilk. Beat at medium speed of electric mixer for 2 minutes. Add eggs and vanilla. Beat at medium speed for 1 minute. Spread batter evenly in prepared pans.

2. Bake for 35 to 40 minutes or until toothpick inserted in center comes out clean. Cool for 10 minutes in pans on rack, then remove from pans and transfer to rack to cool completely. Frost with Banana Butter Frosting (see recipe, below.)

Variations

Frost with Cocoa Butter Frosting (see recipe, page 154) Peanut Butter Frosting (see recipe, page 61) or Chocolate Whipped Cream (see recipe, page 156).

If you will finish eating the cake the same day it is baked, add a layer of sliced bananas between the cake layers.

Banana Butter Frosting

- Makes about 3 cups (750 mL) frosting
- Enough to fill and frost a 9-inch (23 cm) 2-layer cake

½ cup	butter, softened	125 mL
½ cup	mashed ripe banana (about 1 large)	125 mL
4 cups	icing sugar, sifted	1 L
1 tbsp	half-and-half (10%) cream	15 mL

1. In a large mixer bowl, cream butter, mashed banana and half of the icing sugar on medium speed of electric mixer until creamy. Add cream. Add remaining icing sugar gradually, beating until smooth and creamy.

Apple-Filled Cake

An abundance of cinnamon-coated apples make this simple cake moist and not too sweet.

Tips

Use a tart, firm apple, such as Granny Smith.

Slice apples thinly for even cooking.

Keep apples on hand for this and other quick fruit desserts, such as apple crisp.

One apple should make almost 1 cup (250 mL) sliced. Always have one more apple on hand than you think you'll need.

- *Preheat oven to 350°F (180°C)*
- *9-inch (2.5 L) square cake pan, greased*

2	eggs	2
1 cup	granulated sugar	250 mL
½ cup	vegetable oil	125 mL
3 tbsp	apple juice	45 mL
1½ cups	Robin Hood All-Purpose Flour	375 mL
2 tsp	baking powder	10 mL
¼ tsp	salt	1 mL
4 cups	thinly sliced peeled cored apples (about 5)	1 L
½ cup	packed brown sugar	125 mL
2 tsp	ground cinnamon	10 mL

1. Beat eggs and granulated sugar in a large bowl until thoroughly blended. Beat in oil and apple juice.

2. Combine flour, baking powder and salt. Stir into egg mixture, beating just until smooth. Spread half of the batter in prepared pan.

3. Combine apples, brown sugar and cinnamon. Toss lightly to coat. Spread over batter in pan. Cover with remaining batter.

4. Bake for 50 to 55 minutes or until toothpick inserted in center comes out clean. Cool completely in pan on rack.

Strawberry Cream Torte

A buttery cake shell holds a creamy cheese filling with strawberry jam inside. There's no need for icing, but an icing drizzle or dusting of icing sugar adds an appealing finishing touch.

Tips

Place pan on a piece of aluminum foil in the oven to catch any drips that may leak out.

Make sure the cream cheese is at room temperature so it will blend smoothly with the other ingredients.

Use light cream cheese if you want to reduce the calories.

If the strawberry jam seems too sweet, stir in 1 tsp (5 mL) lemon juice.

If there are large pieces of fruit in the jam, chop them a bit for an even consistency.

Stir jam to soften before spooning it over the filling.

• *Preheat oven to 350°F (180°C)*
• *10-inch (25 cm) springform pan, greased*

Crust

1¾ cups	Robin Hood All-Purpose Flour	425 mL
¾ cup	butter, softened	175 mL
½ cup	granulated sugar	125 mL
1 tsp	vanilla	5 mL
½ tsp	baking powder	2 mL
½ tsp	baking soda	2 mL
¼ tsp	salt	1 mL
2	eggs	2

Filling

1	package (8 oz/250 g) cream cheese, softened	1
1	egg	1
¼ cup	granulated sugar	50 mL
1 tsp	vanilla	5 mL
1 tsp	lemon juice	5 mL
1 cup	strawberry jam	250 mL

1. *Crust:* Combine flour, butter, sugar, vanilla, baking powder, baking soda, salt and eggs in a large mixer bowl. Beat at medium speed of electric mixer for about 2 minutes or until smooth. Spread over bottom and 2 inches (5 cm) up side of prepared pan. Set aside.

2. *Filling:* Beat cream cheese, egg, sugar, vanilla and lemon juice in a small bowl on medium speed of electric mixer until smooth and creamy. Spread ¼ cup (50 mL) of the jam over prepared crust. Pour cheese mixture evenly over top. Spoon remaining jam evenly over cheese mixture.

3. Bake for 45 to 55 minutes or until set and light golden. Serve slightly warm or cool.

Variations

Replace strawberry jam with your favorite kind. Apricot, peach, raspberry, plum, pineapple and mixed berry all work well in this recipe.

Decorate the plate with fresh berries for a pretty presentation.

Pineapple Walnut Carrot Cake

*Crushed pineapple adds
color, flavor and moistness
to a traditional favorite.*

Tips

Drain pineapple well. Carrot
cake is moist, and excess
liquid will cause it to fall.

Don't worry if the batter seems
very stiff. During baking, the
carrots release moisture.

Always peel carrots before
shredding them.

Instead of the Cream Cheese
Frosting, drizzle this cake with
an Orange Glaze (see recipe,
page 157) or finish simply
with a dusting of icing sugar.

*Don't limit the use of this
delicious frosting to carrot
cake. It's very versatile. Try it
on spice cake and chocolate
cake, too.*

Tips

When you package frosted
pieces of cake for lunch boxes,
lightly grease the area of the
wrapping that will come into
contact with the frosting.
When the cake is unwrapped,
the frosting will stay on the
cake, not the wrapping.

- *Preheat oven to 350°F (180°C)*
- *10-inch (4 L) tube pan, greased and floured*

1 cup	vegetable oil	250 mL
1½ cups	granulated sugar	375 mL
4	eggs	4
2 cups	Robin Hood All-Purpose Flour	500 mL
2 tsp	baking powder	10 mL
2 tsp	ground cinnamon	10 mL
1½ tsp	baking soda	7 mL
1 tsp	salt	5 mL
2 cups	shredded peeled carrots	500 mL
¾ cup	crushed pineapple, drained	175 mL
¾ cup	chopped walnuts, optional	175 mL

1. Pour vegetable oil into a large mixer bowl. Add sugar gradually, beating on medium speed of electric mixer until well blended. Add eggs, one at a time, beating after each addition. Continue beating until mixture is light.

2. Combine flour, baking powder, cinnamon, baking soda and salt. Add to sugar mixture, beating on medium speed until combined. Stir in remaining ingredients. Pour batter into prepared pan.

3. Bake for 60 to 70 minutes or until toothpick inserted in center comes out clean. Cool for 20 minutes in pan on rack, then remove from pan and transfer to rack to cool completely.

Basic Cream Cheese Frosting

- *Makes about 3 cups (750 mL) frosting*
- *Enough to fill and frost a 9-inch (23 cm) 2-layer cake*

1	package (8 oz/250 g) cream cheese, softened	1
½ cup	butter, softened	125 mL
1 tsp	vanilla	5 mL
3 to 3½ cups	icing sugar, sifted	750 to 875 mL

1. Beat cream cheese, butter and vanilla in a large mixer bowl on medium speed of electric mixer until fluffy. Gradually add icing sugar, beating until light and creamy. If necessary, add icing sugar, 1 tbsp (15 mL), at a time to stiffen.

Orange Cream Cheese Frosting: Omit vanilla. Add 1 tbsp (15 mL) grated orange zest and 2 tbsp (30 mL) orange juice to cheese mixture, alternately with icing sugar.

Pecan Cream Cheese Frosting: Fold 1 cup (250 mL) finely chopped pecans into frosting.

Divine Chocolate Raspberry Cake

**MAKES ABOUT
10 SERVINGS**

Preparation: 20 minutes
Baking: 28 minutes
Chilling: 30 minutes
Freezing: excellent

*Every bite of this luscious
cake is like eating a chocolate
raspberry truffle.*

Tips

You can choose the finish
for this cake to suit your
taste. Use a chocolate glaze
if you're appealing to
chocolate addicts or top with
a dollop of plain or Chocolate
Whipped Cream (see recipe,
page 156). Scatter some fresh
raspberries around the plate.

To add eye appeal to an
unglazed cake, place a doily
on top and sift icing sugar
over top. Remove the doily
and you're left with an
attractive sugar design.
Or decorate with chocolate
cutouts: Melt together 1 cup
(250 mL) each semi-sweet
and white chocolate chips
and 1 tbsp (15 mL) vegetable
oil. Cool slightly. Pour onto
a baking sheet lined with
waxed paper; spread
chocolate about ¼ inch
(5 mm) thick. Chill until
almost set. Press small
cookie cutters into chocolate.
Chill until firm, then lift
cutouts off the paper and
arrange them on the cake
or on serving plates.

- *Preheat oven to 350°F (180°C)*
- *8-inch (1.2 L) or 9-inch (1.5 L) round cake pan, greased and lined with a circle of parchment paper*

Cake

2	squares (each 1 oz/28 g) unsweetened chocolate, chopped	2
½ cup	butter	125 mL
2	eggs	2
½ cup	granulated sugar	125 mL
½ cup	seedless raspberry jam	125 mL
2 tsp	raspberry brandy	10 mL
1	square (1 oz/28 g) semi-sweet chocolate, finely chopped	1
⅔ cup	Robin Hood All-Purpose Flour	150 mL
½ tsp	baking powder	2 mL
¼ tsp	salt	1 mL

Chocolate Glaze, optional

¼ cup	butter	50 mL
4	squares (each 1 oz/28 g) semi-sweet chocolate, chopped	4

1. *Cake:* Melt unsweetened chocolate and butter in top of double boiler or small saucepan over low heat, stirring constantly, until smooth. Remove from heat.

2. Whisk together eggs, sugar, jam, brandy, chopped semi-sweet chocolate and melted chocolate in a large bowl until blended.

3. Combine flour, baking powder and salt. Add to egg mixture, whisking until smooth. Spread batter evenly in prepared pan.

4. Bake for 23 to 28 minutes or until toothpick inserted in center comes out clean. Cool for 10 minutes in pan on rack, then remove cake from pan and transfer to rack to cool completely. When cool, remove paper from bottom of cake.

5. *Glaze (optional):* Melt butter and chocolate in a small saucepan over low heat, stirring until smooth. Cool slightly until mixture starts to thicken and is a soft, spreadable consistency. Leave cake on rack but place a sheet of waxed paper underneath. Pour glaze over top of cake, letting it drip down, covering the sides. Chill to set glaze, about 30 minutes.

Variation

Replace raspberry jam with strained apricot jam and the raspberry brandy with apricot brandy.

Chocolate Toffee Candy Bar Cheesecake

This creamy cheesecake with chopped chocolate-covered toffee bars scattered throughout is rich and decadent.

Tips

If preparing the crust in a food processor, use cold butter cut into pieces.

Place the pan on a piece of aluminum foil in the oven to catch any drips, as the seal on springform pans is often less than perfect.

Run a knife around the edge of the pan to release the cake as soon as it comes out of the oven.

For the best texture, cool cheesecake completely, then chill in the refrigerator for at least 3 hours or overnight.

Cut cheesecakes with a warm wet knife.

Crush chocolate bars in their packages or in a plastic bag using a mallet or a rolling pin.

Skor chocolate bars work well in this recipe, or you can use your favorite brand.

- *Preheat oven to 350°F (180°C)*
- *10-inch (25 cm) springform pan, greased*

Crust

1 cup	Robin Hood All-Purpose Flour	250 mL
1/2 cup	cold butter	125 mL
1/3 cup	packed brown sugar	75 mL
1/3 cup	finely chopped almonds	75 mL

Filling

3	packages (each 8 oz/250 g) cream cheese, softened	3
3/4 cup	granulated sugar	175 mL
1 tbsp	Robin Hood All-Purpose Flour	15 mL
1 tsp	vanilla	5 mL
3	eggs	3
1/3 cup	sour cream	75 mL
3/4 cup	chopped crunchy toffee chocolate bars (3 bars, each 1.4 oz/39 g)	175 mL

1. *Crust:* Combine flour, butter, sugar and almonds in a food processor fitted with a metal blade and process until crumbly. (You can also do this in a mixing bowl, cutting the butter in.) Press firmly over bottom of prepared pan. Bake for 15 to 20 minutes or until light golden.

2. *Filling:* Beat cream cheese, sugar, flour and vanilla in a large bowl on medium speed of electric mixer until smooth. Add eggs, one at a time, beating lightly after each addition. Add sour cream and chocolate toffee pieces. Mix well. Spread mixture evenly over warm crust.

3. Bake for 15 minutes, then reduce temperature to 300°F (150°C) and bake for 45 to 50 minutes longer or until softly set. Remove from oven. Run knife around edge of pan. Cool completely in pan on rack. Chill for 3 hours or overnight before serving.

Variation

For an even more decadent dessert, serve with a drizzle of caramel or chocolate sauce.

Chocolate Cream Hazelnut Meringue Torte

<table>
<tr><td colspan="2">MAKES ABOUT
12 SERVINGS</td></tr>
<tr><td colspan="2">Preparation: 35 minutes
Baking: 35 minutes
Chilling: 1 to 6 hours
Freezing:
not recommended</td></tr>
</table>

One piece of this multilayered dessert will exhaust your weekly dessert quota, but it will definitely be worth every delicious calorie.

Tips

Tortes differ from layer cakes in that they usually have more layers and are quite rich. They are spectacular to look at and can be served in thin slices. This cake definitely meets all those criteria.

Cream of tartar helps keep the beaten egg whites stiff.

Use a food processor or nut grinder to finely chop the nuts.

The Chocolate Cream is delightful. Try using it on other cakes, such as the Chocolate Raspberry Torte (see recipe, page 132) or Best-Ever Banana Cake (see recipe, page 142).

- *Preheat oven to 350°F (180°C)*
- *Two 8-inch (1.2 L) or 9-inch (1.5 L) round cake pans, greased and floured*

Cake

½ cup	butter, softened	125 mL
½ cup	granulated sugar	125 mL
4	eggs, separated	4
1 tsp	vanilla	5 mL
1 cup	Robin Hood All-Purpose Flour	250 mL
1 tsp	baking powder	5 mL
¼ tsp	salt	1 mL
⅓ cup	milk	75 mL
¼ tsp	cream of tartar	1 mL
1 cup	granulated sugar	250 mL
¾ cup	finely chopped hazelnuts	175 mL

Chocolate Cream

¾ cup	granulated sugar	175 mL
⅓ cup	unsweetened cocoa powder, sifted	75 mL
1½ cups	whipping (35%) cream	375 mL

1. *Cake:* Cream butter and ½ cup (125 mL) sugar in a large bowl on medium speed of electric mixer until light. Add egg yolks, one at a time, beating for 1 minute after each addition. Stir in vanilla.

2. Combine flour, baking powder and salt. Add to creamed mixture alternately with milk, making three dry and two liquid additions, beating lightly on low speed after each addition. Spread evenly in prepared pans. Set aside.

3. Beat egg whites and cream of tartar in a small bowl until soft peaks form. Gradually add 1 cup (250 mL) sugar, beating until stiff peaks form. Fold in hazelnuts. Spread over batter.

4. Bake for 30 to 35 minutes or until toothpick inserted in center comes out clean. Cool for 10 minutes in pans on rack, then transfer to rack, meringue-side up. Cool completely.

5. *Chocolate Cream:* Combine sugar and cocoa in a medium bowl. Gradually add whipping cream, stirring until blended, then beat on medium speed of electric mixer until soft peaks form.

6. *Assembly:* Place one cake layer, meringue-side up, on serving plate. Spread half of the Chocolate Cream on top (not on the sides). Repeat layers. Chill for at least 1 hour or for up to 6 hours.

Variation

Replace hazelnuts with almonds or pecans.

Orange Chiffon Cake

Light as a feather, chiffon cakes are especially nice to serve after a hearty meal.

Tips

Chiffon cakes are quite versatile in their presentations. You can cut them in three layers and fill with whipped cream or a butter frosting. Or leave them whole and cover with a simple glaze.

When serving, cut the cake into wedges, and top with fresh fruit and a dollop of whipped cream or yogurt sauce. Macerated berries are especially tasty.

For a quick vanilla sauce, defrost a premium-quality French vanilla ice cream, stirring to obtain a smooth saucelike consistency. Chill until ready to serve.

Don't grease the pan. The batter rises up by sticking to the pan, which it won't do if the sides are greased. Basically, it has to crawl up the sides to achieve its volume.

To separate an egg neatly, break it into a small funnel. The yolk stays in the funnel, and the white passes through.

- *Preheat oven to 350°F (180°C)*
- *10-inch (4 L) tube pan, ungreased*

1¾ cups	Robin Hood All-Purpose Flour	425 mL
¾ cup	granulated sugar	175 mL
1 tbsp	baking powder	15 mL
1 tsp	salt	5 mL
6	eggs, separated	6
1 tbsp	grated orange zest	15 mL
¾ cup	orange juice	175 mL
½ cup	vegetable oil	125 mL
½ tsp	cream of tartar	2 mL
¾ cup	granulated sugar	175 mL

1. Combine flour, ¾ cup (175 mL) sugar, baking powder and salt in a large mixer bowl. Stir well. Add egg yolks, orange zest and juice, and oil. Beat on medium speed of electric mixer until smooth, about 30 seconds.

2. Beat egg whites and cream of tartar in a small bowl until soft peaks form. Gradually add ¾ cup (175 mL) sugar, beating until stiff, shiny peaks form. Fold one-quarter of the egg whites into egg yolk mixture until thoroughly blended. Gently fold in remainder. Pour batter into pan.

3. Bake for 55 to 60 minutes or until toothpick inserted in center comes out clean. Invert pan and cool completely in pan on rack. Run a knife around the edge to loosen, then shake pan to remove cake.

Variation

Lemon Chiffon Cake: Replace orange zest with lemon zest and orange juice with 2 tsp (10 mL) lemon juice plus enough water to make ¾ cup (175 mL) liquid.

Raspberry Almond Cake with Cream Cheese Frosting

A very attractive presentation turns a simple white layer cake into a special treat.

Tips

The cake mellows as it stands, so it improves if it is prepared a day ahead, then garnished when ready to serve.

Separate eggs when they are cold, but let the whites come to room temperature before beating to get the maximum volume.

For a smaller cake, freeze one layer for use at a later date and prepare only half of the frosting.

It is easier to cut cake layers if they are very cold. Chill thoroughly or freeze and partially thaw before slicing. Because chilling makes cakes less fragile, they are less likely to break as you cut them.

- *Preheat oven to 350°F (180°C)*
- *Two 8-inch (1.2 L) round cake pans, greased and floured*

Cake

¾ cup	butter, softened	175 mL
1½ cups	granulated sugar	375 mL
1 tsp	vanilla	5 mL
1 tsp	almond extract	5 mL
2 cups	Robin Hood All-Purpose Flour	500 mL
1 tbsp	baking powder	15 mL
½ tsp	salt	2 mL
1 cup	milk	250 mL
5	egg whites	5

Frosting

2	packages (each 8 oz/250 g) cream cheese, softened	2
6 tbsp	butter, softened	90 mL
1 tsp	vanilla	5 mL
1½ cups	icing sugar, sifted	375 mL

Filling

¾ cup	seedless raspberry jam	175 mL

Garnish

	Fresh raspberries, optional	
1⅓ cups	sliced almonds, toasted	325 mL

1. *Cake:* Beat butter, sugar, vanilla and almond extract in a large bowl on medium speed of electric mixer until light and creamy.

2. Combine flour, baking powder and salt. Add to butter mixture alternately with milk, making three dry and two liquid additions, mixing on low speed lightly after each.

3. Beat egg whites until stiff peaks form. Fold into batter gently until thoroughly combined. Spread batter evenly in prepared pans.

4. Bake for 35 to 40 minutes or until toothpick inserted in center comes out clean. Cool for 10 minutes in pans on rack, then remove from pans and transfer to a rack to cool completely. Cut each layer in half horizontally to make four layers total.

5. *Frosting:* Beat cream cheese, butter and vanilla in a large bowl on high speed of electric mixer until blended. Reduce speed to low and gradually add icing sugar, beating until smooth.

6. *Assembly:* Place one halved cake layer, cut-side up, on plate. Spread about ½ cup (125 mL) frosting over top. Drizzle ¼ cup (50 mL) jam over top. Repeat layering, ending with top cake layer, cut-side down. Spread remaining frosting on top and sides of cake.

7. *Garnish:* Garnish top with fresh raspberries, if using, and press almonds onto the side of cake. Chill until ready to serve.

Variation

Replace raspberry jam and raspberries with strawberry jam and strawberries.

Frostings

This versatile frosting lends itself to a variety of flavours.

Tips

Prepare an extra batch of frosting. Store it in the refrigerator for up to a month and let come to room temperature before using.

Add a little more cream if the frosting is too stiff or a little more icing sugar if too soft to make a spreadable consistency.

This frosting has a light, creamy chocolate color that looks and tastes terrific on dark chocolate cake.

Basic Butter Frosting

- *Makes about 2¾ cups (675 mL) frosting*
- *Enough to fill and frost an 8-inch (20 cm) 2-layer cake*

½ cup	butter, softened	125 mL
4 cups	icing sugar, sifted	1 L
⅓ cup	half-and-half (10%) cream or evaporated milk	75 mL
1 tsp	vanilla	5 mL

1. Beat butter and half of the sugar in a large mixer bowl on medium speed of electric mixer until light. Add cream and vanilla. Gradually add remaining sugar, beating until smooth.

   Lemon or Orange Butter Frosting: Omit vanilla; add 1 tbsp (15 mL) grated lemon or orange zest and 1 tbsp (15 mL) lemon or orange juice.

   Coffee Butter Frosting: Omit vanilla; add 1 tbsp (15 mL) instant coffee granules dissolved in 1 tsp (5 mL) warm water.

   Chocolate Butter Frosting: Melt 2 squares (each 1 oz/28 g) unsweetened chocolate; cool completely. Add to mixture before adding the cream and vanilla. Beat until smooth.

   Cocoa Butter Frosting: Replace ½ cup (125 mL) of the icing sugar with ½ cup (125 mL) unsweetened cocoa powder. Sift together cocoa and icing sugar before beating in.

Chocolate Sour Cream Frosting

- *Makes about 2½ cups (625 mL) frosting*
- *Enough to frost a 9-inch (23 cm) square cake*

¼ cup	butter	50 mL
3	squares (each 1 oz/28 g) semi-sweet chocolate	3
½ cup	sour cream	125 mL
3 cups	icing sugar, sifted	750 mL
2 tbsp	warm water	30 mL
1 tsp	vanilla	5 mL

1. In a small saucepan over low heat, combine butter and chocolate. Heat, stirring constantly, until smooth and melted. Cool slightly, then transfer to a large mixer bowl. Stir in sour cream. Gradually add sugar alternately with warm water, beating on low speed of electric mixer until smooth and creamy. Beat in vanilla. Chill slightly, if necessary, to reach a spreadable consistency.

Whipped Creams

This is a basic, slightly sweetened whipped cream from which you can make many different flavors.

Tips

Chill the bowl, beaters and cream well before beating.

Double the recipe if desired.

Basic Whipped Cream

- *Makes about 2 cups (500 mL) whipped cream*
- *Enough to fill and frost a 9-inch (23 cm) 2-layer cake*

1 cup	whipping (35%) cream	250 mL
2 tbsp	icing sugar, sifted	30 mL

Flavor Variations

1 tsp	vanilla	5 mL
1/2 tsp	almond extract	2 mL
1/2 tsp	rum or brandy extract	2 mL
1/2 tsp	maple extract	2 mL
1/2 tsp	ground cinnamon	2 mL
1 1/2 tsp	grated lemon or orange zest	7 mL
1 1/2 tsp	instant coffee granules	7 mL

1. In a small mixer bowl, beat cream, icing sugar and one of the flavorings on high speed of electic mixer until stiff peaks form.

Variation

Fold 1/4 cup (50 mL) crushed nut brittle, grated chocolate, chopped nuts, fruit or toasted coconut into whipped cream.

Chocolate Whipped Cream

- *Makes about 4 cups (1 L)*
- *Enough to fill and frost a 9-inch (23 cm) 4-layer cake*

2 cups	whipping (35%) cream	500 mL
1/2 cup	granulated sugar	125 mL
1/3 cup	unsweetened cocoa powder, sifted	75 mL

1. In a small mixer bowl, combine cream, sugar and cocoa. Chill for 15 minutes. Beat mixture until stiff peaks form.

Variation

Fold 1 cup (250 mL) crushed crunchy toffee chocolate bars, such as Skor, Heath, Butterfinger or Crispy Crunch into the whipped cream.

Glazes

Glazes are a nice alternative to frostings. They give a simple finishing touch in taste and appearance. They are quick and easy to prepare, too. They are usually drizzled over Bundt and tube cakes and will harden as they cool.

Vanilla or Almond Glaze

2 cups	icing sugar, sifted	500 mL
1 tbsp	butter, softened	15 mL
1 tsp	vanilla or almond extract	5 mL
2 to 3 tbsp	hot water	30 to 45 mL

1. In a small bowl, combine icing sugar and butter. Add vanilla and enough of the hot water to make a smooth, pourable consistency.

   Orange, Lemon or Lime Glaze: Omit vanilla and water. Add 2 tsp (10 mL) grated orange, lemon or lime zest and 2 to 4 tbsp (30 to 60 mL) orange, lemon or lime juice.

   Pineapple-Orange Glaze: Omit vanilla and water. Add 1 tsp (5 mL) grated orange zest and 2 to 4 tbsp (30 to 60 mL) pineapple juice.

   Coffee Glaze: Replace vanilla with 2 tsp (10 mL) instant coffee granules dissolved in 3 tbsp (45 mL) of the hot water.

There are many recipes for chocolate glaze, each a little different but all quite simple to make. They are warm when you spread or drizzle them and firm up as they cool. Here are two favorites.

Basic Chocolate Glaze

1	square (1 oz/28 g) unsweetened chocolate, chopped	1
¼ cup	water	50 mL
1 tbsp	butter	15 mL
2 cups	icing sugar, sifted	500 mL

1. In a small saucepan over low heat, heat chocolate, water and butter, stirring constantly until chocolate is melted and smooth. Remove from heat. Gradually add icing sugar, stirring until smooth. Add a little more water, if necessary, to reach a pourable consistency.

Basic Chocolate Chip Glaze

1 cup	granulated sugar	250 mL
⅓ cup	butter	75 mL
⅓ cup	half-and-half (10%) cream	75 mL
1 cup	semi-sweet chocolate chips	250 mL
½ tsp	vanilla	2 mL

1. In a small saucepan, combine sugar, butter and cream. Cook over medium heat, stirring constantly, until mixture comes to a boil. Boil for 1 minute. Remove from heat. Add chocolate chips and vanilla, stirring until smooth and melted. Pour warm glaze over top of cake, letting it drizzle down sides.

PIES AND PASTRY

◄ *Creamy Peach Crumble Pie*

Creamy Peach Crumble Pie

**MAKES ABOUT
8 SERVINGS**

Preparation: 20 minutes
Baking: 60 minutes
Freezing:
not recommended

The crumbly oat topping and creamy filling bring out the best in fresh peaches.

Tips

Although canned peaches would work in this pie, they don't have the same taste as fresh. It is best to make fruit pies with fresh fruit that is in season. The exception is apples, which are available yearround. In the winter, make non-fruit pies, such as pecan.

Large-flake oats look great in toppings and have a nice oat flavor that is enhanced by butter and brown sugar. If you don't have any, use regular or quick oats in this recipe.

If you have leftover peaches, sauté the peeled slices in a little butter and brown sugar until tender. Add a splash of rum, brandy or orange liqueur and serve warm over ice cream.

When filling an unbaked pie shell with fruit, sprinkle it lightly with fine dry bread crumbs before filling to prevent a soggy crust.

- *Preheat oven to 350°F (180°C)*
- *9-inch (23 cm) pie plate*

Crust

	Pastry for 9-inch (23 cm) single-crust pie (see recipes, pages 176 to 179, or use Robin Hood Flaky Pie Crust Mix)	

Topping

¾ cup	Robin Hood All-Purpose Flour	175 mL
½ cup	packed brown sugar	125 mL
⅓ cup	Robin Hood or Old Mill Large-Flake Oats	75 mL
1 tsp	ground cinnamon	5 mL
⅓ cup	butter	75 mL

Filling

¾ cup	sour cream	175 mL
½ cup	granulated sugar	125 mL
¼ cup	Robin Hood All-Purpose Flour	50 mL
6	medium peaches, peeled, pitted and sliced	6

1. *Crust:* Prepare pastry for unbaked pie shell. Roll out and fit into pie plate.
2. *Topping:* Combine flour, brown sugar, oats and cinnamon in a bowl. Using two knives, a pastry blender or your fingers, cut in butter until mixture resembles coarse crumbs. Set aside.
3. *Filling:* Mix sour cream, sugar and flour in a bowl until smooth. Stir in peaches. Spread in bottom of pie shell. Sprinkle topping evenly over filling. Place pie on a piece of aluminum foil to catch any drips.
4. Bake on bottom rack for 50 to 60 minutes or until peaches are tender. Cool completely on rack.

Variation

Replace half or all of the peaches with apples.

Fresh Strawberry Pie

The fresh strawberries create an explosion of color and flavor in this dynamite pie.

Tips

Drizzle melted chocolate over the filling for a special treat.

The berries can be soft for the cooked sauce but should be firmer for the uncooked portion.

If the berries seem very wet, add another teaspoon (5 mL) of cornstarch.

- *Preheat oven to 400°F (200°C)*
- *9-inch (23 cm) pie plate*

Crust

1 cup	Robin Hood All-Purpose Flour	250 mL
1/2 cup	butter, softened	125 mL
1/4 cup	icing sugar, sifted	50 mL
1/4 cup	ground pecans	50 mL

Filling

5 1/2 cups	fresh strawberries	1.375 L
1 cup	granulated sugar	250 mL
3 tbsp	cornstarch	45 mL
1 tbsp	lemon juice	15 mL

1. *Crust:* Combine flour, butter, icing sugar and pecans, mixing until smooth. Turn out onto a floured board and knead lightly to form a smooth dough. Press firmly into bottom and up sides of pie plate. Prick well with a fork. Chill for 20 minutes.

2. Bake on bottom rack of oven for 12 to 15 minutes or until golden. Cool completely.

3. *Filling:* Cut 2 cups (500 mL) of the strawberries in half. Combine with sugar and cornstarch in a small saucepan. Cook over medium-high heat, stirring constantly, until mixture starts to bubble. Reduce heat to low and cook, stirring often, until berries soften and mixture thickens slightly. Chill to lukewarm.

4. Leave remaining berries whole if small or halve if large. Mix with thickened berry mixture. Cool completely. Pour mixture into baked pie shell. Chill for 1 hour before serving.

Variations

Replace pecans with hazelnuts or almonds.

Replace some of the fresh strawberries with blueberries, raspberries or a mixture of berries.

Chilly Orange Cream Pie

*Don't save this cool,
refreshingly light pie for the
lazy, hazy days of summer.
Enjoy its delicious flavor
year-round.*

Tips

Bake pie shells one or two days ahead for convenience.

Gelatin pies need at least four hours to set in order to slice properly. That makes them good choices for entertaining, as you can prepare dessert the day before you intend to serve it.

Canned mandarin oranges are a convenient choice for this pie. If desired, add slices of fresh orange for an attractive garnish.

Robin Hood Flaky Pie Crust Mix is a busy cook's dream. The ingredients have been premeasured, and the mix makes a very flaky pastry even if you overwork the dough.

If you love lemon, increase the lemon juice to ½ cup (125 mL).

Add 1 tbsp (15 mL) sesame seeds to the pie crust for a nice, nutty flavor.

- *Preheat oven to 425°F (220°C)*
- *9-inch (23 cm) pie plate*

Crust

	Pastry for 9-inch (23 cm) single-crust pie (see recipes, pages 176 to 179, or use Robin Hood Flaky Pie Crust Mix)	

Filling

1	envelope (1 tbsp/15 mL) unflavored gelatin	1
2 tbsp	cold water	30 mL
1	can (10 oz/284 mL) mandarin oranges, drained and coarsely chopped, juice reserved	1
¾ cup	granulated sugar	175 mL
⅓ cup	lemon juice	75 mL
1 cup	whipping (35%) cream	250 mL
	Whipped cream and orange slices, optional	

1. *Crust:* Prepare and bake pie shell according to recipe or package instructions. Cool completely.

2. *Filling:* Mix gelatin and cold water. Let stand for 10 minutes to soften.

3. Pour mandarin juice into a measuring cup and add enough water to make 1 cup (250 mL). In a saucepan, bring mixture to a boil. Add gelatin mixture, stirring until dissolved. Stir in sugar and lemon juice. Mix well. Refrigerate for 2 hours or until mixture just starts to thicken but does not set.

4. Beat cream until soft peaks form. Fold into gelatin mixture gently but thoroughly. Fold in mandarins. Spread evenly in pie shell. Chill for 4 hours or overnight or until set.

Variations

Melt 2 squares (each 1 oz/28 g) semi-sweet chocolate and spread over pastry shell. Let set before filling.

Substitute clementines for the mandarins.

Raspberry Lattice Pie

There are few sights prettier than fresh red raspberries peeking through glistening golden pastry strips in this favorite pie.

Tips

For a rich golden crust, brush lattice with the glaze. A sprinkle of sugar will add sparkle to the pastry.

Start pies in a hot oven (425°F/220°C) and place them on the bottom rack. This quickly creates steam in the pastry, which makes air pockets that push up the flakes of fat-coated starch, creating a flaky crust.

Cool pies before cutting to allow time for the filling to set.

When fluting the edge, keep it high. This helps keep the juices in the pie.

Watch the pie carefully. If the pastry seems to be browning too quickly around the edges, cut the inside from a foil pie plate and place the rim over the pie to prevent over-browning. It stays in place and is reusable.

- *Preheat oven to 425°F (220°C)*
- *9-inch (23 cm) pie plate*

Crust

	Pastry for 9-inch (23 cm) double-crust pie (see recipes, pages 176 to 179, or use Robin Hood Flaky Pie Crust Mix)	

Filling

4 cups	fresh raspberries	1 L
2/3 to 1 cup	granulated sugar, depending on sweetness of fruit	150 to 250 mL
3 tbsp	quick-cooking tapioca or cornstarch	45 mL
1 tbsp	lemon juice	15 mL
2 tbsp	butter	30 mL

Glaze, optional

1	egg yolk	1
2 tsp	water	10 mL
	Granulated sugar	

1. *Crust:* Prepare pastry for double-crust pie. Roll out bottom crust and fit into pie plate.

2. *Filling:* Combine raspberries, sugar, tapioca and lemon juice in a large bowl. Toss gently until fruit is thoroughly coated. Turn into the pastry-lined pie plate and dot with butter.

3. Roll out pastry for top crust. Cut into strips about ½ inch (1 cm) wide. Arrange strips about 1 inch (2.5 cm) apart on top of the filling, weaving lengthwise and crosswise strips to form a lattice. Press strips against the edge of the bottom pastry and seal. Flute edge.

4. *Glaze (optional):* Beat egg yolk and water in a small bowl. Brush lightly over lattice strips. Sprinkle with sugar.

5. Bake on bottom rack of oven for 15 minutes, then reduce temperature to 350°F (180°C) and bake for 25 to 35 minutes longer or until crust is golden and fruit is tender and bubbly.

Best Blueberry Pie

**MAKES ABOUT
8 SERVINGS**

Preparation: 25 minutes
Baking: 1 hour
Freezing: excellent

Blueberries are a plentiful treat during Canadian summers. Enjoy the bounty in this simple double-crust pie.

Tips

If using frozen fruit, thaw just enough to separate the berries. Replace the flour with cornstarch, which has twice as much thickening power — it's necessary to accommodate the additional juice in the frozen fruit. Also, increase the baking time by about 20 minutes. Watch carefully and cover the top with aluminum foil during baking if it's browning too quickly.

For a nicely browned top, brush the crust with an egg glaze (see Glaze, page 164).

As an added safeguard, press the floured tines of a fork into the fluted edge that rests on the plate rim. This keeps the fruit in place and helps seal in the juices.

If you have trouble rolling and placing the top crust on a pie (or you just want a fun alternative to a plain top), cut the pastry into attractive shapes with a cookie cutter and arrange the pieces, slightly overlapping, over the filling.

- *Preheat oven to 425°F (220°C)*
- *9-inch (23 cm) pie plate*

Crust

	Pastry for 9-inch (23 cm) double-crust pie (see recipes, pages 176 to 179 or use Robin Hood Flaky Pie Crust Mix)	

Filling

5 cups	fresh or frozen blueberries (see tips, left)	1.25 L
¾ cup	granulated sugar	175 mL
⅓ cup	Robin Hood All-Purpose Flour	75 mL
2 tsp	grated lemon zest	10 mL
1 tbsp	lemon juice	15 mL
2 tbsp	butter	30 mL

1. *Crust:* Prepare pastry for double-crust pie. Roll out bottom crust and fit into pie plate.
2. *Filling:* Combine blueberries, sugar, flour and lemon zest and juice. Toss gently until fruit is thoroughly coated. Turn into the pastry-lined pie plate and dot with butter.
3. Roll out pastry for top crust. Arrange over filling. Seal and flute edge. Slash top crust to allow steam to escape. Place pie on a piece of aluminum foil to catch drips.
4. Bake on bottom rack of oven for 15 minutes, then reduce heat to 350°F (180°C) and bake for 35 to 45 minutes longer or until crust is golden and fruit is tender and bubbly.

Variations

Replace half of the blueberries with raspberries.

A pinch of ground nutmeg or ginger adds an intriguing hint of flavor to fruit pies.

Chocolate Peanut Butter Cream Pie

*This luscious dessert is like a
chocolate peanut butter cup
dressed up as a pie.*

Tips
Use smooth peanut butter
in the filling to maintain
a creamy texture.

Sift the icing sugar after
measuring and add it
gradually to the cheese
mixture. Adding it all at once
makes it more difficult to
blend smoothly.

When adding melted butter
to recipes, unless otherwise
specified, the butter should
be cooled but still liquid.

To get the maximum volume
when whipping cream, chill
the bowl and beaters.

Decorate the top of this pie
with quartered chocolate
peanut butter cups.

- *Preheat oven to 425°F (220°C)*
- *9-inch (23 cm) pie plate*

Crust

	Pastry for 9-inch (23 cm) single-crust pie (see recipes, pages 176 to 179, or use Robin Hood Flaky Pie Crust Mix)	

Filling

1¼ cups	smooth peanut butter	300 mL
1	package (8 oz/250 g) cream cheese, softened	1
¾ cup	icing sugar, sifted	175 mL
2 tbsp	butter, melted	30 mL
2 tsp	vanilla	10 mL
1¼ cups	whipping (35%) cream	300 mL
¼ cup	icing sugar, sifted	50 mL

Glaze

⅓ cup	whipping (35%) cream	75 mL
3	squares (each 1 oz/28 g) semi-sweet chocolate, chopped	3

1. *Crust:* Prepare and bake pie shell according to recipe or package instructions. Cool completely.

2. *Filling:* Beat peanut butter and cream cheese in a large bowl on medium speed of electric mixer until smooth. Gradually add ¾ cup (175 mL) icing sugar, melted butter and vanilla; mix well.

3. Beat whipping cream and ¼ cup (50 mL) icing sugar until stiff peaks form. Stir one-quarter of the whipped cream into peanut butter mixture and mix thoroughly. Fold in remaining cream gently but thoroughly. Spoon into prepared crust. Chill for 1 hour or until firm.

4. *Glaze:* Bring cream to a boil in a small saucepan over low heat. Remove from heat. Add chocolate, stirring until melted and smooth. Cool slightly. Pour over filling, tilting pie to cover top completely. Chill for at least 1 hour or overnight to set glaze.

Variation

For an even more decadent treat, chop two chocolate bars with peanut butter filling and spread them evenly over the baked pie shell before adding the filling.

Easy Bumbleberry Pie

Preparation: 30 minutes
Baking: 65 minutes
Freezing: excellent

This mixture of apples and berries brings out the best in all the fruits. The pie looks fabulous as well.

Tips

Toss apples with the lemon juice as soon as you slice them to prevent browning.

After the filling is mixed, let it stand for 5 minutes, then mix it again before adding it to the pastry. This gives the flour and sugar a better chance to become thoroughly blended with the fruit, which helps the filling thicken during baking.

- *Preheat oven to 425°F (220°C)*
- *9-inch (23 cm) pie plate*

Crust

| | Pastry for 9-inch (23 cm) double-crust pie (see recipes, pages 176 to 179, or use Robin Hood Flaky Pie Crust Mix) | |

Filling

¾ cup	granulated sugar	175 mL
6 tbsp	Robin Hood All-Purpose Flour	90 mL
4 cups	sliced peeled cored apples	1 L
1 cup	raspberries	250 mL
1 cup	blueberries	250 mL
1 tbsp	lemon juice	15 mL
2 tbsp	butter	30 mL

1. *Crust:* Prepare pastry for double-crust pie. Roll out bottom crust and fit into pie plate.

2. *Filling:* Mix sugar and flour in a large bowl. Add apples, raspberries, blueberries and lemon juice. Toss gently until fruit is thoroughly coated. Turn into the pastry-lined pie plate and dot with butter.

3. Roll out pastry for top crust. Arrange over filling. Seal and flute the edge. Slash the top to allow steam to escape. Place pie on a piece of aluminum foil to catch drips.

4. Bake on bottom rack of oven for 15 minutes, then reduce temperature to 350°F (180°C) and bake for 40 to 50 minutes longer or until crust is golden and apples are tender and bubbly.

Variation

Replace apples with peaches.

Walnut Raspberry Tart

**MAKES ABOUT
12 SERVINGS**

Preparation: 30 minutes
Baking: 45 minutes
Freezing: excellent
(without topping)

*This tart is a real dazzler.
The tender, buttery crust and
cinnamon-sugared walnut
filling combined with a
raspberry-and-cream topping
has great taste, texture and
eye appeal.*

Tips

Prepare the tart a day ahead,
then add the topping when
you are ready to serve.

A shortbread crust usually
needs to be kneaded with
your hands. Work the dough
to make it come together
smoothly rather than adding
more butter, which will cause
it to shrink down the sides
of the pan and become too
crisp when baked.

Chop the walnuts in fairly
chunky pieces, not finely.

- *Preheat oven to 400°F (200°C)*
- *10-inch (25 cm) fluted flan pan with removable bottom*

Crust

½ cup	butter, softened	125 mL
¼ cup	granulated sugar	50 mL
1½ cups	Robin Hood All-Purpose Flour	375 mL
¼ tsp	salt	1 mL
1	egg, beaten	1

Filling

2	eggs	2
1	egg yolk	1
1 cup	packed brown sugar	250 mL
½ cup	Robin Hood All-Purpose Flour	125 mL
¾ tsp	ground cinnamon	3 mL
½ tsp	baking powder	2 mL
2 cups	walnut pieces, coarsely chopped	500 mL

Topping

¾ cup	red currant jelly	175 mL
4 cups	fresh raspberries	1 L
1 cup	whipped cream, optional	250 mL

1. *Crust:* Cream butter and sugar in a large bowl until light and creamy. Add flour, salt and egg. Mix well then knead lightly to form a smooth dough. Press into bottom and 1 inch (2.5 cm) up side of pan.

2. Bake on bottom rack of oven for 8 to 10 minutes or until very light golden. Reduce heat to 350°F (180°C).

3. *Filling:* Beat eggs, egg yolk and brown sugar in a small bowl on medium speed of electric mixer until light and fluffy. Add flour, cinnamon and baking powder and mix until blended. Stir in walnuts. Pour into crust.

4. Bake at 350°F (180°C) for 30 to 35 minutes longer or until filling is set. Cool completely in pan on rack.

5. *Topping:* Melt jelly in a small saucepan over low heat. Add berries, stirring to coat. Spread evenly over top of cooled tart filling. Serve with dollops of whipped cream, if using.

Variations

Use a combination of raspberries and blackberries in the topping.

Replace the red currant jelly with raspberry or strawberry jelly. Red apple jelly is fine, too.

Fabulous Fruit Flan

MAKES ABOUT 8 SERVINGS

Preparation: 35 minutes
Baking: 10 minutes
Freezing: not recommended

This all-year-round dessert changes its look constantly depending on what fruits are in season. Enjoy fresh berries in the summer and canned fruit in the winter.

Tips

When using canned fruits, such as mandarin oranges and peach slices, set them on a paper towel to drain well before arranging them over the filling. Do not use frozen fruit in this flan, as is it too soft and wet.

Make this flan as simple (all one fruit) or as colorful and elaborate (several kinds of fruit) as you like.

Prepare the crust a few days ahead for easy entertaining.

Because this crust is like shortbread, only butter will do. Work the dough with your hands until it melds into a smooth ball.

If using red fruit, such as berries, use red currant jelly for the glaze.

Serve this flan at room temperature for best results. If it has been chilling in the refrigerator, bring it to room temperature to serve.

- *Preheat oven to 425°F (220°C)*
- *9-inch (23 cm) fluted flan pan with removable bottom*

Crust

1¼ cups	Robin Hood All-Purpose Flour	300 mL
2 tbsp	icing sugar, sifted	30 mL
½ cup	butter, softened	125 mL

Filling

1	package (8 oz/250 g) cream cheese, softened	1
½ cup	icing sugar, sifted	125 mL
1 tsp	vanilla	5 mL
½ cup	whipping (35%) cream	125 mL
3 cups	fruit	750 mL

Glaze, optional

½ cup	apricot jam, put through a sieve	125 mL
1 tbsp	lemon juice	15 mL

1. *Crust:* Combine flour and icing sugar. Cream butter in a bowl and gradually blend in flour mixture. Use your hands to form a smooth dough. Press evenly onto bottom and up side of pan; prick well with fork and chill for 15 minutes.

2. Bake on bottom rack of oven for 7 to 10 minutes or until light golden. Cool completely in pan on rack.

3. *Filling:* Beat cream cheese, icing sugar and vanilla until smooth. Whip cream until stiff peaks form and fold into cheese mixture. Spread evenly in baked crust.

4. Arrange fruit attractively over filling.

5. *Glaze (optional):* If desired, melt jam and lemon juice together until smooth and brush over fruit. Serve at room temperature.

Variation

Use your favorite fresh or canned fruit: strawberries, raspberries, blueberries, blackberries, kiwifruit, grapes, apricots, mandarins, pineapple, peaches and so on; they're all scrumptious.

Lemon Meringue Pie

This is the ultimate pie, a favorite with lemon lovers everywhere.

Tips

Serve lemon meringue pie the same day you make it for the best taste and appearance.

With a homemade lemon filling, you can control the tartness. If you like a pucker-up taste, increase the lemon juice to ¾ cup (175 mL) and decrease the water to 1¼ cups (300 mL).

Use fresh lemons, not packaged juice, for the best flavor. One lemon will give you about ¼ cup (50 mL) juice and 2 tsp (10 mL) grated zest.

This meringue takes a little more time to prepare than some other versions, but the results are worth it. The cornstarch stabilizes the meringue so it won't weep. The lower baking temperature produces a beautiful, evenly browned crust.

- *Preheat oven to 425°F (220°C)*
- *9-inch (23 cm) pie plate*

Crust

	Pastry for 9-inch (23 cm) single-crust pie (see recipes, pages 176 to 179, or use Robin Hood Flaky Pie Crust Mix)	

Filling

1½ cups	cold water	375 mL
1 cup	granulated sugar	250 mL
¼ cup	cornstarch	50 mL
Pinch	salt	Pinch
6	egg yolks	6
1 tbsp	grated lemon zest	15 mL
½ cup	lemon juice	125 mL
2 tbsp	butter	30 mL

Meringue

⅓ cup	cold water	75 mL
1 tbsp	cornstarch	15 mL
½ cup	granulated sugar	125 mL
¼ tsp	cream of tartar	1 mL
4	egg whites	4

1. *Crust:* Prepare and bake pie shell according to recipe or package instructions. Cool completely.

2. *Filling:* Combine water, sugar, cornstarch and salt in a large saucepan. Bring to a simmer over medium heat, whisking constantly. When mixture starts to simmer and turn translucent, add egg yolks, two at a time, whisking after each addition until thoroughly blended. Whisk in lemon zest and juice and butter. Bring mixture to a boil, whisking constantly. Remove from heat. Cover surface with plastic wrap to keep warm and prevent a skin from forming. Set aside.

3. *Meringue:* Mix water and cornstarch in a small saucepan. Bring to a simmer, whisking constantly. When mixture starts to simmer and turn translucent, remove from heat. Cool while going on to next step.

4. Preheat oven to 325°F (160°C). Mix sugar and cream of tartar. Beat egg whites in a medium bowl until frothy. Add sugar mixture, 1 tbsp (15 mL) at a time, beating until soft peaks form. Add cornstarch mixture, 1 tbsp (15 mL) at a time, beating until stiff peaks form.

The filling should be hot when you add it to the shell and cover it with meringue. If meringue is placed on a cool filling, it can cause condensation or weeping under the meringue.

Spread the meringue so it adheres to the pastry to prevent it from shrinking as it cooks.

5. If necessary, return lemon filling to low heat for 1 minute or until hot. Pour hot filling into baked pie shell. Immediately spread meringue over the filling, sealing it to the crust. Make peaks using the back of a spoon.

6. Bake for 15 to 20 minutes or until golden. Cool completely in plate on rack. Serve the same day.

Mixed Nut Tart

*If you like nuts, you'll love
this tart, which is loaded with
them. It has a similar flavor
to pecan pie*

Tips

Buy deluxe mixed nuts with
no peanuts or make your
own blend using pecans,
almonds, hazelnuts, cashews
and Brazil nuts.

Use nuts that are similar in
size. If using large Brazil nuts,
cut them in half.

Take the time to turn some
of the nuts in the filling right
side up for the most
attractive presentation.

Use salted nuts. The
combination of sweet and
salty is particularly appealing.

Pastry made with butter
shrinks more and is not
as flaky as that made
with shortening.

To transfer dough to the pan,
drape it over the rolling pin or
fold it in half for easy moving.

- Preheat oven to 400°F (200°C)
- 11-inch (27 cm) fluted flan pan with removable bottom

Crust

1½ cups	Robin Hood All-Purpose Flour	375 mL
2 tbsp	granulated sugar	30 mL
¼ tsp	salt	1 mL
½ cup	cold shortening or butter	125 mL
4 to 5 tbsp	cold water	60 to 75 mL

Filling

2	eggs	2
½ cup	packed brown sugar	125 mL
½ cup	corn syrup	125 mL
3 tbsp	butter, melted	45 mL
2 tsp	vanilla	10 mL
2 cups	deluxe mixed nuts (11 oz/300 g)	500 mL
	Whipped cream, optional	

1. *Crust:* Combine flour, sugar and salt in a mixing bowl. Using a pastry blender, two knives or your fingers, cut in shortening until mixture resembles coarse crumbs. Add water, 1 tbsp (15 mL) at a time, mixing lightly with a fork until dough comes together. Add just enough water to hold dough together. Press into a ball.

2. Roll dough out on lightly floured surface to a 14-inch (35 cm) round. Transfer to pan. Press into bottom and up side of pan. Fold overhang in and press against side of pan to form a rim slightly taller than the edge of the pan. Prick bottom with a fork.

3. Bake for 15 minutes or until set but not golden. Reduce temperature to 375°F (190°C).

4. *Filling:* Whisk eggs, brown sugar, corn syrup, butter and vanilla in a medium bowl until smoothly blended. Stir in nuts. Pour mixture into tart shell.

5. Bake on bottom rack of oven for 25 to 30 minutes or until set and golden. Cool completely in pan on rack. Serve with whipped cream, if using.

Variation

If you prefer, use a mixture of nuts that contains peanuts, but keep the peanuts to a minimum for the best flavor and appearance.

Basic Pastry

This-tried-and-true recipe makes tender, flaky pastry every time.

Tips

If you are concerned about your consumption of trans fats, replace ¼ cup (50 mL) of the shortening with cold butter. Trans fats raise LDL (bad cholesterol), while lowering HDL (good cholesterol). Although butter is high in saturated fat, it is a healthier choice because it raises HDL as well as LDL.

Robin Hood Cake-and-Pastry Flour helps take the worry out of making pastry, as it is more forgiving of little mistakes. If you are using all-purpose flour, handle the dough as little as possible, because too much handling will make it tough.

A pastry cloth and rolling pin cover are worthwhile investments. They eliminate sticking, which means when rolling it out you only need to use a minimum amount of extra flour, which makes the dough tough.

Use a pastry blender to cut in the shortening and don't make the mixture too fine. Flaky pastry is created when the lumps of fat melt during baking.

- *9-inch (23 cm) pie plate*

Single Crust

1 cup + 2 tbsp	Robin Hood Cake-and-Pastry Flour	280 mL
½ tsp	salt	2 mL
½ cup	cold shortening	125 mL
2 to 3 tbsp	cold water	30 to 45 mL

Double Crust

2¼ cups	Robin Hood Cake-and-Pastry Flour	550 mL
¾ tsp	salt	3 mL
¾ cup	cold shortening	175 mL
4 to 6 tbsp	cold water	60 to 90 mL

1. Combine flour and salt in a mixing bowl. Using two knives, a pastry blender or your fingers, cut in shortening until mixture is uniform and resembles large peas. Don't overblend.

2. Sprinkle with water, 1 tbsp (15 mL) at a time, mixing lightly with a fork after each addition. Add just enough water to hold dough together. Press into a ball. Chill for 15 to 30 minutes for easy rolling.

3. Divide dough into 2 portions for double-crust pie. Flatten into round disc(s). Place 1 disc on a floured surface or pastry cloth.

4. Roll out dough to a uniform thickness (about ⅛ inch/0.3 cm), starting in the center and rolling, spoke-fashion, toward the edge with light, even strokes. If dough sticks, dust the bottom of the pastry or the board lightly with flour. Roll pastry loosely around the rolling pin, then unroll over the pie plate; ease into the plate without stretching. Trim dough ½ inch (1 cm) beyond the edge of the pie plate.

5. For a single crust, fold under the edge and flute.

6. For a double crust, fill bottom crust, then roll out remaining dough as for bottom crust and flip over filling. Fold edge of top crust under the overhang of bottom crust; seal and flute edge. Cut slits in the center of the top crust to allow steam to escape.

Variations

Replace ¼ cup (50 mL) shortening with cold butter. Shortening makes the pastry tender, flaky and easy to handle, while butter adds flavor and color.

All-Purpose Flour: Use 1 cup (250 mL) for a single crust and 2 cups (500 mL) for a double crust.

When assembling double-crust pies, you can flute the edges by pinching the evenly trimmed top and bottom crusts together in a crimped pattern, or simply seal them together using the tines of a fork.

Start pies in a hot oven (425°F/220°C) and place them on the bottom rack. This quickly creates steam in the pastry, which makes air pockets that push up the flakes of fat-coated starch, creating a flaky crust.

For convenience, make pastry dough ahead of time. Unrolled pastry dough can be stored in the refrigerator for up to 3 days or frozen for up to 6 months. Thaw frozen dough overnight in the refrigerator before rolling it out.

Baking Pastry

The following general directions are for baking pastry. If there are specific directions in your recipe, follow those.

Double Crust: Cut slits in top crust or prick with a fork. Bake in a 425°F (220°C) oven for 40 to 50 minutes or until the top is golden.

Unbaked Shell (for fillings such as custard, pumpkin or quiche): Do not prick the dough. Fill and bake in a 450°F (230°C) oven for 10 minutes. Reduce heat to 350°F (180°C) and bake for 30 to 40 minutes longer.

Baked Shell (lemon or cream filling): Prick the dough all over with a fork. Bake in a 425°F (220°C) oven for 12 to 15 minutes. Cool then fill.

To Bake Blind: Pie crusts tend to shrink when they are baked because the strands of gluten, which have been stretched by rolling, retract when heated. Here's a foolproof way to bake a pastry shell without shrinkage. Cut a 12-inch (30 cm) circle of aluminum foil or parchment paper. Fit into pastry shell. Fill with pie weights or dried beans. Bake on bottom rack in 425°F (220°C) oven for 10 minutes. Cool for 5 minutes, then remove beans. Reduce heat to 350°F (180°C) and bake for 15 to 20 minutes longer or until golden.

Oil Pastry

Here is an easy way to make pastry that is very tender and tasty. If you are trying to reduce your consumption of trans and/or saturated fats, using oils, such as olive and canola, in place of shortening and butter, is a healthy choice.

Tips

Pastry made with oil is not as flaky as that made with shortening or butter, but it is very tender and easy to mix.

Using liquid oils (such as safflower, sunflower, canola and olive) instead of solid fats (such as lard, shortening and solid margarine) will help you to reduce the saturated and trans fats in your diet.

When making savory recipes, add dried herbs to the pastry for enhanced flavor. Try basil, oregano, parsley and dill — whatever complements the filling. Grated or shredded cheese, such as Parmesan or Cheddar (about ½ cup/125 mL, added to the dry ingredients), also works well.

For dessert pastries, try adding sesame seeds, cinnamon, nutmeg, ginger, grated chocolate, orange or lemon zest, or finely chopped nuts to the dry ingredients, to taste, when making this pastry.

- *9-inch (23 cm) pie plate*

Single Crust

1 cup + 2 tbsp	Robin Hood All-Purpose Flour	280 mL
½ tsp	salt	2 mL
6 tbsp	vegetable oil	90 mL
2 tbsp	cold water	30 mL

Double Crust

2¼ cups	Robin Hood All-Purpose Flour	550 mL
1 tsp	salt	5 mL
¾ cup	vegetable or canola oil	175 mL
¼ cup	cold water	50 mL

1. Combine flour and salt in a mixing bowl.

2. Combine oil and water. Add to flour all at once. Stir lightly with a fork until the dough comes together, then shape into a ball. If making a double-crust pie, divide into two portions. Using your hand, flatten slightly into disc(s). Place one disc of dough between two large squares of waxed paper.

3. Place paper and dough on a moistened surface to prevent paper from moving. Roll out to a uniform thickness (about ⅛ inch/0.3 cm), starting in center and rolling, spoke-fashion, toward the edge with light, even strokes until dough reaches the desired size. Peel off top paper and flip dough over onto pie plate. Gently peel off the remaining paper. Ease dough into the plate without stretching. Trim dough ½ inch (1 cm) beyond the edge of the pie plate.

4. For a single crust, fold under the edge and flute.

5. For a double crust, fill bottom crust, then roll out remaining dough as for top crust and flip over filling. Fold edge of top crust under the edge of bottom crust; seal and flute. Cut slits in center of top crust to allow steam to escape. Bake as directed in recipe.

Easy-as-Pie Pastry

If you make a lot of pies, this larger-batch recipe makes life easy. It makes enough pastry for five 9-inch (23 cm) pie shells, or two double-crust pies and one single-crust pie.

Tips

The egg and vinegar tenderize the pastry and make it very easy to work with.

Although shortening can be stored at room temperature, it works better in pastry if it is cold.

For convenience, prepare shells or pies ahead and refrigerate or freeze them. Rolled pastry dough can be kept in the fridge for up to 3 days or frozen for up to 6 months. Wrap tightly in plastic before freezing. It isn't necessary to thaw rolled dough before baking.

5 cups	Robin Hood All-Purpose Flour	1.25 L
1 ½ tsp	salt	7 mL
1	package (1 lb/454 g) shortening, chilled (2 ⅓ cups/575 mL)	1
1	egg	1
1 tbsp	vinegar	15 mL
½ cup	cold water	125 mL

1. Combine flour and salt in a large mixing bowl.

2. Using two knives, a pastry blender or your fingers, cut in shortening until mixture is uniform and resembles large peas. Don't overblend.

3. Beat egg and vinegar in a measuring cup. Add enough cold water to make ¾ cup (175 mL) liquid and add all at once to flour mixture. Stir with fork until dough holds together, then form into a ball using your hands.

4. Roll out for use in recipe.

DESSERTS

Cream Puffs

It's a challenge to purchase prepared cream puffs or chocolate éclairs filled with real whipped cream, because they need to be eaten soon after the puffs are filled. Serve these to your guests and you'll be a star.

Tips

Cream puffs and éclairs are made from the same *choux* pastry dough and are filled and topped in a similar way; they are just shaped differently. Cream puffs are round mounds, and éclairs are long tubes. For best results, use a pastry bag to make éclairs. When making cream puffs, just drop the dough onto the prepared baking sheet.

Be sure to have your eggs at room temperature before adding them to the dough.

Prepare cream puffs ahead of time and assemble just before serving.

Serve these delectable morsels on a dessert plate, drizzled with chocolate sauce. For a change, fill puffs with ice cream.

- *Preheat oven to 400°F (200°C)*
- *Baking sheet, greased*

Puffs

1 cup	water	250 mL
½ cup	butter	125 mL
1 cup	Robin Hood All-Purpose Flour	250 mL
Pinch	salt	Pinch
4	eggs	4

Filling

4 cups	sweetened whipped cream	1 L

Topping

2 cups	chocolate, caramel or fruit sauce	500 mL

1. *Puffs:* Combine water and butter in a medium saucepan over medium heat; bring to a rolling boil. Add flour and salt all at once. Stir vigorously over low heat for 1 minute or until mixture pulls away from the side of the pan and forms a ball. Remove from heat and cool for 5 minutes.

2. Add eggs, one at a time, beating vigorously after each addition on high speed of an electric mixer or with a wooden spoon until smooth and glossy. Drop dough by scant ¼ cupfuls (50 mL), 2 inches (5 cm) apart, onto prepared baking sheet.

3. Bake for 30 to 35 minutes or until puffed and golden. Cut a small slit in the side of each puff to allow steam to escape. Bake for 2 minutes longer. Transfer from pan to rack and cool completely.

4. *Filling:* To serve, cut puff in half horizontally. Fill with whipped cream.

5. *Topping:* Top with warm or cool sauce. Serve immediately.

Variations

Éclairs: Spoon cream puff dough into a pastry bag fitted with a ½-inch (1 cm) round tip. Pipe 2-inch (5 cm) strips, 2 inches (5 cm) apart, onto prepared baking sheet. Bake and assemble as for cream puffs.

For a party, try finishing the puffs with Chocolate Glaze (see recipe, page 157) or a sprinkle of icing sugar, rather than with the sauce, to simplify serving.

If you're serving these as a plated dessert, fill them with ice cream for a change.

Make smaller puffs for bite-size treats.

Raspberry Hazelnut Cream Crêpes

With a stack of prepared crêpes in the freezer, this dessert is a snap.

Tips

To store cooked crêpes, cool them completely, then stack each one between squares of waxed paper. Store in an airtight plastic bag and freeze for up to 3 months. Defrost overnight in the refrigerator or for 2 hours at room temperature.

Prepare filling and sauce the day before, then assemble the crêpes when you are ready to serve.

Light cream cheese works very well in this filling.

Freshly ground nuts have the best flavor. Use a food processor or a nut grinder to make the job easy. Toast nuts lightly to bring out their flavor.

Serve the sauce warm or cool.

Crêpes

1	batch Basic Crêpe Batter (see recipe, page 250)	1

Filling

1	package (8 oz/250 g) cream cheese, softened	1
¼ cup	icing sugar, sifted	50 mL
1 tsp	vanilla	5 mL
1 cup	whipping (35%) cream, whipped until stiff peaks form	250 mL
½ cup	ground hazelnuts	125 mL

Raspberry Sauce

1	package (15 oz/425 g) frozen whole raspberries in syrup, thawed	1
	Cranberry juice	
⅓ cup	granulated sugar	75 mL
3 tbsp	cornstarch	45 mL
1 tbsp	lemon juice	15 mL

1. *Crêpes:* Prepare crêpes; set aside.

2. *Filling:* Beat together cream cheese, icing sugar and vanilla in a bowl until smooth. Fold in whipped cream and hazelnuts.

3. *Raspberry Sauce:* Drain raspberries, reserving juice. Add cranberry juice to raspberry juice to make 2 cups (500 mL). Combine sugar, cornstarch and juice mixture in saucepan. Cook over medium heat, stirring constantly, until mixture comes to a boil. Stir in lemon juice and raspberries. Keep warm or cool to room temperature.

4. *Assembly:* Fill crêpes with filling. Roll up. Top with warm or cool sauce.

Variations

Replace raspberries with sliced strawberries.

Replace ground hazelnuts with ground pecans or almonds.

Bumbleberry Cream-Filled Crêpes

Here's a smashing dessert crêpe that is delicious made with any seasonal berries.

Tips

Six-inch (15 cm) crêpes are a perfect size to handle and to serve. You can make larger 8-inch (20 cm) crêpes if you have the proper pan. Larger ones work well on a buffet table as a single serving, supplemented with other desserts. If you're serving smaller crêpes, two usually constitute a serving.

Reserve the most attractive fruit for garnish. A mint leaf adds a nice finishing touch.

If you use strawberries in the filling, garnish each serving with a whole berry dipped in chocolate and a drizzle of chocolate sauce.

For convenience, make a sugar shaker for dusting baked goods. Fill a large salt shaker with icing sugar and a few grains of rice to keep the sugar dry.

Crêpes

1	batch Basic Crêpe Batter (see recipe, page 250)	1

Filling

2/3 cup	raspberries	150 mL
2/3 cup	blueberries	150 mL
2/3 cup	sliced strawberries	150 mL
1 cup	whipping (35%) cream	250 mL
2 tbsp	icing sugar, sifted	30 mL
1 tsp	vanilla	5 mL
1/2 cup	strawberry jam	125 mL
	Icing sugar	
	Fresh berries	

1. *Crêpes:* Prepare crêpes; set aside.
2. Combine raspberries, blueberries and strawberries. Whip cream, icing sugar and vanilla in a bowl until stiff peaks form. Fold in berry mixture. Spread each crêpe with a thin layer of jam. Spoon filling down the center of each; roll up. Place two crêpes, seam-side down, on a dessert plate. Sprinkle with icing sugar and garnish with fresh berries. Serve immediately.

Variation

Use whatever berries you prefer. You can't go wrong with this recipe.

Raspberry Clafouti

Preparation: 15 minutes
Baking: 35 minutes
Freezing:
not recommended

Clafouti is usually made with tart cherries, but this raspberry version seems even more delicious than the traditional one. Clafouti is also one of the quickest desserts in this book, so if you're short on time, try this.

Tips

Use only fresh fruit in clafouti. Frozen has too much moisture and produces a soggy pink dessert.

Serve warm.

Garnish with a dollop of whipped cream for a special treat and enjoy plain for a lighter, everyday dessert.

Use a glass or ceramic pie plate for the best appearance. They are also easy to clean.

Check your pan size. You need a regular 10-inch (25 cm) pie plate or a 9-inch (23 cm) deep-dish pie plate.

- *Preheat oven to 375°F (190°C)*
- *10-inch (25 cm) pie plate, greased*

Fruit

3 cups	fresh raspberries	750 mL
¼ cup	granulated sugar	50 mL

Batter

3	eggs	3
¾ cup	milk	175 mL
2 tbsp	orange liqueur (such as Cointreau or Grand Marnier)	30 mL
2 tbsp	butter, melted	30 mL
¾ cup	Robin Hood All-Purpose Flour	175 mL
¼ cup	granulated sugar	50 mL
½ tsp	baking powder	2 mL
¼ tsp	salt	1 mL

Topping

⅓ cup	granulated sugar	75 mL

1. *Fruit:* Scatter raspberries over bottom of prepared pie plate. Sprinkle sugar over top.

2. *Batter:* Whisk eggs, milk, liqueur and melted butter in a medium bowl. Combine flour, sugar, baking powder and salt. Gradually add to egg mixture, whisking constantly until smooth. Pour evenly over berries.

3. Bake for 30 to 35 minutes or until set, puffed and golden. Let cool for 10 minutes in pan on rack.

4. *Topping:* Sprinkle with ⅓ cup (75 mL) sugar. Cut into wedges and serve warm.

Variation

Replace raspberries with blackberries or pitted tart cherries.

Apple Peach Blueberry Crisp

Not only is this tasty dessert easy to make, it is also low in fat, cholesterol and calories — a winner on all fronts. Change it to accommodate seasonal fruits and your family's tastes.

Tips

Vary the fruit but keep the total amount to 5 cups (1.25 L).

You may have to adjust the sugar and flour in the filling depending upon how sweet and juicy the fruit is. Use more sugar if the fruit is less sweet, more flour if it is juicy.

For convenience, prepare several batches of the topping ahead. Pack in individual containers or plastic bags and refrigerate for up to 2 weeks.

Serve this crisp warm with a big scoop of vanilla ice cream or a dollop of whipped cream. If you prefer a lighter version, top with vanilla yogurt.

You can use Robin Hood Whole Wheat Flour and large-flake oats in this recipe. Both are healthy ingredient choices.

- *Preheat oven to 375°F (190°C)*
- *6-cup (1.5 L) baking dish, greased*

Crisp Topping

¾ cup	Robin Hood or Old Mill Oats	175 mL
⅓ cup	Robin Hood All-Purpose Flour	75 mL
½ cup	packed brown sugar	125 mL
1 tsp	ground cinnamon	5 mL
¼ cup	butter	50 mL

Fruit

2 cups	sliced peeled cored apples	500 mL
2 cups	sliced peeled pitted peaches	500 mL
1 cup	blueberries	250 mL
½ cup	granulated sugar	125 mL
3 tbsp	Robin Hood All-Purpose Flour	45 mL
1 tbsp	lemon juice	15 mL

1. *Crisp Topping:* Combine oats, flour, brown sugar and cinnamon in a mixing bowl. Using two knives, a pastry blender or your fingers, cut in butter until mixture resembles coarse crumbs. Set aside.

2. *Fruit:* Combine apples, peaches, blueberries, sugar, flour and lemon juice in a bowl. Mix thoroughly. Let stand for 5 minutes then mix again. Turn into prepared baking dish. Sprinkle topping evenly over fruit.

3. Bake for 35 to 40 minutes or until fruit is tender.

Variation

Almost any fruit works well in this recipe. Leave softer fruits, such as berries, whole or in larger pieces and cut firmer fruits, such as apples, into thin slices so they will cook to tender in approximately the same time.

Triple-Berry Shortcake

*Quicker and easier to prepare
than the biscuit-type cake,
this version of the classic
dessert is often preferred
because it's light and tender.*

Tips

Prepare the cake a day
ahead or keep one on
hand in the freezer. Thaw
before assembling.

Fresh fruit in season is
sensational, but frozen
berries, including those
packed in syrup, are also
delicious in this cake.

Coarse granulated sugar,
which is often available in
bulk stores, adds a special
touch to the top of shortcake.

- *Preheat oven to 400°F (200°C)*
- *8-inch (2 L) square cake pan, greased*

Shortcake

2 cups	Robin Hood All-Purpose Flour	500 mL
1/2 cup	granulated sugar	125 mL
1 tbsp	baking powder	15 mL
1/2 tsp	baking soda	2 mL
1/2 tsp	salt	2 mL
1/2 cup	butter	125 mL
1 cup	buttermilk	250 mL

Filling

Triple-berry mixture (any combination
of strawberries, raspberries, blackberries
and/or blueberries)
Whipped cream

1. *Shortcake:* Combine flour, sugar, baking powder, baking soda
   and salt in a mixing bowl. Using a pastry blender, two knives
   or your fingers, cut in butter until mixture resembles coarse
   crumbs. Add buttermilk to flour mixture, stirring just until
   moistened. Spread dough in prepared pan.

2. Bake for 17 to 23 minutes or until light golden. Cool in pan
   on rack.

3. *Filling:* To serve, cut cake into 6 rectangles; cut each in half
   horizontally. Spoon berries over bottom half; add a spoonful of
   whipped cream. Repeat layering, ending with a generous dollop
   of whipped cream.

Variations

Although this cake is made with a mixture of berries, strawberries,
raspberries, blueberries or blackberries on their own look and
taste great. For a change, try using sliced peaches.

Replace whipped cream with slightly softened vanilla ice cream.

Peach Pastry Squares

*These delicious squares taste
like a fresh peach tart. They
are very easy to make and ideal
for feeding a crowd, making
them a great potluck dessert.*

Tips

To peel peaches, dip
them in boiling water for
30 seconds. Immediately
plunge into a bowl of ice
water for a few seconds.
The skin should peel off easily.

Look for freestone peaches,
which are easier to slice than
clingstone varieties.

A jelly roll pan is like a cookie
sheet with 1/2-inch (1 cm)
sides. Be sure you have
the right size; this is the
smaller version.

Don't peel and slice the
peaches until you are ready
to bake. Exposure to air
turns them brown. Toss with
a little lemon juice to prevent
browning, if necessary.

For convenience, you can
use a food processor fitted
with a metal blade to make
the crust. Pulse the dry
ingredients, then add cold
butter and pulse until
the mixture resembles coarse
crumbs. Add the egg and
pulse until blended.

- *Preheat oven to 400°F (200°C)*
- *15- by 10 (2 L) jelly roll pan, greased*

Crust

2 1/2 cups	Robin Hood All-Purpose Flour	625 mL
2/3 cup	granulated sugar	150 mL
1/2 tsp	salt	2 mL
1 cup	butter	250 mL
1	egg, beaten	1

Topping

1/3 cup	granulated sugar	75 mL
1 tsp	ground cinnamon	5 mL
6 cups	sliced peeled pitted peaches (about 8)	1.5 L
1	egg, beaten	1
1 cup	sour cream	250 mL
1 tbsp	granulated sugar	15 mL

1. *Crust:* Combine flour, sugar and salt in a large bowl. Using two knives, a pastry blender or your fingers, cut in butter until mixture resembles coarse crumbs. Add egg and mix lightly to blend. Press firmly into prepared pan to form a thin, even layer.

2. Bake on bottom oven rack for 10 to 15 minutes or until golden.

3. *Topping:* Combine sugar and cinnamon. Add to peaches and toss well. Arrange evenly over crust.

4. Bake for 15 minutes longer. Reduce temperature to 350°F (180°C).

5. Combine egg, sour cream and sugar. Drizzle over peaches. Bake for 10 minutes longer or just until fruit is tender and topping is set. Serve warm or cool.

Variation

Replace peach slices with sliced nectarines, plums or apples. A mixture of any two of these fruits is also tasty.

Lemon Sponge Pudding

With a soufflé-like crust resting on a creamy yet tangy lemon sauce, this delicious dessert is the ultimate comfort food.

Tips

When serving, be sure to dip the spoon all the way down to the bottom of the dish so that each helping is a blend of the crusty top and saucy bottom.

Garnish each plate with fresh berries for an attractive finish.

This very light dessert is a great choice when you want a little something to end a hearty meal.

Plan to serve this the same day it is prepared. In fact, for optimum taste and texture, it is best served warm from the oven.

- *Preheat oven to 350°F (180°C)*
- *8-cup (2 L) baking dish, greased*
- *Larger pan to hold baking dish*

1 cup	granulated sugar	250 mL
1/3 cup	Robin Hood All-Purpose Flour	75 mL
1 1/2 tbsp	grated lemon zest	25 mL
1/4 tsp	salt	1 mL
1 1/2 cups	half-and-half (10%) cream	375 mL
1/3 cup	lemon juice	75 mL
3	egg yolks, beaten	3
3	egg whites	3

1. Combine sugar, flour, lemon zest and salt in a large bowl. Add cream, lemon juice and egg yolks, whisking until smooth.

2. Beat egg whites in a bowl until stiff peaks form. Gently fold into batter. Carefully pour into prepared baking dish. Set dish in a large pan filled with hot water to 1-inch (2.5 cm) depth.

3. Bake for 40 to 45 minutes or until top is set and golden. Serve warm.

Variation

Replace lemon juice and zest with orange or lime. A combination of lemon and lime is also good.

BREADS

◄ *Orange Cranberry Spiral*

Orange Cranberry Spiral

MAKES 2 LOAVES (ABOUT 12 SLICES PER LOAF)

Preparation: 65 minutes
Rising: 65 minutes
Baking: 35 minutes
Freezing: excellent

This loaf looks amazingly complicated but is actually very easy and fun to shape. Quick-rise yeast makes it faster to prepare than traditional breads.

Tips

A glaze of egg and milk before baking gives this loaf a beautiful, shiny golden surface.

Quick-rise yeast is finely granulated yeast that is mixed directly with the other dry ingredients. It produces a quick first rise.

To be really fancy, add a drizzle of orange icing on top.

After brushing the strips with butter, sprinkle lightly with cinnamon-sugar. It looks and tastes great!

Replace dried cranberries with raisins.

- *Preheat oven to 350°F (180°C) during second rising*
- *Two 9-inch (23 cm) springform pans, greased*

Dough

5 to 6 cups	Robin Hood Best for Bread Homestyle White or All-Purpose Flour	1.25 to 1.50 L
1/3 cup	granulated sugar	75 mL
4 1/2 tsp	quick-rise instant yeast (2 envelopes, each 1/4 oz/8 g)	22 mL
1 tsp	salt	5 mL
3/4 tsp	ground nutmeg	3 mL
1 3/4 cups	milk	425 mL
1 1/2 cups	dried cranberries	375 mL
3/4 cup	butter	175 mL
1 tbsp	grated orange zest	15 mL
1	egg, beaten	1

Filling and Glaze

2 tbsp	butter, melted	30 mL
1	egg	1
1 tbsp	milk	15 mL

1. *Dough:* Combine 2 cups (500 mL) of the flour, sugar, yeast, salt and nutmeg in a large mixer bowl.

2. Heat milk, dried cranberries, butter and orange zest in a saucepan over medium heat until mixture is hot (125°F/50°C) and butter is melted. Add to flour mixture along with egg. Beat on low speed of electric mixer for 1 minute, then on high speed for 3 minutes. Stir in enough of the remaining flour to make a soft dough. Turn out onto a floured surface. Knead dough for about 10 minutes, adding enough flour to make dough smooth and elastic. Divide dough in half. Shape each portion into a ball. Cover and let rest for 20 minutes.

3. *Filling and Glaze:* To shape bread, roll one ball of dough into a 16- by 12-inch (40 x 30 cm) rectangle. Cut lengthwise into six 2-inch (5 cm) wide strips. Brush with 1 tbsp (15 mL) of the melted butter. Roll up one strip loosely and place, cut side up in center of prepared pan. Coil remaining strips loosely around the center roll, covering the bottom of pan. Repeat with remaining dough and melted butter to make a second loaf.

4. Cover with a tea towel and let rise in a warm place (75 to 85°F/24 to 29°C) until doubled in bulk, about 45 minutes. Beat egg and milk together in a small bowl. Brush over loaves.

5. Bake on center rack of oven for 30 to 35 minutes or until golden. Cover with foil for last 10 minutes if the top is becoming too brown. Cool in pans for 20 minutes, then turn out onto rack and cool completely.

Cheery Cherry Bread

This ruby-studded loaf is festive enough for the holiday season but delicious all year round. You have to try this to believe how great it is.

Tips

Use candied cherries, not maraschino, which are much wetter and quite different in flavor.

The cherries will leak moisture when you're kneading the dough, so don't be alarmed if you need to add more flour during this step.

For a browner crust, brush the top with melted butter just before baking.

For a soft crust, brush the top of the loaf with melted butter as soon as it comes out of the oven.

- Preheat oven to 350°F (180°C) during second rising
- One 9- by 5-inch (2 L) loaf pan, greased

1 tsp	granulated sugar	5 mL
1 cup	warm water (105°F to 115°F/40°C to 46°C)	250 mL
2¼ tsp	active dry yeast (1 envelope, ¼ oz/8 g)	11 mL
3 to 3½ cups	Robin Hood Best for Bread Homestyle White or All-Purpose Flour	750 to 875 mL
1 tbsp	butter, softened	15 mL
⅓ cup	granulated sugar	75 mL
1 tsp	salt	5 mL
½ tsp	ground cinnamon	2 mL
¼ tsp	ground nutmeg	1 mL
1 cup	whole candied cherries	250 mL

1. Dissolve 1 tsp (5 mL) sugar in warm water in a large bowl. Sprinkle with yeast; let stand for 10 minutes. Stir well. Add 1 cup (250 mL) of the flour, ⅓ cup (75 mL) sugar, butter, salt, cinnamon and nutmeg to dissolved yeast mixture. Beat with a wooden spoon or on medium speed of an electric mixer until smooth and elastic. Stir in cherries.

2. Gradually stir in 2 cups (500 mL) of the remaining flour. If necessary, add more flour to make a soft dough that leaves sides of the bowl and forms a ball. Turn out onto a lightly floured surface. Form into a ball. Knead, adding enough of the remaining flour to make the dough smooth, elastic and no longer sticky, about 10 minutes. Place in a lightly greased bowl and turn to grease top. Cover with plastic wrap. Let rise in a warm place (75 to 85°F/24 to 29°C) until doubled, 1½ to 2 hours.

3. Punch down dough. Turn out onto a lightly floured surface. Cover and let rest for 10 minutes.

4. *Shaping:* Shape dough into a loaf. Place in prepared loaf pan. Cover with a tea towel and let rise in a warm place until dough doubles in bulk, 1½ to 2 hours.

5. Bake on bottom rack of oven for 45 to 55 minutes or until top is golden and loaf sounds hollow when tapped on the bottom. Remove from pan immediately and cool on rack.

Variation

Use red or green cherries or a combination of both.

Multigrain Seed Bread

Moist, dense and hearty, this loaf is a healthy choice for sandwiches and toast.

Tips

If you like the top crusty, spritz it lightly with water three times during baking.

Enhance the appearance of any grainy loaf by brushing the top with milk and sprinkling with oats just before baking.

- *Preheat oven to 375°F (190°C) during second rising*
- *Two 8½- by 4½-inch (1.5 L) or 9- by 5-inch (2 L) loaf pans, greased*

1 tsp	granulated sugar	5 mL
2 cups	warm water (105°F to 115°F/40°C to 46°C)	500 mL
2¼ tsp	active dry yeast (1 envelope, ¼ oz/8 g)	11 mL
¼ cup	fancy molasses	50 mL
2 tbsp	vegetable oil	30 mL
1 cup	Robin Hood Best for Bread or regular Whole Wheat Flour	250 mL
⅔ cup	Robin Hood or Old Mill Oats	150 mL
⅔ cup	sunflower seeds, toasted	150 mL
⅓ cup	flaxseeds	75 mL
⅓ cup	Robin Hood Red River Cereal	75 mL
1½ tsp	salt	7 mL
3 to 3½ cups	Robin Hood Best for Bread Homestyle White or All-Purpose Flour	750 to 875 mL

1. Dissolve sugar in warm water in a large bowl. Sprinkle with yeast; let stand for 10 minutes. Stir in molasses and oil.

2. Combine 1 cup (250 mL) flour, oats, sunflower seeds, flaxseeds, cereal and salt. Stir into yeast mixture. Stir in enough of the 3 to 3½ cups (750 mL to 875 mL) white flour to form a slightly sticky dough. Turn out onto a lightly floured surface. Knead for 8 to 10 minutes, adding enough of the remaining flour to make dough smooth and elastic. Place in a greased bowl and turn to grease the top. Cover with plastic wrap. Let rise in a warm place (75 to 85°F/24 to 29°C) until doubled in bulk, 1 to 1½ hours.

3. Punch down dough. Divide in half. Shape each half into a loaf. Place in prepared pans. Cover with a tea towel and let rise in a warm place until doubled in bulk, about 1 hour.

4. Bake on bottom rack of oven for 25 to 30 minutes or until top is golden and loaf sounds hollow when tapped on the bottom. Remove from pans and cool on rack.

Variation

Dinner rolls: After the first rising, shape dough into 15 balls and place on a greased baking sheet, about 2 inches (5 cm) apart. Cover and let rise until doubled in size, about 1 hour. Bake in 375°F (190°C) oven until golden, about 20 minutes.

Double Cheese Bread

*Double the cheese means
double the flavor.*

Tips

Use freshly grated Parmesan cheese for the best flavor.

When you add cubes of cheese to a yeast dough, the bread will have holes where the cheese melts. If you use shredded cheese, you won't have this effect. The choice is yours.

Individual mini-loaves are cute. Divide dough into six portions and place in six 5¾- by 3¼-inch (500 mL) pans. Reduce rising and baking times by 10 minutes each.

Recipes for breads usually give a range for the amount of flour. Start with the least and add only as much as is necessary to make a smooth dough.

On hot, humid days bread dough will take more flour than on cool, dry days.

- Preheat oven to 375°F (190°C) during second rising
- Two 8½- by 4½-inch (1.5 L) loaf pans, greased

1 tsp	granulated sugar	5 mL
1½ cups	warm water (105°F to 115°F/40°C to 46°C)	375 mL
2¼ tsp	active dry yeast (1 envelope, ¼ oz/8 g)	11 mL
⅓ cup	vegetable oil	75 mL
1 tsp	salt	5 mL
1 tsp	hot sauce, or to taste	5 mL
1	egg, beaten	1
2½ cups	shredded old Cheddar cheese	625 mL
½ cup	grated Parmesan cheese	125 mL
4¼ to 4¾ cups	Robin Hood Best for Bread Homestyle White or All-Purpose Flour	1.05 to 1.175 L

1. Dissolve sugar in warm water in a large bowl. Sprinkle with yeast; let stand for 10 minutes. Stir well. Beat in oil, salt, hot sauce and egg. Stir in 1 cup (250 mL) of the Cheddar cheese and Parmesan cheese. Beat well.

2. Stir in 2 cups (500 mL) of the flour. Add more flour until mixture becomes too stiff to stir. Turn out onto a lightly floured surface. Knead for 8 to 10 minutes, adding enough of the remaining flour to make the dough smooth and elastic. Place in greased bowl and turn to grease top. Cover with plastic wrap. Let rise in warm place (75 to 85°F/24 to 29°C) until doubled in bulk, about 1 hour.

3. Punch down dough. Turn out onto a lightly floured surface. Knead in remaining Cheddar cheese until well distributed. Divide into six equal portions. Shape each portion into a ball. Place three balls side by side in the bottom of each greased pan. Cover with a tea towel. Let rise in a warm place until doubled in bulk, 50 to 60 minutes.

4. Bake on bottom rack of oven for 30 to 35 minutes or until golden and loaves sound hollow when tapped on the bottom. Remove from pans immediately and cool on rack.

Variations

For a "chunky cheese" look, shred 1½ cups (375 mL) of the Cheddar cheese and cut the rest into cubes to make 1 cup (250 mL). Add the cubed cheese and the remaining ½ cup (125 mL) of the shredded cheese to the dough in Step 3.

Add diced cooked bacon and/or chives to the dough along with the second portion of cheese.

Old-Fashioned Cloverleaf Potato Rolls

Moist and flavourful, this traditional favorite will never go out of style.

Tips

In addition to a tender texture, mashed potatoes give yeast bread extra moistness and a subtle, rich, creamy flavor.

Grandmothers made extra mashed potatoes so they would have them on hand to make these rolls. If you prefer, you can make them using instant mashed potatoes for convenience.

Use a thermometer to check the temperature of the liquid. If it's too hot, the yeast will be killed. If it's too cool, the action of the yeast will slow down.

If you prefer a shiny top, brush the rolls lightly with butter or an egg wash just before baking.

Sprinkle sesame or poppy seeds over top, if desired.

- *Preheat oven to 400°F (200°C) during second rising*
- *Two 12-cup muffin pans, greased*

1¼ cups	milk	300 mL
½ cup	butter	125 mL
½ cup	mashed potatoes	125 mL
4¾ to 5 cups	Robin Hood Best for Bread Homestyle White or All-Purpose Flour	1.175 to 1.25 L
¼ cup	granulated sugar	50 mL
2¼ tsp	quick-rise instant yeast (1 envelope, ¼ oz/8 g)	11 mL
1½ tsp	salt	7 mL
1	egg, beaten	1
	Melted butter, optional	

1. Heat milk, butter and mashed potatoes in a saucepan over medium heat until mixture is hot (125°F/50°C) and butter is melted.

2. Combine 3 cups (750 mL) of the flour, sugar, yeast and salt in a large bowl. Stir in milk mixture and egg. Stir vigorously with a wooden spoon until blended. Gradually add enough of the remaining flour to make a soft dough. Turn out onto a floured surface and knead dough for about 10 minutes, adding enough flour to make the dough smooth and elastic. Cover and let rest for 20 minutes.

3. *Shaping:* Divide dough into eight portions. Cut each portion into nine pieces to make 72 pieces total. Shape each piece into a ball. Place 3 balls in the bottom of each prepared muffin cup. Repeat, using all the balls to fill the 24 cups. Cover with a tea towel and let stand in a warm place (75 to 85°F/24 to 29°C) until doubled in size, about 1 hour. Brush with melted butter, if using.

4. Bake on center rack of oven for 10 to 12 minutes or until golden. Remove from pans immediately. Cool for 10 minutes on rack.

Variation

Try other shapes, such as snails, spirals, crescents and small balls but remember to keep them all about the same size to ensure that the dough rises and bakes uniformly.

Lemon Poppy Seed Loaf

MAKES 1 LOAF

Preparation: 15 minutes
Baking: 65 minutes
Freezing: excellent

The tart taste of lemon together with the crunch of poppy seeds makes this delicious loaf a real winner.

Tips

Be sure to remove the zest first, then cut the lemon in half to juice.

Remove only the yellow part of the zest. The white pith will be bitter.

To extract the maximum amount of juice, warm lemons slightly before juicing by immersing them in hot water for 30 seconds. One lemon will yield at least 2 tbsp (30 mL) juice.

- *Preheat oven to 350°F (180°C)*
- *8¹/₂- by 4¹/₂-inch (1.5 L) loaf pan, greased*

Loaf

¹/₃ cup	butter, softened	75 mL
1 cup	granulated sugar	250 mL
2	eggs	2
1¹/₂ cups	Robin Hood All-Purpose Flour	375 mL
1¹/₂ tsp	baking powder	7 mL
1 tsp	grated lemon zest	5 mL
¹/₂ tsp	salt	2 mL
¹/₂ cup	milk	125 mL
2 tbsp	poppy seeds	30 mL

Lemon Glaze

¹/₄ cup	granulated sugar	50 mL
2 tbsp	lemon juice	30 mL

1. *Loaf:* Cream butter and sugar in a large mixer bowl on medium speed of electric mixer until fluffy. Add eggs, one at a time, beating well after each addition.

2. Combine flour, baking powder, lemon zest and salt. Add to creamed mixture alternately with milk, beating lightly after each addition. Stir in poppy seeds. Spread in prepared pan.

3. Bake for 55 to 65 minutes or until toothpick inserted in center comes out clean. Remove from oven. While still warm in pan, poke holes with toothpick or fork in top of loaf, 1 inch (2.5 cm) apart.

4. *Lemon Glaze:* Heat sugar and lemon juice in a small saucepan or microwave until sugar is dissolved. Brush glaze over loaf. Cool for 15 minutes in pan, then turn out onto rack and cool completely.

Variations

Omit poppy seeds, if desired.

Substitute ¹/₂ cup (125 mL) chopped pecans, walnuts or hazelnuts for the poppy seeds.

Date-and-Nut Loaf

MAKES 1 LOAF

Preparation: 20 minutes
Baking: 75 minutes
Freezing: excellent

This loaf, which was a favorite in the 1920's, remains popular and has stood the test of time.

Tips

Because it is so moist, this loaf is easy to slice very thinly. Enjoy it lightly buttered or spread with cream cheese. It is also good toasted.

Buy pitted dates that are fairly soft for easy cutting.

Spray knife with cooking spray or lightly oil to prevent dates from sticking.

- *Preheat oven to 325°F (160°C)*
- *One 9- by 5-inch (2 L) loaf pan, greased*

1 cup	chopped pitted dates	250 mL
1 cup	boiling water	250 mL
1 tsp	baking soda	5 mL
1 cup	packed brown sugar	250 mL
1/4 cup	butter, melted	50 mL
1	egg, beaten	1
1 3/4 cups	Robin Hood All-Purpose Flour	425 mL
1 tsp	baking powder	5 mL
1/2 tsp	salt	2 mL
3/4 cup	chopped walnuts	175 mL

1. Combine dates, boiling water and baking soda in a large bowl. Stir well; let cool. Stir in brown sugar, butter and egg, mixing until blended.

2. Combine flour, baking powder and salt. Stir into date mixture along with walnuts. Mix well. Spread in prepared pan.

3. Bake for 65 to 75 minutes or until toothpick inserted in center comes out clean. Cool for 15 minutes in pan, then turn out onto rack and cool completely.

Variation

Add 1 tbsp (15 mL) grated orange or lemon zest to the batter.

Rhubarb Bread

MAKES 2 LOAVES

Preparation: 10 minutes
Baking: 60 minutes
Freezing: excellent

If you don't know what to do with all that fresh rhubarb in the garden, here's an ideal way to use it up. If you're not a gardener, it's worth purchasing rhubarb for this mouthwatering recipe.

Tips

Fresh rhubarb is preferable to frozen, which is softer and wetter no matter how much you try to dry it out. If you use frozen rhubarb, thaw and pat dry with paper towels to remove excess moisture before using in baking.

For foolproof removal of loaves, line the pan bottom and sides with greased aluminum foil or parchment paper. To remove, simply lift the loaves out of the pan — they won't stick. Remove paper and let cool.

If you are making a gift of this or any other bread, leave it in the pan. Cool completely, then wrap pan and loaf in colorful plastic wrap or an airtight bag. Attach a recipe card with the recipe written on it.

- *Preheat oven to 350°F (180°C)*
- *Two 9- by 5-inch (2 L) loaf pans, greased*

Loaf

1½ cups	packed brown sugar	375 mL
1 cup	buttermilk	250 mL
⅔ cup	vegetable oil	150 mL
1	egg	1
2 tsp	grated orange zest	10 mL
2½ cups	Robin Hood All-Purpose Flour	625 mL
1 tsp	baking soda	5 mL
1 tsp	salt	5 mL
1¾ cups	chopped rhubarb	425 mL
½ cup	chopped pecans	125 mL

Topping

½ cup	granulated sugar	125 mL
1 tbsp	butter, softened	15 mL
2 tsp	grated orange zest	10 mL

1. *Loaf:* Combine brown sugar, buttermilk, oil, egg and orange zest in a large bowl. Mix well.

2. Combine flour, baking soda and salt. Add to sugar mixture, mixing until smooth. Fold in rhubarb and pecans. Spread batter in prepared pans, dividing evenly.

3. *Topping:* Mix sugar, butter and orange zest together with a fork until blended. Sprinkle over batter.

4. Bake for 55 to 60 minutes or until toothpick inserted in center comes out clean. Cool for 15 minutes in pan, then turn out onto rack and cool completely.

Variations

Replace half of the rhubarb with sliced strawberries.

Although the color of the finished loaf isn't as attractive, adding 1 tsp (5 mL) ground cinnamon to the batter along with the salt adds terrific flavor.

Mini Banana Loaves

These mini-loaves are a nice size to give as gifts. They also make a great item for bake sales.

Tips

Use ripe bananas for the best flavor in loaves and muffins. Plan ahead by purchasing bananas in advance of baking and allowing them to ripen.

You can freeze mashed bananas, but keep in mind that they are much wetter than freshly mashed. The extra moisture will affect the recipe by producing a soggy loaf that is sunken in the center. To avoid this problem, bake banana loaves with fresh bananas and freeze them. Reserve frozen mashed bananas for smoothies and shakes.

- Preheat oven to 350°F (180°C)
- Six 5¾- by 3¼-inch (500 mL) mini-loaf pans, greased

3 cups	mashed ripe banana (about 7 large)	750 mL
½ cup	lemon juice	125 mL
⅔ cup	butter, softened	150 mL
1 cup	granulated sugar	250 mL
4	eggs	4
1 tsp	vanilla	5 mL
3¾ cups	Robin Hood All-Purpose Flour	925 mL
2 tsp	baking soda	10 mL
1½ tsp	baking powder	7 mL
1 tsp	salt	5 mL
¾ tsp	ground nutmeg	3 mL

1. Combine mashed banana and lemon juice in a bowl; set aside.
2. Cream butter and sugar in a large bowl until light and creamy. Add eggs, one at a time, beating lightly after each addition. Add banana mixture and vanilla. Stir well.
3. Combine flour, baking soda, baking powder, salt and nutmeg. Stir into banana mixture gradually, mixing until smooth. Spread in prepared pans, dividing evenly.
4. Bake for 40 to 45 minutes or until toothpick inserted in center comes out clean. Cool for 15 minutes in pans, then turn out onto rack and cool completely.

Variations

Add 1 cup (250 mL) dried cranberries to the batter.

Add 1 cup (250 mL) chopped nuts to the batter.

Add ⅔ cup (150 mL) flaked coconut to the batter.

Wheaten Bread

This healthy bread stays moist for days. It has lots of flavor on its own but makes great sandwiches, too.

Tips

The batter will be very stiff.

Store whole wheat flour in the freezer. At room temperature, it has a shelf life of only 3 months.

If you don't have buttermilk, here is a substitute. To make 1 cup (250 mL) buttermilk, mix 1 tbsp (15 mL) vinegar or lemon juice with enough milk to make 1 cup (250 mL). Let stand for 5 minutes, then stir.

Sprinkle a little (1 tbsp/15 mL) whole wheat flour on top of the batter before baking to give the loaf a healthy, homemade look.

- *Preheat oven to 350°F (180°C)*
- *One 8½- by 4½-inch (1.5 L) loaf pan, greased*

1½ cups	Robin Hood All-Purpose Flour	375 mL
1½ cups	Robin Hood Whole Wheat Flour	375 mL
½ cup	granulated sugar	125 mL
2 tsp	baking powder	10 mL
1 tsp	baking soda	5 mL
1 tsp	salt	5 mL
1 cup	buttermilk	250 mL
¾ cup	milk	175 mL

1. Combine white and whole wheat flours, sugar, baking powder, baking soda and salt in a mixing bowl. Add buttermilk and milk. Mix well.

2. Spread batter in prepared pan.

3. Bake for 30 minutes, then lower oven temperature to 325°F (160°C) and bake for 20 to 25 minutes longer or until toothpick inserted in center comes out clean. Cool for 10 minutes in pan, then turn out onto rack and cool completely.

Variation

Add 2 tbsp (30 mL) each flaxseeds and sesame seeds.

Popovers that Pop

MAKES 12 POPOVERS

Preparation: 10 minutes
Baking:
40 minutes
Freezing:
not recommended

These popovers, which make a great substitute for Yorkshire pudding, stay puffed, unlike Yorkshire pudding, which starts to deflate as soon as it comes out of the oven. They also have a delicious butter-and-egg flavor. Serve these tasty treats with roast beef and gravy or enjoy them with soup or salad in place of rolls.

Tips

The key to making popovers puff is to start them in a hot oven and reduce the heat after they have cooked for a while. If the initial heat is too low, they will never puff.

A little hot fat in each cup aids the puffing and adds flavor.

Use a wire whisk to get the batter smooth.

Don't peek. If you open the door during baking, the popovers will collapse.

- *Preheat oven to 400°F (200°C)*
- *12-cup muffin pan, ungreased*

¼ cup	butter, melted	50 mL
1 cup + 2 tbsp	Robin Hood All-Purpose Flour	280 mL
4	eggs	4
1 cup	milk	250 mL
1 tsp	salt	5 mL

1. Put 1 tsp (5 mL) melted butter in each muffin cup. Place in oven for 5 minutes to heat.

2. Combine flour, eggs, milk and salt in a small bowl, beating until thick and smooth. Pour batter into heated pan, filling cups about half full.

3. Bake for 20 minutes, then reduce heat to 375°F (190°C) and bake for 10 to 15 minutes longer or until puffed. Remove from pan immediately.

Variation

Replace butter with oil or melted beef fat.

KIDS'
FAVORITES

Cranberry Apricot Granola

*It's always a treat to find
a healthy snack and/or
breakfast that tastes so good.*

Tips

Try this granola as a dessert.
Top it with ice cream or
frozen yogurt and finish
with a drizzle of maple syrup
or honey.

Use any dried fruit you like in
this recipe. You can add other
ingredients, such as fresh
berries, to granola just before
serving and enjoy a different
breakfast every morning.

Be sure your pan has sides
that are about 1½ inches
(4 cm) high so the ingredients
won't spill over while you
are stirring.

- *Preheat oven to 300°F (150°C)*
- *13- by 9-inch (3.5 L) baking pan, ungreased*

2 cups	Robin Hood or Old Mill Large-Flake Oats	500 mL
1½ cups	bran flake cereal, slightly crushed	375 mL
½ cup	flaked coconut	125 mL
½ cup	chopped dried apricots	125 mL
½ cup	dried cranberries	125 mL
⅓ cup	sunflower seeds	75 mL
⅓ cup	packed brown sugar	75 mL
¼ cup	vegetable oil	50 mL
3 tbsp	apple or orange juice	45 mL
1 tsp	vanilla	5 mL

1. Combine oats, bran flakes, coconut, apricots, cranberries, sunflower seeds and brown sugar in a large bowl. Mix well.
2. Combine oil, juice and vanilla. Add to cereal mixture. Toss until thoroughly mixed. Spread out in pan.
3. Bake for 30 to 35 minutes, stirring frequently until lightly golden. Cool completely in pan on rack. Store in airtight containers or plastic bags in a cool place for up to 1 month.

Variations

Add fruit and nuts to suit your taste, such as raisins, dates, dried apples or cherries.

Use water in place of juice.

Double-Decker Granola Bars

Preparation: 20 minutes
Baking: 30 minutes
Freezing: excellent

*Two granola-like mixtures
make up the crust and topping
of this delightful bar.*

Tips

Use regular clover honey
for making cookies and
bars. Some varieties, such
as buckwheat, have a
strong flavor that can
be overpowering.

If your honey has crystallized,
heat it gently in a pan of
hot water until the
crystals dissolve.

For added fiber, use whole
wheat flour instead of
all-purpose.

- *Preheat oven to 325°F (160°C)*
- *8-inch (2 L) square cake pan, greased*

Crust

1/2 cup	Robin Hood All-Purpose or Whole Wheat Flour	125 mL
1/2 cup	Robin Hood or Old Mill Oats	125 mL
3 tbsp	packed brown sugar	45 mL
1/4 tsp	baking powder	1 mL
3 tbsp	butter, melted	45 mL

Topping

1/4 cup	butter, melted	50 mL
2 tbsp	packed brown sugar	30 mL
2 tbsp	honey	30 mL
1/2 cup	Robin Hood or Old Mill Oats	125 mL
1/2 cup	finely chopped nuts	125 mL
1/3 cup	flaked coconut	75 mL
1/4 cup	sunflower seeds	50 mL
1/4 cup	raisins	50 mL

1. *Crust:* Combine flour, oats, brown sugar and baking powder in a medium bowl. Add melted butter. Mix well. Press firmly into prepared pan. Bake for 10 minutes or until light golden at edges and set.

2. *Topping:* Combine melted butter, brown sugar and honey in a medium bowl. Stir until well blended. Add oats, nuts, coconut, sunflower seeds and raisins. Mix well. Spread mixture over crust. Press down gently.

3. Bake for 15 to 20 minutes longer or until golden and set. Cool completely in pan on rack, then cut into bars.

Variations

Use any nuts you have on hand or a combination of them. Just be sure they are finely chopped to make cutting the bars easy.

Replace the raisins with dried cranberries, chopped pitted dates or chopped dried apricots.

Oats-and-Seeds Bars

Preparation: 10 minutes
Baking: 12 minutes
Freezing: excellent

These delicious bars make a nutritious treat to pack in children's knapsacks for a school snack, a hike or a bicycle ride.

Tips

Melted chocolate on top tastes great, but leave the bars plain if you intend to pack or store them.

Dark brown sugar has a mild molasses flavor; golden brown sugar tastes more like butterscotch. Both work well in this recipe.

If you don't feel like cutting these bars, try breaking them into irregular shapes. It's easier than cutting them.

- *Preheat oven to 375°F (190°C)*
- *15- by 10-inch (2 L) jelly roll pan, greased*

¾ cup	butter	175 mL
1¼ cups	packed brown sugar	300 mL
1½ tsp	vanilla	7 mL
2¼ cups	Robin Hood or Old Mill Oats	550 mL
½ cup	sesame seeds	125 mL
¼ cup	flaxseeds	50 mL
¾ tsp	baking powder	3 mL

1. Melt butter in a large saucepan. Stir in brown sugar and vanilla. Cook over medium heat, stirring often, for 2 minutes or until mixture is bubbly. Remove from heat and stir in oats, sesame seeds, flaxseeds and baking powder; mix well. Press firmly with the back of a spoon into prepared pan.

2. Bake for 7 to 12 minutes or until golden. Cool completely in pan on rack. Cut into bars or break into pieces.

Variations

Replace flaxseeds with sunflower seeds.

Add ¼ cup (50 mL) sunflower seeds.

Soft 'n' Chewy Chocolate Oat Squares

These chewy bars combine two perennial favorites, chocolate and peanut butter, with an abundance of nutritious oats to make a treat that kids enjoy and parents endorse.

Tips

Quick-cooking oats work well in these squares, but you can use whatever variety you have on hand.

To remove bars easily from the pan, line the pan completely with greased aluminum foil or parchment paper. Once the bars have cooled completely, lift them out of the pan and place on a cutting board. Remove the paper and cut into bars. Bars and squares are much easier to cut after they have been removed from the pan.

If you plan to pack these bars in lunches, omit the topping.

- *Preheat oven to 350°F (180°C)*
- *13- by 9-inch (3.5 L) cake pan, greased*

Squares

½ cup	butter, softened	125 mL
1 cup	packed brown sugar	250 mL
½ cup	corn syrup	125 mL
½ tsp	salt	2 mL
1 tsp	vanilla	5 mL
4 cups	Robin Hood or Old Mill Oats	1 L
½ cup	creamy peanut butter	125 mL

Topping

8	squares (each 1 oz/28 g) semi-sweet chocolate	8
¼ cup	butter	50 mL

1. *Squares:* Cream butter and brown sugar in a large bowl until light and creamy. Add corn syrup, salt, vanilla and oats. Mix well. Spread mixture evenly in prepared pan.

2. Bake for 13 to 18 minutes or until set and golden. Cool slightly on rack. Spread peanut butter evenly over top.

3. *Topping:* Heat chocolate and butter in a saucepan over low heat, stirring until smooth. Spread over peanut butter. Cool until chocolate is set, then cut into squares.

Variations

For a lighter treat, prepare only half of the chocolate topping and drizzle it over the peanut butter.

To add kid appeal, sprinkle mini M&M's on top of the bars.

No-Bake Marshmallow Oat Balls

Kids enjoy shaping these into balls as much as Mom enjoys having healthy homemade treats for them to eat.

Tips

Choose marshmallows carefully. The fresher and softer they are, the easier it is to melt them.

Cook butter and marshmallows over low heat. Be patient — if you try to hurry, they'll burn on the bottom.

To keep calories down, use unsweetened coconut.

Use wet hands to shape the mixture into balls. This will help keep it from sticking to every finger.

• *Baking sheet or tray, lined with waxed paper*

Oat Balls

6 cups	miniature marshmallows	1500 mL
¼ cup	butter	50 mL
2½ cups	Robin Hood or Old Mill Oats	625 mL
1½ cups	chopped walnuts	375 mL
1 cup	flaked coconut	250 mL

Garnish, optional

2	squares (each 1 oz/28 g) semi-sweet chocolate optional	2

1. *Oat Balls:* Heat marshmallows and butter together in a large saucepan over low heat, stirring, until melted. Remove from heat. Stir in oats, nuts and coconut. Mix well.

2. With wet hands, shape mixture into small balls. Place on prepared baking sheet.

3. *Garnish (optional):* Melt chocolate and drizzle over balls. Let set. Store uncovered at room temperature for up to 1 week.

Variations

Add finely chopped dried apricots, dates or dried cranberries to taste.

For a special treat, press a chocolate kiss candy on top in place of the chocolate drizzle.

Oat Pancakes with Cinnamon Honey Butter

A wonderful weekend treat the whole family can enjoy making and eating. Keep a supply of the Cinnamon Honey Butter on hand. It's great on toast and waffles, too.

Tips

Prepare honey butter ahead. Refrigerate, then bring to room temperature to use.

These pancakes are light but hearty. With bacon or sausage, they are a meal in themselves.

To test pan for the correct temperature (375°F /190°C), heat over medium-high heat. Sprinkle a few drops of cold water on the surface. When the drops bounce and evaporate, it's ready to use.

Save any leftover pancakes. Cool completely, wrap well and store in the freezer. Pop them into the toaster for a quick breakfast.

Try these pancakes with chunky applesauce on the side.

- *Preheat griddle to 375°F (190°C)*
- *Griddle or skillet, lightly greased*

Cinnamon Honey Butter

1 cup	butter, softened	250 mL
1 cup	honey	250 mL
2 tsp	ground cinnamon	10 mL

Pancakes

2 cups	milk	500 mL
1½ cups	Robin Hood or Old Mill Oats	375 mL
1 cup	Robin Hood All-Purpose Flour	250 mL
2 tbsp	brown or granulated sugar	30 mL
2 tbsp	baking powder	30 mL
¾ tsp	salt	3 mL
3	eggs	3
¼ cup	vegetable oil	50 mL

1. *Cinnamon Honey Butter:* Beat butter, honey and cinnamon until smooth and blended. Set aside.

2. *Pancakes:* Mix milk and oats in a small bowl. Set aside until milk is absorbed.

3. Combine flour, sugar, baking powder and salt in a mixing bowl. Stir well.

4. Add eggs and oil to oat mixture. Beat well. Add oat mixture to flour mixture all at once, mixing until smooth.

5. Spoon batter by ¼ cupfuls (50 mL) onto griddle. Cook for 2 to 3 minutes or until bubbles break on the surface and bottoms are golden; turn and cook for 1 to 2 minutes or until bottoms are lightly browned. Serve hot with Cinnamon Honey Butter.

Variations

If you're a big fan of cinnamon, add ½ tsp (2 mL) to the batter.

Serve with maple syrup instead of the Cinnamon Honey Butter.

Toonie Pancakes

*Children enjoy making these
mini-pancakes. They don't
take long to cook, and kids
can have fun trying them with
different syrups and toppings.*

Tips

To test pan for the correct
temperature (375°F /190°C),
heat over medium-high heat.
Sprinkle a few drops of cold
water on the surface.
When the drops bounce and
evaporate, it's ready to use.

To keep cooked pancakes
warm, place them in a single
layer on a baking sheet.
Cover loosely with foil and
keep in a warm oven
(200°F/100°C).

If the batter thickens as it
stands, thin with a little milk
to the proper consistency.

You can also make regular-
size pancakes using ¼ cup
(50 mL) batter for each. They
will take a bit longer to cook.

- *Preheat griddle to 375°F (190°C)*
- *Griddle or skillet, lightly greased*

1⅓ cups	Robin Hood All-Purpose Flour	325 mL
2 tbsp	granulated sugar	30 mL
1 tbsp	baking powder	15 mL
½ tsp	salt	2 mL
1	egg	1
1¼ cups	milk	300 mL
3 tbsp	melted butter or vegetable oil	45 mL
	Butter	
	Maple syrup	

1. Combine flour, sugar, baking powder and salt. Set aside

2. Beat egg, milk and melted butter in a medium bowl. Add dry ingredients. Whisk until smooth.

3. Pour batter by tablespoonfuls (15 mL) onto prepared griddle. Cook for 2 minutes or until bubbles break on the tops and bottoms are golden; turn and cook for 1 to 2 minutes or until bottoms are golden. Serve warm with butter and syrup.

Variations

As soon as you put the batter on the griddle, sprinkle the pancakes with mini chocolate chips.

Try serving plain pancakes with butter and cinnamon-sugar.

Apple Crumble Muffin Bites

MAKES 30 MINI-MUFFINS

Preparation: 20 minutes
Baking: 15 minutes
Freezing: excellent

Healthy snacks in small sizes, like these tasty muffin bites, are a perfect solution for school lunch boxes.

Tips

Applesauce replaces some of the fat in this recipe, making these tiny muffins a no-guilt healthy snack.

You can make a dozen regular-size muffins with the same recipe. Bake for approximately 20 minutes.

Either sweetened or unsweetened applesauce will work in this recipe.

Use quick-cooking, not large-flake, oats in this recipe.

Increase the fiber by using all or half Robin Hood Whole Wheat Flour in place of the all-purpose.

Shred apples on the coarse side of a grater. Using one that is too fine will make the job much more difficult.

- *Preheat oven to 400°F (200°C)*
- *Three 12-cup mini-muffin pans, greased or lined with paper liners*

Topping

1/2 cup	Robin Hood or Old Mill Quick-Cooking Oats	125 mL
1/4 cup	packed brown sugar	50 mL
2 tbsp	butter, melted	30 mL
1/4 tsp	ground cinnamon	1 mL

Batter

1 1/4 cups	Robin Hood All-Purpose Flour	300 mL
1 cup	Robin Hood or Old Mill Quick-Cooking Oats	250 mL
1/3 cup	packed brown sugar	75 mL
1 tbsp	baking powder	15 mL
1/2 tsp	salt	2 mL
1/2 tsp	ground cinnamon	2 mL
1	egg	1
1 cup	shredded peeled apple (about 2)	250 mL
2/3 cup	applesauce	150 mL
1/3 cup	milk	75 mL
1/4 cup	vegetable oil	50 mL

1. *Topping:* Combine oats, brown sugar, melted butter and cinnamon in a small bowl. Mix well; set aside.

2. *Batter:* Combine flour, oats, brown sugar, baking powder, salt and cinnamon. In a large bowl, beat egg, apple, applesauce, milk and oil. Add dry ingredients and stir just until moistened. Spoon into prepared pans. Sprinkle with topping.

3. Bake for 12 to 15 minutes or until tops spring back when lightly touched. Cool for 5 minutes in pan, then transfer to rack and cool completely.

Variation

Add raisins or dried cranberries (about 1 cup/250 mL) to the batter.

Fruit Puff

Serve this unique dish for breakfast, brunch or dessert. Fill with any fresh or canned fruit to fit the season or the ingredients you have on hand.

Tips

Let children watch this puff while it bakes. It's like a monster that puffs and then collapses when it comes out of the oven.

Have icing sugar in a small sieve ready to sprinkle on top just before serving.

Children love to drizzle maple syrup over top of this puff, which is like a pancake.

You can halve the recipe to make one puff, if desired.

Plan to serve your puff as soon as it comes out of the oven.

- *Preheat oven to 425°F (220°C)*
- *Two 9-inch (23 cm) pie plates*

3 tbsp	butter	45 mL
4	eggs	4
1 cup	milk	250 mL
1 tsp	grated lemon zest	5 mL
1 cup	Robin Hood All-Purpose Flour	250 mL
2 tbsp	granulated sugar	30 mL
½ tsp	salt	2 mL
	Fresh berries (such as strawberries, raspberries and/or blueberries)	
	Icing sugar	

1. Divide butter evenly between two pie plates. Place plates in oven while preparing the batter.

2. Place eggs, milk and lemon zest in a blender and process until blended. Add flour, sugar and salt and blend until smooth. Pour batter into hot butter in pie plates, dividing evenly.

3. Bake for 18 to 25 minutes or until puffed and golden. Remove from oven. Fill with fruit. Dust with icing sugar. Cut puff into wedges and serve immediately.

Variation

Enjoy this dessert year-round using canned fruit, such as sliced peaches.

Banana Softies

These cakelike squares are particularly appealing to young children, who enjoy their soft texture and mellow flavor.

Tips

To make measuring easier, measure any oil that is required first. Then measure honey in the same cup. It will slip out cleanly and easily.

Kids love to mash bananas. It's especially easy to do when the bananas are very ripe. Just squish them on a plate with the tines of a fork.

Add some nuts or mini chocolate chips (about ½ cup/125 mL) to the batter.

- *Preheat oven to 350°F (180°C)*
- *8-inch (2 L) square cake pan, greased*

1	ripe banana, mashed	1
2 tbsp	packed brown sugar	30 mL
2 tbsp	vegetable oil	30 mL
2 tbsp	liquid honey	30 mL
1	egg white	1
1 tsp	vanilla	5 mL
⅓ cup	Robin Hood All-Purpose Flour	75 mL
½ tsp	baking soda	2 mL
½ tsp	ground cinnamon	2 mL
1¼ cups	Cranberry Apricot Granola (see recipe, page 210)	300 mL

1. Combine banana, brown sugar, oil, honey, egg white and vanilla in a large bowl. Beat with a wooden spoon until smooth. Combine flour, baking soda and cinnamon. Add to banana mixture along with granola. Mix well. Spread mixture evenly in prepared pan.

2. Bake for 15 to 20 minutes or until set and golden. Cool completely in pan on rack, then cut into squares.

Raspberry Almond Bars

**MAKES ABOUT
2 DOZEN BARS**

Preparation: 20 minutes
Baking: 30 minutes
Freezing: excellent

These are the best granola bars you will ever eat. Even better, they are so easy to make that children can make them by themselves and Mom can put them in the hot oven.

Tips

Increase the fiber by using Robin Hood Whole Wheat Flour instead of all-purpose.

To measure brown sugar accurately, pack it firmly into a dry measuring cup. Level off the top and turn the cup onto a piece of waxed paper. The sugar should hold its shape when the cup is removed.

- *Preheat oven to 350°F (180°C)*
- *9-inch (2.5 L) square cake pan, greased*

1¾ cups	Robin Hood or Old Mill Oats	425 mL
1 cup	Robin Hood All-Purpose or Whole Wheat Flour	250 mL
1 cup	packed brown sugar	250 mL
1 tsp	baking powder	5 mL
¼ tsp	salt	1 mL
¾ cup	butter, melted	175 mL
¾ cup	raspberry jam	175 mL
½ cup	sliced almonds	125 mL

1. Combine oats, flour, brown sugar, baking powder and salt in a large bowl. Mix well. Stir in melted butter. Press two-thirds of mixture into prepared pan. Spread with jam. Add almonds to remainder and sprinkle over jam, patting down lightly.

2. Bake for 25 to 30 minutes or until golden. Cool completely in pan on rack, then cut into bars.

Variation

Replace raspberry jam with strawberry or apricot jam.

Kaleidoscope Cookies

*These colorful cookies are fun
to make and attractive to look
at — and they taste great, too!*

Tips

Use bright primary colors for
the most impact. For some
occasions, such as Easter,
pastels may be more
appropriate. Let children
decide what to use.

This is a good cookie to
involve younger children in
making, because there is no
wrong way to blend the balls
of dough. Every cookie will
have a different look.

Paste cake-decorating colors
are quite strong compared
to regular liquid colorings.
If using, add 1 drop at a
time and work into the
dough — a very small
amount will give you a
vibrant color.

You can prepare a few rolls
of dough ahead and
refrigerate them to bake at
another time. Baking cookies
is a good after-school project
that lets kids prepare their
own snack.

Preheat oven to 350°F (180°C)
Cookie sheet, ungreased

½ cup	butter, softened	125 mL
½ cup	icing sugar, sifted	125 mL
1 cup	Robin Hood All-Purpose Flour	250 mL
4	food coloring bottles or tubes — red, blue, green and yellow	4

1. Cream butter and icing sugar in a medium bowl until smooth and creamy. Gradually add flour, mixing until a smooth dough forms.

2. Divide dough into four equal portions. Using a different color for each portion, work in enough food coloring to make a deep color. Work dough with hands to incorporate color thoroughly. Divide each piece of colored dough in half. Shape each into a ball. You'll have eight balls, two of each color.

3. Place two different colored balls side by side on a board, then arrange the remaining balls on top of them, alternating colors and pressing them together. Roll into a 8-inch (20 cm) long log. Chill for 1 hour or until dough is firm enough to slice.

4. Cut log into thin slices, about ¼ inch (5 mm) thick, and place slices on cookie sheet, about 1 inch (2.5 cm) apart.

5. Bake for 10 to 12 minutes or until cookies are set and just starting to brown around edges. Cool for 5 minutes on sheet, then transfer to rack and cool completely.

Apple Pecan Cake

Let kids do the mixing themselves. This cake doesn't require a mixer — all you need is a wooden spoon and a little effort.

Tips

This is a good cake for snacks and lunch boxes. Kids will enjoy eating their apple a day in a cake.

There's not much fat in this cake, which keeps well because it's so moist.

The raw cake mixture will be thick and pasty — not your normal cake batter.

Serve this cake warm with ice cream and caramel sauce for a delicious dessert.

Use Golden Delicious or Granny Smith apples, which hold their shape, for the best result.

- *Preheat oven to 350°F (180°C)*
- *8-inch (2 L) square cake pan, greased*

2 cups	diced peeled apple (about 2 or 3)	500 mL
1	egg, beaten	1
2/3 cup	granulated sugar	150 mL
1/2 cup	coarsely chopped pecans	125 mL
1/4 cup	vegetable oil	50 mL
1 cup	Robin Hood Whole Wheat Flour	250 mL
1 tsp	baking soda	5 mL
1 tsp	ground cinnamon	5 mL
1/2 tsp	salt	2 mL
1/4 tsp	ground nutmeg	1 mL

1. Beat apple, egg, sugar, pecans and oil thoroughly in a large bowl.

2. Combine flour, baking soda, cinnamon, salt and nutmeg. Add to apple mixture. Stir well to blend. Spread evenly in prepared pan.

3. Bake for 40 to 45 minutes or until toothpick inserted in center comes out clean. Let cool for 10 minutes in pan on rack, then serve warm, or transfer cake to rack to cool completely.

Variations

Replace pecans with walnuts.

Replace whole wheat flour with Robin Hood All-Purpose Flour.

Mix-in-the-Pan Chocolate Cake

*This cake is especially suited
to kids. They love the easy
cleanup as much as the cake.*

Tips

Don't be surprised — there
is no egg in this cake. Keep
it in mind if you bake for
people with egg allergies.

You can mix the cake with
a fork right in the pan or in
a bowl with a whisk. Either
way, no mixer is required.

To pour melted butter easily,
put the measured amount
in a glass measure and melt
it in the microwave. The
measure has a spout for easy
pouring.

If your frosting recipe makes
more than you need, store
any extra in the refrigerator
for up to 2 weeks. Bring
to room temperature
before using.

- *Preheat oven to 350°F (180°C)*
- *8-inch (2 L) square cake pan, ungreased*

1½ cups	Robin Hood All-Purpose Flour	375 mL
1 cup	granulated sugar	250 mL
¼ cup	unsweetened cocoa powder, sifted	50 mL
1 tsp	baking powder	5 mL
1 tsp	baking soda	5 mL
½ tsp	salt	2 mL
⅓ cup	butter, melted	75 mL
1 tbsp	vinegar	15 mL
1 cup	warm water	250 mL

1. Combine flour, sugar, cocoa, baking powder, baking soda and salt in pan. Stir well to blend. Make two holes in flour mixture. Pour melted butter into one hole, vinegar into the other. Pour water over top. Mix well with a fork until smooth.

2. Bake for 35 to 40 minutes or until toothpick inserted in center comes out clean. Cool completely in pan on rack.

Variations

Replace warm water with brewed coffee.

Leave cake plain or frost with Cocoa Buttercream Frosting (see recipe, below) or Basic, Coffee or Chocolate Butter Frosting (see recipes, page 154).

Cocoa Buttercream Frosting

- *Makes about 3 cups (750 mL) frosting*
- *Enough to fill and frost a 9-inch (23 cm) 2-layer cake*

3 cups	icing sugar	750 mL
¾ cup	unsweetened cocoa powder	175 mL
⅔ cup	butter, softened	150 mL
5 to 6 tbsp	half-and-half (10%) cream or milk	75 to 90 mL
1½ tsp	vanilla	7 mL

1. Sift icing sugar and cocoa together; set aside. In a large mixer bowl, beat butter on medium speed until smooth. Gradually add cocoa mixture alternately with cream, beating until smooth and creamy. (Add only enough of the cream to make a soft, spreadable consistency.) Beat in vanilla. Gradually add a little more cream if frosting is too stiff or a little more icing sugar if frosting is too soft.

Pizza in a Pan

This tasty dish has all the flavors of pizza without the bread crust. It can be eaten with a spoon, which makes it easier for young kids.

Tips

You can vary this versatile dish to suit your family's tastes.

Add crusty rolls for lunch and a green salad for dinner.

If your pasta sauce has lots of flavor, you may not need more seasoning, but if it doesn't you can always add herbs, such as oregano, garlic, basil and hot peppers, if you wish.

Use a pasta sauce that is thick and chunky. If it is on the thin side, decrease the amount slightly.

- *Preheat oven to 400°F (200°C)*
- *13- by 9-inch (3.5 L) baking dish, greased*

---

1 lb	Italian sausage, mild or hot	500 g
1	onion, chopped	1
¾ cup	chopped sweet green pepper	175 mL
8 oz	fresh mushrooms, sliced	250 g
1½ cups	seasoned tomato sauce	375 mL
¾ cup	sliced pitted black olives	175 mL
8	slices mozzarella cheese	8
2	eggs	2
1 cup	milk	250 mL
1 cup	Robin Hood All-Purpose Flour	250 mL
1 tbsp	vegetable oil	15 mL
¼ tsp	salt	2 mL
⅓ cup	grated Parmesan cheese	75 mL

1. Remove casings from sausage. Crumble meat into a large skillet and cook over medium-high heat for 3 minutes. Add onion, green pepper and mushrooms. Continue cooking, stirring occasionally, for 10 minutes or until vegetables are tender and sausage is browned. Drain off fat. Stir in tomato sauce and olives. Spread evenly in prepared pan. Arrange cheese slices over top.

2. Combine eggs, milk, flour, oil and salt in a blender and process until smooth. (You can also do this in a bowl, with a whisk.) Pour evenly over cheese slices. Sprinkle with Parmesan cheese.

3. Bake for 25 to 30 minutes or until top is golden. Let cool for 10 minutes, then cut into squares and serve warm.

Variations

Replace sausage with ground beef, pork or chicken.

For convenience, replace fresh mushrooms with a can of sliced mushrooms, well drained.

Use a zesty pasta sauce and hot sausage for a spicy dish that is likely to appeal to teenagers. For younger children, keep it mild and pass the hot sauce as an option.

SAVORIES

Mushroom, Asparagus and Pepper Quiche

If you're cooking for vegetarians, here's a meal they are sure to enjoy. Light but filling, it makes a delicious brunch, lunch or dinner.

Tips

For a nonvegetarian meal, treat this as a vegetable side dish and serve with pork chops, chicken or ham. For a vegetarian meal, add soup, salad and rolls.

This quiche is a delicious way to get children to enjoy their vegetables.

Cheese is a good source of protein and calcium. However, it is also high in fat. If you're serving this alongside another protein, such as meat or fish, use a lower-fat cheese. Many varieties, such as Cheddar, Swiss, provolone and mozzarella, are now available in reduced-fat versions.

- *Preheat oven to 425°F (220°C)*
- *9-inch (23 cm) pie plate*

Crust

	Pastry for 9-inch (23 cm) single-crust pie (see recipes, pages 176 to 179, or use Robin Hood Flaky Pie Crust Mix)	

Filling

1 tbsp	Dijon mustard	15 mL
1 tbsp	vegetable oil	15 mL
1	small onion, chopped	1
1 lb	fresh asparagus, trimmed and coarsely chopped	500 g
1½ cups	sliced mushrooms	375 mL
Half	large sweet red pepper, cut in strips	Half
1½ cups	shredded Swiss cheese	375 mL
3	eggs	3
1 cup	milk	250 mL
3 tbsp	finely chopped fresh dill (or 1 tsp/5 mL dried dillweed)	45 mL
½ tsp	salt	2 mL
¼ tsp	black pepper	1 mL

1. *Crust:* Prepare pastry for unbaked pie shell. Roll out and fit into pie plate.

2. *Filling:* Spread mustard evenly over pastry. Heat oil in a large skillet over medium-high heat. Sauté onion, asparagus, mushrooms and red pepper until pepper is tender-crisp, about 5 minutes. Remove from heat. Spread evenly in pie shell. Sprinkle cheese over top.

3. Beat eggs, milk, dill, salt and pepper in a bowl until blended. Pour over vegetable mixture.

4. Bake for 10 minutes, then reduce heat to 350°F (180°C) and bake for 30 to 35 minutes longer or until filling is set and pastry is golden. Cool for 10 minutes, then slice and serve warm.

Variations

Replace asparagus with broccoli or green beans.

Omit red pepper; reduce asparagus to 12 oz (375 g) and add 1 cup (250 mL) diced cooked ham, smoked chicken, shrimp or salmon.

Chunky Ham-and-Vegetable Quiche

**MAKES ABOUT
6 SERVINGS**

Preparation: 25 minutes
Cooking: 5 minutes
Baking: 45 minutes
Freezing:
not recommended

This delicious quiche is also good served cold. Chilled leftovers make wonderful picnic fare.

Tips

Bake pies on the bottom oven rack to ensure that the bottom crust browns before the filling soaks through.

Before baking, brush pastry with a lightly beaten egg white. This helps prevent a soggy crust.

For added flavor, spread a little Dijon mustard on the pastry shell.

Sauté vegetables in a hot pan to seal in the moisture and flavour. If the heat is too low, moisture comes out of the vegetables and they simmer, losing flavor.

• *Preheat oven to 425°F (220°C)*
• *10-inch (25 cm) pie plate or quiche pan*

Crust

| | Pastry for 9-inch (23 cm) single-crust pie (see recipes, pages 176 to 179, or use Robin Hood Flaky Pie Crust Mix) | |

Filling

2 tbsp	vegetable oil	30 mL
2 cups	sliced mushrooms	500 mL
¾ cup	sliced sweet red pepper (1 small)	175 mL
¾ cup	sliced sweet green pepper (1 small)	175 mL
½ cup	chopped onion	125 mL
1 cup	diced ham	250 mL
3	eggs	3
1¼ cups	half-and-half (10%) cream	300 mL
⅓ cup	grated Parmesan cheese	75 mL
1 tsp	dried basil leaves	5 mL
	Salt and pepper to taste	

1. *Crust:* Prepare pastry for unbaked pie shell. Roll out and fit into pie plate.

2. *Filling:* Heat oil in a large skillet over medium-high heat. Sauté mushrooms, peppers and onions until peppers are tender-crisp, about 5 minutes. Stir in ham. Spread mixture evenly over pastry.

3. Beat eggs, cream, Parmesan cheese, basil, salt and pepper in a bowl until blended. Pour over ham mixture.

4. Bake for 10 minutes, then reduce heat to 350°F (180°C) and bake for 30 to 35 minutes longer or just until filling is set and pastry is golden. Cool for 10 minutes, then slice and serve warm.

Variation

Replace ham with diced cooked chicken or eight slices bacon, cooked and diced.

Chicken Pot Pie

**MAKES ABOUT
8 SERVINGS**

Preparation: 30 minutes
Baking: 30 minutes
Freezing: excellent

It's worth having leftover chicken or turkey so you can make this old-fashioned favorite. We've lightened it up by using only a top crust and lots of filling.

Tips

Add a bit of sage or thyme to the pastry when you are using it with poultry.

Although this is only a single-crust pie, you'll need to make a double-crust recipe to fit the larger surface of the shallow casserole dish.

If you don't have leftover chicken, poach six to eight boneless skinless chicken breasts for this recipe.

Potatoes with the skin on are a good source of fiber. When peeled, potatoes lose half of their fiber.

To thaw frozen peas quickly, put them in a colander and run hot water over them.

You can reduce the salt and fat in many savory dishes by using herbs, such as thyme, oregano, chives, rosemary, celery or parsley leaves, as flavor enhancers. Choose one or two that complement the dish.

- *Preheat oven to 425°F (220°C)*
- *12-cup (3 L) shallow casserole or baking dish, greased*

Crust

	Pastry for 9-inch (23 cm) double-crust pie (see recipes, pages 176 to 179, or use Robin Hood Flaky Pie Crust Mix)	

Filling

2 cups	quartered potatoes (3 medium)	500 mL
1½ cups	chopped peeled carrot	375 mL
1 tbsp	butter	15 mL
2 cups	sliced mushrooms	500 mL
1 cup	chopped onion	250 mL
1	can (10 oz/284 mL) condensed cream of mushroom soup	1
2 tbsp	Robin Hood All-Purpose Flour	30 mL
1 tsp	dried thyme leaves	5 mL
¾ tsp	dry mustard	3 mL
½ tsp	dried oregano leaves	2 mL
4 cups	chopped cooked chicken	1 L
1 cup	frozen green peas, thawed	250 mL

Glaze, optional

1	egg yolk	1
1 tbsp	milk	15 mL

1. *Crust:* Prepare pastry for double-crust pie. Set aside.
2. *Filling:* Cook potatoes and carrots in boiling salted water just until tender, about 15 minutes. Drain, reserving ¾ cup (175 mL) cooking liquid for the sauce. Meanwhile, heat butter in a large skillet over medium-high heat; sauté mushrooms and onion just until tender.
3. Combine soup, flour, thyme, mustard and oregano and reserved vegetable liquid, stirring until smooth. Stir in chicken, mushroom mixture, potatoes, carrots and peas. Pour into prepared casserole.
4. Roll out pastry to fit top of casserole. Place over filling. Flute edges. Cut slits in the center to allow steam to escape.
5. *Glaze (optional):* Beat egg yolk and milk until blended. Brush over pastry.
6. Bake for 30 minutes or until crust is golden and filling is hot.

Variations

Use leftover holiday turkey to make a turkey pot pie.

If you prefer, divide the mixture between two casseroles (each 6 cups/1.5 L) and bake as per recipe. Or make six to eight individual pot pies. Decrease baking time by about 5 minutes.

Deep-Dish Lamb Pot Pie

*A hearty lamb stew topped
with a unique biscuitlike
pastry makes a delicious,
warming winter meal. This
pie is also delicious made with
veal, pork or beef shoulder.*

Tips

The flavor of stews is usually
better the next day, so
prepare the filling ahead
and chill overnight. You can
also lower the fat content
by removing the fat that
hardens on top before
placing the filling in the
crust. Reheat before placing
in the casserole.

Use only the white and very
pale green parts of leeks.
The dark green portion is
tough and woody even
when cooked.

Leeks are usually quite gritty
between the layers and need
to be cleaned thoroughly.
Cut in half lengthwise and
wash well, separating the
layers. Pat dry before slicing.

Red meats are a good source
of iron. Most fish are, too.

Pot pies are meals in
themselves since the meat
and vegetables are all in the
same dish. Add a green
vegetable or salad and bread
to complete the meal.

- *Preheat oven to 375°F (190°C)*
- *8-cup (2 L) deep casserole*

Stew

2 tbsp	vegetable oil	30 mL
1½ lbs	boneless lamb shoulder, trimmed and cut in ¾-inch (1.5 cm) cubes	750 g
4	medium carrots, peeled and cut in ¼-inch (0.5 cm) slices	4
3	medium leeks (white and light green parts only) cleaned and cut in ¼-inch (0.5 cm) slices	3
2 tbsp	Robin Hood All-Purpose Flour	30 mL
2 cups	chicken stock	500 mL
3	potatoes, peeled and cut in ½-inch (1 cm) cubes	3
2	bay leaves	2
1½ tsp	salt	7 mL
1 tsp	dried rosemary	5 mL
¼ tsp	black pepper	1 mL

Pastry

1 cup	Robin Hood All-Purpose Flour	250 mL
½ tsp	each baking soda and salt	2 mL
3 tbsp	butter	45 mL
1	egg yolk	1
⅓ cup	buttermilk	75 mL

1. *Stew:* Heat oil in a large saucepan over medium-high heat. Add lamb. Cook, stirring, until well browned, about 10 minutes. Add carrots and leeks. Cook, stirring, until leeks start to brown, about 5 minutes. Sprinkle with flour and toss to coat. Stir in stock, potatoes, bay leaves, salt, rosemary and pepper. Bring to a boil, then reduce heat to low, cover and simmer, stirring occasionally, for 1½ hours or until meat is tender. Skim foam from surface, if necessary. Remove bay leaves. Transfer mixture to casserole or chill overnight (see Tips, left).

2. *Pastry:* Combine flour, baking soda and salt in a mixing bowl. Using two knives, a pastry blender or your fingers, cut in butter until mixture resembles coarse crumbs. Beat egg yolk and buttermilk together. Add to flour mixture. Toss with a fork until mixture comes together. Turn out on a lightly floured surface, knead briefly, then pat or roll out dough to fit top of casserole. Pastry should be about ½ inch (1 cm) thick.

3. *Assembly and baking:* Pour hot stew into casserole. Place pastry over top. Press to seal against inside rim of casserole. Bake for 30 to 35 minutes or until pastry is golden.

Multilayered Dinner

**MAKES ABOUT
6 SERVINGS**

Preparation: 25 minutes
Baking: 45 minutes
Freezing:
not recommended

The leftovers, served cold, are almost as delicious as this pie when it is hot out of the oven.

Tips

Prepare the parts the day before for easy assembly the next day.

Increase the vegetable layers and omit the ham for a vegetarian meal.

Healthy eating on its own isn't enough. Combine a nutritious diet with regular physical activity.

If you eat a variety of foods, choosing from each of the food groups every day, you'll likely get the nutrients you need.

A quiche pan with straight sides produces an attractive result, but a pie plate works well, too.

- *Preheat oven to 400°F (200°C)*
- *9-inch (23 cm) deep-dish pie plate or quiche pan*

Crust

	Pastry for 9-inch (23 cm) double-crust pie (see recipes, pages 176 to 179, or use Robin Hood Flaky Pie Crust Mix)	

Filling

1	package (10 oz/300 g) frozen chopped broccoli, thawed	1
½ cup	chopped green onion	125 mL
3 tbsp	chopped fresh basil	45 mL
8 oz	sliced ham	250 g
8 oz	sliced Cheddar cheese	250 g
1	sweet red pepper, cut in strips	1
4	eggs, beaten	4
	Salt and black pepper to taste	

1. *Crust:* Prepare pastry for double-crust pie. Roll out bottom crust and fit into pan.

2. *Filling:* Combine broccoli, onion and basil. Lay ham slices over pastry. Cover with a layer of cheese, broccoli mixture, then the red pepper strips.

3. Reserve small amount of egg (about 1 tbsp/15 mL) to brush over top crust. Slowly pour remaining egg evenly into pie. Roll out top crust and arrange over filling. Seal and flute edges. Brush with reserved egg. Cut slits in center of top crust to allow steam to escape.

4. Bake for 35 to 45 minutes or until pastry is golden.

Variations

Use any cheese or meat, keeping in mind the colors of the layers for an attractive pie, as well as the flavor combinations.

Replace frozen broccoli with 2 cups (500 mL) cooked and chopped fresh broccoli.

Tasty Traditional Tourtière

Tourtière, a French-Canadian meat pie traditionally associated with the holiday season, is so appetizing it has traveled well beyond the Quebec border. It freezes well, so keep a few in your freezer.

Tips

Everyone who makes tourtière has his or her individual style. The combination of meat, spices and thickener varies from cook to cook. Try this recipe to start, then add your own touches, such as shredded carrot, tomatoes or a hint of cinnamon instead of cloves.

Use lean ground meat to avoid excess fat in the filling.

If you're making several pies at one time, make the filling the day before for convenience.

Serve tourtière with red or green chowchow (similar to chili sauce) or a good chutney.

- *Preheat oven to 400°F (200°C)*
- *9-inch (23 cm) pie plate*

Pastry

	Pastry for 9-inch (23 cm) double-crust pie (see recipes, pages 176 to 179, or use Robin Hood Flaky Pie Crust Mix)	

Filling

1 lb	lean ground pork	500 g
8 oz	ground veal	250 g
1	onion, chopped	1
1	potato, grated	1
¼ cup	water	50 mL
1 tbsp	beef bouillon concentrate	15 mL
½ tsp	salt	2 mL
¼ tsp	ground savory or thyme	1 mL
¼ tsp	black pepper	1 mL
¼ tsp	ground cloves	1 mL

1. *Pastry:* Prepare pastry for double-crust pie. Set aside.
2. *Filling:* Combine pork, veal, onion, potato, water, bouillon concentrate, salt, savory and pepper in a large saucepan. Cook over medium heat, stirring constantly, until meat is no longer pink and liquid is absorbed, about 15 minutes. Stir in cloves. Cool slightly.
3. Roll out half of the pastry and fit into pie plate. Fill with meat mixture. Roll out remaining pastry and arrange over filling. Seal and flute edges. Slash center of top crust to allow steam to escape.
4. Bake on bottom oven rack for 25 to 30 minutes or until pastry is golden.

Variations

Use ground turkey or chicken in place of the veal.

Omit grated potato. Stir ¾ cup (175 mL) mashed potato into the cooked meat mixture.

Tuna Soufflé

*Light as a feather and low in
fat, this delicious soufflé
makes a fabulous dinner.
Serve with fresh asparagus
and sliced tomatoes.*

Tips

Use tuna that is packed in
broth or water. It's lower
in fat than oil-packed tuna
but still high in flavor.

When beating egg whites,
be sure the bowl and
beaters are clean. Any trace
of oil will prevent the egg
whites from stiffening.

Beat egg whites just until
they form stiff peaks but are
still moist. If they become
dry, they are difficult to fold
into other mixtures.

Soufflés must be served as
soon as they come out of
the oven, as they immediately
begin to collapse. Keep this
in mind when you're
planning your timetable.

As a safeguard, wrap a
greased 3-inch (7.5 cm) foil
collar around the top of your
soufflé dish to support the
soufflé as it rises above the
rim of the dish.

- *Preheat oven to 375°F (190°C)*
- *7-inch (18 cm) soufflé dish, greased*

3 tbsp	butter	45 mL
1/3 cup	finely chopped onion	75 mL
1/4 cup	Robin Hood All-Purpose Flour	50 mL
1 cup	milk	250 mL
6	eggs, separated	6
2	cans (each 6 oz/170 g) tuna, drained and flaked	2
2 tbsp	lemon juice	30 mL
1 tbsp	tomato paste	15 mL
1 tsp	dried oregano leaves	5 mL
1/2 tsp	salt	2 mL

1. Melt butter in a medium saucepan over medium heat. Add onion and cook, stirring, until softened, about 3 minutes. Add flour and mix well. Gradually add milk, stirring until smooth. Cook, stirring constantly, until mixture comes to a boil and thickens. Remove from heat. Cool slightly, about 10 minutes. Add egg yolks, one at a time, beating well after each addition. Stir in tuna, lemon juice, tomato paste, oregano and salt. Mix well.

2. Beat egg whites until stiff but moist peaks form. Fold into tuna mixture. Pour into prepared dish.

3. Bake for 50 to 55 minutes or until puffed, set and golden. Serve immediately.

Variations

Serve the soufflé with hollandaise sauce or a creamy mushroom sauce.

Replace tomato paste with Dijon mustard.

Sausage Rolls

**MAKES ABOUT
30 SAUSAGE ROLLS**

Preparation: 25 minutes
Cooking: 5 minutes
Baking: 20 minutes
Freezing: excellent

*Although sausage rolls are
widely available in the frozen
foods section of grocery stores,
nothing can match the great
flavor of homemade. To ease
preparation, use Robin Hood
Flaky Pie Crust Mix, which
is very simple to use.*

Tips

The shredded Cheddar
cheese adds flavor and eye
appeal to the rolls, but you
can make them plain, too.

Add dried herbs, such as basil
and oregano to the pastry.

Making your own sausage
rolls can be almost as
convenient as buying them
since they can be prepared
ahead and frozen. Thaw,
then warm to serve.

For a better seal, moisten
the corners of the pastry
square with water before
pressing together.

* *Preheat oven to 450°F (230°C)*
* *Baking sheet, ungreased*

1 lb	pork or beef breakfast sausages	500 g
	Pastry for 9-inch (23 cm) double-crust pie (see recipes, pages 176 to 179, or use Robin Hood Flaky Pie Crust Mix)	
½ cup	shredded Cheddar cheese	125 mL
	Mustard	

1. Parboil sausages in boiling water for 5 minutes. Drain and set aside to cool. Cut in half crosswise.

2. Prepare pastry as directed, adding cheese to dry ingredients.

3. Roll out pastry, one half at a time, on lightly floured surface to ⅛ inch (0.3 cm) thickness. Cut into 2¼-inch (5.5 cm) squares. Spread a little mustard diagonally from corner to corner of the square. Place sausage half in the center of the square to cover part of the mustard. Fold the two corners on the other diagonal over to meet each other and seal. Place on baking sheet.

4. Bake for 15 to 20 minutes or until pastry is golden. Serve warm.

Variation

Use cocktail wieners for a change.

Mushroom Turnovers

**MAKES ABOUT
30 TURNOVERS**

Preparation: 30 minutes
Cooking:
about 10 minutes
Baking: 15 minutes
Freezing: excellent

*These bite-size turnovers
can be made ahead for easy
entertaining. They are a good
vegetarian addition to cocktail
party platters.*

Tips

Use this cream cheese pastry
for savory turnovers and tarts.

These turnovers can be frozen
baked or unbaked. Choose
the method that fits your
schedule — both work well.
To freeze baked turnovers,
cool completely, wrap well
with plastic wrap and freeze
for up to 1 month. Reheat
from frozen in a 300°F
(150°C) oven for 10 to
15 minutes. To freeze
unbaked turnovers, prepare
up to and including Step 3.
Freeze until firm in single
layer on tray lined with
plastic wrap, then transfer to
airtight containers and freeze
for up to 1 month. Bake at
400°F (200°C) for 15 to
18 minutes.

Line baking sheet with
parchment paper for easy
cleanup.

A cutter with a fluted edge
is nice but not a necessity.

- *Preheat oven to 400°F (200°C)*
- *Baking sheet, ungreased*
- *3-inch (7.5 cm) round cookie or biscuit cutter, preferably fluted*

Pastry

½ cup	butter, softened	125 mL
4 oz	cream cheese, softened	125 g
1½ cups	Robin Hood All-Purpose Flour	375 mL
½ tsp	salt	2 mL

Filling

2 tbsp	butter	30 mL
8 oz	fresh mushrooms, finely chopped	250 g
⅓ cup	finely chopped onion	75 mL
2 tbsp	Robin Hood All-Purpose Flour	30 mL
1 tbsp	dry sherry	15 mL
¼ tsp	each salt and black pepper	1 mL
¼ cup	sour cream	50 mL

Glaze

1	egg yolk	1
1 tbsp	water	15 mL

1. *Pastry:* Cream butter and cream cheese in a bowl until smoothly blended. Add flour and salt, mixing to form a stiff dough. Divide in half. Wrap and chill while preparing filling.

2. *Filling:* Heat butter in a large skillet over medium-high heat; sauté mushrooms and onion until mushrooms lose their liquid, about 5 minutes. Stir in flour. Add sherry, salt and pepper. Cook, stirring, until mixture is dry, about 2 minutes. Remove from heat. Stir in sour cream. Set aside to cool.

3. Working with half of the pastry at a time, roll out thinly, to scant ⅛ inch (0.3 cm) thickness. Cut out circles with cutter. Place a rounded teaspoonful (5 mL) of filling in the center of each pastry round. Fold in half to form a semi-circle. Press edges to seal. Place on baking sheet.

4. *Glaze:* Combine egg yolk and water to blend. Brush over tops.

5. Bake for 12 to 15 minutes or until golden. Serve warm, or cool completely and freeze (see Tips, left).

Variations

Use a mixture of white mushrooms and more-exotic varieties, such as shiitake, oyster and cremini for superb flavor.

Add 1 tbsp (15 mL) finely chopped chives to the pastry.

Double-Crust Chicken and Cheese Pizza Sandwich

This tasty pizza is also easy to eat, which makes it ideal for those days when everyone is on the run. It's also good cold and makes a nice change from sandwiches for lunch.

Tips

For added fiber, replace half of the all-purpose flour with Robin Hood Whole Wheat Flour.

Prepare a few extra crusts. They will keep for up to 2 days in the refrigerator and freeze well, too.

Adjust the filling to suit your taste or to use up ingredients you have on hand — almost any kind of cheese will do. For a vegetarian version, you can replace the meat with 2 cups (500 mL) diced roasted vegetables.

For an attractive finish, sprinkle sesame seeds over the glaze before baking.

To prevent the dough from sticking to your hands, oil your fingers lightly before pressing it into the pan.

- *Preheat oven to 400°F (200°C)*
- *Pizza pan or baking sheet, greased*

Pizza Crust

2½ to 3 cups	Robin Hood All-Purpose Flour	625 to 750 mL
2¼ tsp	quick-rise yeast (1 envelope, ¼ oz/8 g)	11 mL
¾	salt	3 mL
1 cup	water	250 mL
2 tbsp	olive oil	30 mL

Filling

2	eggs, beaten	2
2 cups	shredded Gouda cheese	500 mL
2 cups	diced cooked chicken	500 mL
½ cup	chopped sweet green pepper	125 mL
¼ cup	chopped fresh basil	50 mL
	Hot sauce and black pepper to taste	

Glaze

1	egg	1
1 tbsp	milk	15 mL

1. *Pizza Crust:* Combine 2 cups (500 mL) of the flour, yeast and salt in a large bowl. Heat water and oil together until hot (125°F/50°C). Stir into flour mixture for about 2 minutes. Add enough remaining flour to make a soft dough. Turn out onto a lightly floured surface and knead for about 4 minutes, adding more flour as needed to make the dough smooth and elastic. Shape into a ball; cover and let rest for 10 minutes.

2. *Filling:* Combine eggs, cheese, chicken, green pepper, basil, hot pepper sauce and black pepper. Mix well.

3. Divide dough in half. Roll or press one half into a 12-inch (30 cm) circle on pan. Spread filling evenly over dough, leaving a narrow border. Roll or stretch remaining dough to same size. Place over filling. Seal and flute edges. Prick top with fork to allow steam to escape. Cover loosely with aluminum foil. Bake for 45 minutes. Remove foil.

4. *Glaze:* Beat egg and milk until blended. Brush over crust. Bake, uncovered, for 10 to 15 minutes longer or until crust is golden brown. Let stand for 10 minutes, then cut into wedges.

Variations

Replace chicken with roasted vegetables, ham, turkey or smoked chicken.

Quick-Fix Pizzas

Once you see how easy it is to make these delicious treats, you'll never order pizza again.

Tips

Try the toppings called for the first time you make these pizzas, then use your favorites or be creative next time — almost anything goes.

Remember that baking times vary with the size of the pizza. The smaller the pizza, the less time it takes to bake; the larger, the longer. Watch carefully — the crust should be crisp and golden and the filling hot.

To make one pizza, cut the Pizza Crust recipe in half.

Letting the dough rise until it doubles in bulk produces a more "bready" crust.

Dusting the pans with cornmeal gives a nice texture to the crust and prevents it from sticking. If you don't have cornmeal, parchment paper also works well.

- *Preheat oven to 400°F (200°C)*
- *Two pizza pans or baking sheets, greased and sprinkled with cornmeal*

Pizza Crust

1	batch Pizza Crust (see recipe, page 243)	1

Toppings

Zucchini Pesto Pizza

3 tbsp	basil pesto	45 mL
2	medium zucchini, thinly sliced and grilled	2
1	large sweet red pepper, roasted and sliced	1
1 tbsp	olive oil	15 mL
1/2 cup	feta cheese, crumbled	125 mL

Greek Pizza

1 tbsp	olive oil	15 mL
Half	red onion, sliced	Half
2	cloves garlic, minced	2
1 2/3 cups	diced fresh tomatoes	400 mL
1/2 cup	feta cheese, crumbled	125 mL
1/3 cup	sliced black olives, optional	75 mL
1/4 cup	chopped fresh basil leaves	50 mL

1. *Pizza Crust:* Prepare dough for pizza crust as per Step 1, page 243.

2. Cover with plastic wrap and let rise in a warm place for 30 to 60 minutes or until doubled in bulk. Punch dough down and turn out onto a lightly floured surface. Divide in half to prepare the two suggested pizzas, or in increments to suit the size of pizza you want to make. Stretch or roll out dough. Place on prepared pans.

TOPPINGS

Zucchini Pesto Pizza: Spread pesto over dough. Scatter zucchini and red pepper over top. Drizzle with olive oil. Bake for 15 minutes. Sprinkle cheese over top and bake for 5 minutes longer or until crust is golden on the bottom.
Greek Pizza: Heat oil in skillet over medium heat. Add onion and garlic and cook, stirring, until tender, about 5 minutes. Stir in tomatoes, feta cheese, olives and basil. Spread over crust. Bake for 20 minutes or until crust is golden on the bottom.

Variations

The possibilities are endless. Vary the size of the crust and topping to suit the occasion and your tastes.

Supply each of your guests with an individual-size crust, set out a variety of toppings and let people create their own pizza.

Pizza Quiche Tidbits

These bite-size squares offer the best of both quiche and pizza: a flaky bottom and pizza toppings.

Tips

For easy entertaining, make these ahead, then reheat when ready to serve.

Prepared pasta sauce varies considerably. Choose one that is thick and flavourful.

Use a zesty pasta sauce that contains hot peppers if your guests like spicy foods.

Don't be surprised — these tidbits puff in the oven, then deflate on standing.

- *Preheat oven to 425°F (220°C)*
- *9-inch (2.5 L) square baking pan, greased*

3	eggs	3
¾ cup	milk	175 mL
⅔ cup	Robin Hood All-Purpose Flour	150 mL
2 tbsp	finely chopped onion	30 mL
1 tbsp	vegetable oil	15 mL
½ cup	thick pasta sauce	125 mL
1 tsp	dried oregano leaves	5 mL
1 tsp	dried basil leaves	5 mL
½ cup	diced pepperoni	125 mL
½ cup	diced sweet green pepper	125 mL
1 cup	shredded mozzarella cheese	250 mL

1. Beat eggs, milk and flour until smooth. Stir in onion and oil. Pour into prepared pan.

2. Combine pasta sauce, oregano and basil. Pour over egg mixture to produce a marbled effect. Sprinkle pepperoni, green pepper, then cheese over top.

3. Bake for 25 minutes or until puffed and golden. Cool for 5 minutes, then cut into small squares. Serve warm.

Variations

Vary the toppings as you would for pizza: replace pepperoni with diced ham or chicken or add olives and sun-dried tomatoes. You can even combine Cheddar and mozzarella cheeses — the possibilities are endless.

Almond Cheese Gougère Wreath

**MAKES ABOUT
10 SERVINGS**

Preparation: 15 minutes
Baking: 50 minutes
Freezing:
not recommended

*Serve this tasty cheese-
flavored puff as an appetizer
with a full-bodied red wine.*

Tips

If they are available, use
sliced almonds with the skins
on to add color to the top.

Always use freshly ground
pepper in savory dishes.
You'll be amazed at the
difference in flavor compared
to the preground variety.

Check your oven
temperature with an
accurate thermometer. It's
essential that these start at
a high temperature to make
them puff.

Always use large eggs
when baking.

- *Preheat oven to 450°F (230°C)*
- *Baking sheet, greased*

1 cup	water	250 mL
1/2 cup	butter	125 mL
1/4 tsp	salt	1 mL
1/4 tsp	freshly ground black pepper	1 mL
1 cup	Robin Hood All-Purpose Flour	250 mL
4	eggs	4
1 1/2 cups	shredded Gruyère cheese	375 mL
1/3 cup	sliced almonds	75 mL

1. Combine water, butter, salt and pepper in a heavy saucepan.
   Bring to a boil over high heat. Remove from heat. Add flour all
   at once. Beat vigorously with a wooden spoon until mixture is
   smooth and pulls away from the side of the pan to form a ball.
   Return to low heat and beat for 1 minute longer. Remove from
   heat and let cool for 2 minutes.

2. Add eggs, one at a time, beating vigorously after each addition
   until smooth. Stir in 1 1/4 cups (300 mL) of the cheese. Drop
   batter by heaping spoonfuls (8 large or 12 smaller) onto
   prepared baking sheet to form a circle about 8 inches (20 cm)
   in diameter. (The edges of the drops should touch). Sprinkle
   remaining cheese and almonds over top.

3. Bake for 10 minutes, then reduce heat to 350°F (180°C) and
   bake for 30 to 40 minutes longer or until firm and golden
   brown. Remove from oven and immediately poke holes all
   around ring with a fork or the tip of a sharp knife to let steam
   escape. Cool for 10 minutes before serving.

Variation

Replace Gruyère with Swiss cheese.

Sesame Cheese Thins

These crispy wafers pack a whopping cheese flavor and make a delicious appetizer or snack.

Tips

Prepare a few rolls of dough and keep them on hand in the refrigerator. You can quickly bake some thins and have a great appetizer to serve with a glass of wine before dinner.

Use an old (sharp) cheese for the best flavor. Five- or six-year-old Cheddars are particularly good in this recipe.

For variety, use black sesame seeds instead of white, or a mixture of the two. Black sesame seeds are available in Asian grocery stores.

For a zestier result, add 1/2 tsp (2 mL) chili powder along with the paprika.

To store, let wafers cool completely and keep in airtight containers.

- *Preheat oven to 425°F (220°C)*
- *Baking sheet, ungreased*

2 cups	shredded old Cheddar cheese	500 mL
1/4 cup	butter, softened	50 mL
2/3 cup	Robin Hood All-Purpose Flour	150 mL
1/2 tsp	baking powder	2 mL
1/2 tsp	paprika	2 mL
1/4 tsp	salt	1 mL
2 dashes	hot pepper sauce	2 dashes
3 tbsp	sesame seeds	45 mL

1. Cream cheese and butter in a large bowl until smooth and creamy. Combine flour, baking powder, paprika and salt. Add to creamed mixture along with hot pepper sauce. Using two knives, a pastry blender or your fingers, blend mixture until it resembles coarse crumbs. Turn out onto a lightly floured board and knead lightly to form a smooth dough.

2. Shape dough into a log about 9 inches (23 cm) long and 1 inch (2.5 cm) in diameter. Roll in sesame seeds, pressing seeds firmly into dough. Wrap in waxed paper and refrigerate until firm, 2 hours or overnight.

3. Cut dough into 1/8-inch (0.5 cm) thick slices. Arrange on baking sheet. Bake for 8 to 10 minutes or until edges are lightly browned. Serve warm or at room temperature.

Basic Crêpe Batter

MAKES ABOUT EIGHTEEN 6-INCH (15 CM) CRÊPES

Preparation: 10 minutes

Chilling: 1 hour
or overnight

Cooking: about
3 minutes per crêpe

Freezing: excellent

This crêpe batter is versatile and can be used in both sweet and savory dishes.

Tips

Make these crêpes in a blender, a mixer or by hand — whatever suits your fancy.

Prepare a batch of crêpes to have on hand. Cool completely, then stack between squares of waxed paper and refrigerate for up to 2 days or freeze for up to 3 months.

Don't stack warm crêpes or they'll stick together. To cool, turn out onto a tea towel in a single layer.

There are many ways to enjoy crêpes. Fill them (see recipes, pages 183, 184, 250 and 251), brush with butter and sugar and roll up, spread with jam and fold into quarters, or fold and serve with or in a warm sauce.

If you don't have a dedicated crêpe pan, be sure to use a nonstick skillet when making crêpes.

• *Crêpe pan or nonstick skillet, lightly greased*

3	eggs	3
1¼ cups	milk	300 mL
¾ cup	Robin Hood All-Purpose Flour	175 mL
2 tbsp	butter, melted	30 mL
1 tbsp	granulated sugar	15 mL
¼ tsp	salt	1 mL

BLENDER METHOD

1. Combine eggs, milk, flour, butter, sugar and salt in blender container. Blend until smooth, about 1 minute.

2. Cover batter and chill for at least 1 hour or overnight.

MIXER OR WHISK METHOD

1. Beat eggs until light. Gradually add milk and flour alternately, making three dry and two liquid additions, beating until smooth. Beat in butter, sugar and salt, mixing until smooth.

2. Cover batter and chill for at least 1 hour or overnight.

3. *To cook:* Heat prepared pan over medium-high heat. Remove from heat; immediately pour heaping 2 tbsp (30 mL) of batter into hot pan. Lift and tilt pan to cover bottom with a thin layer of batter. Return pan to heat. Cook until bottom is lightly browned, 1 to 2 minutes. Turn crêpe over and brown other side. Repeat with remaining batter. Enjoy warm or let cool in a single layer on a tea towel to use in other recipes.

Chicken and Mushroom Crêpes

Preparation: 40 minutes
Baking: 25 minutes
Freezing:
not recommended

Because half of the preparation can be done ahead, crêpes make a particularly easy yet elegant dinner. Keep a stack of crêpes in the freezer to make entertaining easy anytime.

Tips

Don't be afraid of crêpes. They look difficult but are really just pancakes made thinner.

You can buy special crêpe pans, but a small nonstick skillet works very well. A lightweight one works best, as you have to pick it up and turn it so the batter coats the bottom evenly.

The batter recipe makes 18 crêpes. Freeze the extra for another use.

- *Preheat oven to 350°F (180°C)*
- *Baking dish, buttered*

Crêpes

1	batch Basic Crêpe Batter (see recipe, page 250)	1

Filling

3 tbsp	vegetable oil	45 mL
1	large onion, chopped	1
3 cups	sliced fresh mushrooms	750 mL
1½ cups	sliced celery	375 mL
2½ cups	diced cooked chicken	625 mL

Sauce

⅓ cup	butter	75 mL
⅓ cup	Robin Hood All-Purpose Flour	75 mL
2½ cups	milk	625 mL
2 tsp	Worcestershire sauce	10 mL
2 tbsp	finely chopped fresh parsley	30 mL
1 tsp	dried oregano or basil leaves	5 mL
1 tsp	salt	5 mL
¼ tsp	black pepper	1 mL

1. *Crêpes:* Prepare crêpes; set aside.

2. *Filling:* Heat oil in a large nonstick skillet over medium-high heat. Sauté onion, mushroom and celery until celery is softened, about 5 minutes. Add chicken and stir until heated through. Keep warm.

3. *Sauce:* Melt butter in a medium saucepan. Add flour, stirring until smooth. Gradually add milk and Worcestershire sauce. Cook over medium heat, stirring constantly, just until mixture comes to a boil and thickens, about 5 minutes. Remove from heat. Stir in parsley, oregano, salt and pepper. Mix half of the sauce with filling; reserve remainder for topping.

4. *Assembly:* Fill crêpes with chicken filling, dividing evenly. Place, seam-side down, in a single layer in prepared baking dish. Cover with remaining sauce.

5. Bake for 20 to 25 minutes or until heated through.

Variations

Add 1 cup (250 mL) shredded Swiss cheese to the sauce.

Substitute cooked turkey or ham for the chicken.

Index